Essay I...

P9-DUH-563

GRACES OF HARMONY

GRACES
OF HARMONY

Alliteration, Assonance, and Consonance
in Eighteenth-Century British Poetry

PERCY G. ADAMS

THE UNIVERSITY OF GEORGIA PRESS
ATHENS

Library of Congress Catalog Card Number: 76–1144
International Standard Book Number: 0–8203–0399–2

The University of Georgia Press, Athens 30602

Set in 11 on 13 point Times Roman type
Printed in the United States of America

FOR POLLY

Contents

Preface

This is a book about the sound of poetry. In it I attempt to treat consonant and vowel echoes that occur not in rhymes but in stressed syllables anywhere in the lines. Most such echoes can be classified under the terms alliteration, assonance, and consonance and are not only more subtle than rhymes but have perhaps been historically more important to poets of all nations. One assumption behind this book, then, is that most poets have written for the speaking voice, Hopkins being only one to insist that all his verse was "made for performance," not just "reading with the eye but loud" (*Letters to Bridges*, 1935, p. 246). And even Susanne Langer's theories about poetry's not needing a speaking voice, that the most "musical" poems can be heard "inwardly" (*Feeling and Form*, 1953, pp. 277–79), seem to demand some kind of inner ear. But her theories seem strangely out of place with the dramatic Shakespeare, with Milton who dictated in a sonorous voice, with Pope and Swift who read to each other, with Tennyson who loved to perform for his friends, and today most of all with poets such as Wilbur, Dickey, Giovanni, and Merwin in such demand for reading his or her own poems aloud or with every poet's poems being professionally tape recorded. My appeal here, then, is to the ear of the reader rather than to his eye.

Although primarily about poetry of the period 1660–1800, *Graces of Harmony* necessarily includes historical treatments of alliteration, assonance, and consonance and provides definitions that may help to bring a bit more order into discussions of those terms. Much has been written heretofore about alliteration, almost nothing about asso-

nance or consonance, even though vowel repetitions may
be the most acoustically attractive of all, as poets from
Homer to Dryden to Poe to Verlaine have known, and
consonance has long been a favorite with poets who
worked to achieve pleasant sounds with language, like
Blake, Emily Dickinson, and Dylan Thomas. And since I
hope to show here that eighteenth-century poets were as
successful as those of other periods in achieving such effects, I have gone before 1660 and after 1800 in order to
make certain comparisons, to describe the tradition inherited by Dryden, and to discover not only what his immediate successors passed on but how significant they all
have been in the history of poetic sounds. Pope is not the
only poet of the period who appeals to the ear. It is hoped
then that such a study will be valuable to all readers of
poems as well as to students of the eighteenth century.

   This book, like every book, is the product of more than
one person. Some parts of it have been read before groups
of the Modern Language Association and published. Con-
sequently I wish to thank, with pleasure, *Texas Studies in
Literature and Language*, the *Journal of English and Germanic Philology*, and the *Publications of the Modern Language Association* for permission to use material from four
articles which they have published for me and which, in
altered form, has been reproduced here. Certain of their
readers, as well as certain of my listeners, have made wise
and thoughtful suggestions.

   For my other books it has also been a pleasure to thank
great libraries in this country and in Europe, but for this
study I am more indebted to colleagues, other friends, and
students who have sharpened or modified my theories or
read all or portions of the manuscript. There are, for example, students like that wonderful Chinese poet, Stephen
Liu, who publishes in two languages, and others like Kenneth Cherry, Phillip Anderson, Rita White, and B. J. Frye,
who have applied some of my theories to studies of their

own. Two graduate assistants have gone far beyond the call of duty in collecting, typing, and arranging notes. One is Pat Bruington; the other is Bettie McDavid Mason, whose enthusiasm, specialized knowledge, and talent as a writer have been of inestimable value: she and her husband Jim have read the entire manuscript, modestly but persistently finding ways to save me time or improve my work. Among the colleagues who have helped, sometimes without knowing it, are Professors Thomas A. Kirby, Nicholas Von Kreisler, and Donald Stanford of the Louisiana State University; George T. Wright, poet and now Chairman of English at the University of Minnesota; F. DeWolfe Miller, Eric Stockton, Richard Kelly, and especially John Hurt Fisher of the University of Tennessee; O. B. Hardison, now Director of the Folger Library, whose encouragement breathed new life into my work; the late Harold Orton of Leeds University, Editor of the British Linguistic Atlas, and my colleague for three years; Neil Isaacs, formerly at Tennessee, now at the University of Maryland; and the late Stephen Mooney, a fine poet who was so sensitive to the sounds of words. Then there are Paul Hunter, Chairman of English at Emory University, whose suggestions have been more invaluable than even he can know; Aubrey Williams, of the University of Florida, who has also read the manuscript and given friendly criticism; Nathaniel B. Smith, now at the University of Georgia, whose knowledge of Old French and Old Provençal poetry has stimulated and helped me; and Frank Goodwyn, one of my oldest friends, Professor of Spanish at the University of Maryland, and a student of phonic echoes and rhyme in Spanish poetry of the Siglo de Oro. Nor could a writer ask for better, more patient, more imaginative editing and handling of his book than the editors of the Georgia Press have devoted to mine; I cannot thank Kenneth Cherry and Thomas T. Tuggle enough. And never has my wife Polly been so understanding as a proof reader and critic: her editorial eye, practiced hand, and patient insistence have saved me from many a slip in a book that lends itself to such varied kinds of slips. No one of these, however, can be charged with any of my errors of omission or commission, of fact or judgment, that trained specialists or other keen-eyed readers may find.

But while official readers for journals have lent encouragement and while colleagues, friends, and captive audiences have been patient, this book could never have been written without the grants provided by three generous sources: the Louisiana State University Graduate School headed by its then most capable Dean Max Goodrich; the American Council of Learned Societies, whose fellowships have saved so many of us; and the University of Tennessee Better English Fund, established by a great friend and humanitarian, John C. Hodges. May *Graces of Harmony* do them no dishonor.

Abbreviations

Ab&Ac	*Absalom and Achitophel*
Arbuth	*Epistle to Dr. Arbuthnot*
"Battle"	"Battle of the Summer-Islands"
Conq	*The Conquest of Granada*
Dun	*Dunciad*
Es on Crit	*Essay on Criticism*
Es on Man	*Essay on Man*
Georg	*Georgics*
GP	General Prologue (to the *Canterbury Tales*)
Ham	*Hamlet*
H&P	*The Hind and the Panther*
KT	The Knight's Tale
Macb	*Macbeth*
MacF	*Mac Flecknoe*
MND	*Midsummer Night's Dream*
Moral Ep	*Moral Epistles*
MV	*Merchant of Venice*
NPT	Nun's Priest's Tale
PL	*Paradise Lost*
Rape	*The Rape of the Lock*
Rel L	*Religio Laici*
R&J	*Romeo and Juliet*
"St. Js's P"	"On St. James's Park"
T&C	*Troilus and Criseyde*
WF	*Windsor Forest*

GRACES OF HARMONY

I

Definitions and the Tradition

The "Music" of the Words

"Sometimes when I am writing, the music of the words I am trying to shape takes me far beyond the words"—Spender.

The sounds that their words produce must be an important matter to poets since they seem agreed that what many of them call "music" is an indispensable quality of a poem. Dryden was never tired of saying that the beauty of Virgil's "figurative, elegant, and sounding words" was his "most eminent" grace, an opinion echoed many times by other students of poetry, as when William Empson asserted that "Vergil remains the most melodious of poets." The words of a poem, Ezra Pound argued, "are charged over and above their plain meaning, with some musical property, which directs the bearing or trend of that meaning." Believing that "a poet may gain much from the study of music," T. S. Eliot has even suggested that his own experience led him to the opinion that among poets in general "a poem, or a passage of a poem, may tend to realize itself first as a particular rhythm before it reaches expression in words, and that this rhythm may bring to birth the idea and the image." Conrad Aiken "describes himself as groping for musical effects from the beginning of his poetic career." And Stephen Spender insists that the two "final qualities of a poet" are inspiration and song, song being defined as "the music which a poem as yet unthought of will assume." Some poets, Verlaine being one, have gone so far as to place "la musique avant toute chose." [1]

Although these and many other poets, Coleridge and Hopkins, Mallarmé and Valéry among them, have through

the centuries employed the analogy between the sound of
music and the sound of the language in a poem, and while
critics from the Renaissance to our day have followed
them in making the analogy, we are now being warned
that wherever possible one should avoid such terms
as "music," "musical," "melody," even "counterpoint"
when talking of the acoustic properties of poems.[2] In
music, Calvin Brown reminds us, harmony involves pitch
while in poetry it can refer only to a "general pleasantness
of sound."[3] John Hollander points to two different ways of
studying the relationship between poetry and music—
"how poetry is *like* sound, and how poetry can often be
about sound." In its extreme form the first way is that of the
formalist critic while the second approach, Hollander's
own, is that of the historian of ideas.[4] Nevertheless, while
one can today avoid confusing the acoustic, or phonic,
quality of poetry with the "pitch relationships of simul-
taneously produced tones" unique to music, one cannot
avoid the fact that so many poets have found "music" in
the language they use, and one need not—especially today—avoid the attempt to combine at least a modified for-
malism with aesthetics in the hope of explaining a little
better the relationship between the poet's "discursive" and
his acoustic, that is, his "musical," meaning.

This "music" of poetry derives from many sources.
Chief among them is the fact that the elements of language
create pleasing sounds—what Dryden, Pope, and Dr.
Johnson called "harmony of numbers"—by the repetition
of the expected and the artful use of the unexpected, that is,
by a rhythm which is more or less regular in its repetition of
stressed sounds yet not so regular that it is monotonous.
But while rhythm is by common agreement the most important of the repetitive devices in poetry, it is not the only
one. The length of a line of poetry can be repeated; that is,
each line can have a given number of accents, even syl-

lables. Or two successive lines, as in Psalm 19 or Greek recitative poetry, can balance, complement, parallel each other; one repeats or reverses the other's structure. Or as with Greek lyricists, the makers of ballads, traditional poets like Gascoigne, or writers of free verse like Whitman, one can employ incremental repetition, that is, repetition of part of a phrase; or anaphora, the repetition of words at the beginning of lines or thought groups.

Among the most popular of ear-appealing devices in poetry are the repetitions of smaller sound groups. Rhyme, for example, whether end or internal, is the recurrence of a final vowel-plus-consonant sound in stressed syllables that are near enough to each other for the listener's ear to catch the echo. Although rhyme is sometimes found in early Latin and other poems, it has not always been popular, having come to poetry as a regular ornament apparently with the troubadours of Provence and the minnesingers of Germany.[5] Or one can also blatantly or subtly repeat a consonant, a consonant cluster, a vowel, or a diphthong. When in stressed, strategic positions, such echoes of small sound units have been among the most important to poets of all ages and all nations and can normally be described with the terms *alliteration, assonance,* and *consonance.* But while the devices have always been popular, the terms themselves have not always been in use; and because even now they are defined in a confusing variety of ways, it is necessary to attempt new definitions.

Alliteration is the repetition of the sound of an initial consonant or consonant cluster in stressed syllables close enough to each other for the ear to be affected, perhaps unconsciously, by the repetition. This definition is today not only the most widely accepted,[6] but it is the only logical one if we also employ the terms *assonance* and *consonance.* One must remember, however, that for centuries *alliteration* meant the echo of almost any, even if usually an initial, phone. A student of *Beowulf* and other Germanic poems will, of course, still include in his definition the repetition of initial vowels, as in

egsode eorlas, sytthan aerest wearth,   (*Beowulf*, 6)

where the initial stressed vowels are not even alike. It is for this reason that in the Princeton *Encyclopedia of Poetry and Poetics*, the article "Alliteration," written by a Germanic scholar,[7] defines the term as "any repetition of the same sound(s) or syllable in two or more words of a line (or line group)" and adds, "In Germanic alliterative metre . . . or 'Stabreim' any vowel can alliterate with any other. . . . Alliteration may, however, include with notable effect the repetition of consonants, vowels or consonant-vowel combinations in medial or even final position ('That brave vibration . . .'—Robert Herrick)."

Such a broad use of the word is perfectly historical. In 1656, for example, one writer called alliteration "a figure in Rhetoric, repeating and playing on the same letter," a definition which the eighteenth century accepted, as when Charles Churchill, writing of those who unsuccessfully "pray'd / For apt Alliteration's artful aid," was obviously including in his definition not only initial vowels but unstressed vowels.[8] This kind of letter repetition, as well as that in the line from *Beowulf*, has sometimes been called *vocalic alliteration*. There is also the term *eye alliteration*, which can include Churchill's *a*'s, or the repetition of any initial consonant which is pronounced differently in two different words, such as *p* and *ph* in *pall* and *physic*. But since to many poets—Spender, Verlaine, Dylan Thomas, or Pope, for example—the sound of words is more important than is their appearance, all such vague or ambiguous uses of alliteration might well be avoided—the repetition not only of initial vowels, or of initial letters when a sound is not repeated, but the repetition of sounds of obvious weak stress. Today, then, the term is popularly and appropriately limited to the echo of initial consonants or consonant clusters in stressed syllables, as in Emily Dickinson's "The cricket sang / And set the sun," Ransom's little Lady "lying so primly propped," or Dryden's

> Thy force, infus'd, the fainting Tyrians prop'd;
> And haughty Pharoah found his Fortune stop'd,

from *Absalom and Achitophel* (842–43), where in one couplet there are six initial [f] sounds in stressed syllables, one beginning a medial syllable, another spelled *Ph*, all helping to emphasize peaks in the iambic rhythm.

Alliteration, so defined, has been a common poetic device in nearly all nations and all periods. Hebrew and Sanscrit, without any rhyme, employed it, at least sparingly, while Greek poets such as Homer and Aeschylus made as frequent use of alliteration as have British and American poets. Whether or not the more primitive Latin folk poetry had much alliteration has been argued, but the sophisticated later Latins, at least, made it an important sound effect. Sometimes the use was extreme, as with Ennius. Sometimes it was thick but artistic, as with Lucretius. His *De Rerum Natura*, known so well by British poets such as Dryden, Pope, and James Thomson, has every kind of sound repetition, alliteration being only one of the most prominent, as in this typical line,

> Semina quae faciunt flammae fulfere colores.   (6.21)

One modern student, in fact, believes that Lucretius "revelled in alliteration" to such an extent that with him the device "can scarcely be called 'artful'!" Virgil, even more of an influence, could write many lines with four initial consonants accented, as in the *Ecologues* (8.68),[9]

> Docite ab urbe domum, mea carmina, ducite Daphnim.

In European poetry written since the middle ages the Germans have employed alliteration, although perhaps less than the poets of certain other nations.[10] Heine, for example, has relatively little, Goethe more, as in the first line of "Hochzeitlied,"

> Wir singen und sagen von Grafen zu gern.

On the other hand it is agreed that the Provençal poets liked abundant and varied alliteration,[11] but it is just as often said that French and other so-called syllabic poets did not like it, that in fact in the great French seventeenth century it died out completely and was even considered "mauvaise,"[12] being revived only with the romanticists. Such an opinion is, however, not supported by the facts, for while certain early nineteenth-century writers of France—Musset, Vigny, Hugo—may have used alliteration more, and the later *symbolistes*, the followers of Poe, and the exponents of "pure poetry" like Verlaine perhaps still more, the French contemporaries of Dryden and Pope by no means eschewed it. Boileau, for example, has frequent two-syllable alliterations and a number of lines in which three, even four, strong syllables begin with the same consonant, such as these successive ones from *L'Art poétique* (I):

> N'offrit plus rien de rude à l'oreille épurée,
> Des traits d'esprit semés de temps en temps pétillent.

La Fontaine, who both admired and translated the sound-conscious Virgil, also showed "a calculated handling of alliteration and assonance,"[13] as in this line:

> Les petits ont pati des sottises des grands.

And since the French dramatists of the seventeenth century, especially Corneille and Racine, employed rhetorical ornament of all kinds,[14] it is not surprising to find that they too have considerable alliteration, as when the order comes in Racine's *Andromaque*, "Va, cours; mais crains encore d'y trouver Hermione" (4.5), or when Thésée in *Phèdre* (5.3) says to Aricie,

Non, vous voulez en vain couvrir son attentat;
Votre amour vous aveugle en faveur de l'ingrat.

Even more than the Germans and the French, the Welsh poets have been enduringly alliterative—and in the most complex of ways. While Irish poetry has adopted rhyme as well as a rhythm similar to that of English, the Welsh have retained their highly decorative *cynghanedd*, in which, W. H. Gardner explains, "the rules of alliteration are much stricter than in English. Words of more than one syllable alliterate when *all* their consonants, except the final ones, are the same and in the same order. Thus *moonlight* requires a word like *manly* (m-nl-). Again, the accent must fall on corresponding syllables . . . ; thus bullock:bellow (but not below)."[15] This intricate system of consonantal repetition was perhaps an even greater influence on Gerard Manley Hopkins than were Greek and Roman poetry with their many kinds of word, syllable, and phonal echoes. All of these poetries—classical, German, French, Welsh—as well as many others such as Italian, Spanish, and Russian have been more or less alliterative; and, as this book will demonstrate, English has always been one of the most alliterative.

There is a variety of opinions about how poets have used or should use their initial consonants.[16] One theory, not widely held, is that harmonious alliteration is achieved not only by repeating the same consonant but also by employing different consonants that are phonetically related because of their place and manner of articulation. That is to say, a pleasureable sound is said to result if several syllables near each other begin with, or even contain, a number of labials (p,b), or dentals (t,d), or velars (k,g). Another opinion, negative but more popular, complains that the echoing of initial consonants can be excessive, that "in civilized poetry, alliteration at the expense of sincere expression often defeats the objectives of poetry: cf. Poe,

Swinburne." A positive companion to this opinion argues that "alliteration is no mere 'ornament' of versification: it is a real and powerful adjunct when properly employed." Such an argument, however, would be just as defensible if for *alliteration* one substituted the word *assonance*.

Although there have been a dozen book-length studies of alliteration as used in English poetry before Dryden,[17] there is apparently none that treats assonance as used by any poet or group of poets writing in any language. Such a neglect is all the more surprising if one remembers how many poets have agreed that vowels are more "harmonious," or "sonorous," than consonants. There are at least three possible reasons why prosodists, as well as other readers of poetry, have failed to emphasize assonance so much as they have talked of alliteration.

In the first place alliteration, being initial, is much more apparent to the eye than is assonance, which is not normally initial; and since most readers apparently do not follow the ancient plea to read poetry aloud to the ear and not silently to the eye alone, they see the alliteration but fail to hear the assonance.

In the second place, since vowel sounds in all Indo-European languages have through the centuries often undergone dramatic changes in pronunciation while consonant sounds have remained relatively though not completely stable, readers of poetry necessarily feel insecure with vowels of centuries other than their own. Furthermore, twentieth-century readers apparently do not always recognize the vowel echoes of earlier poets unless those echoes occur in rhymes, just as English readers may have trouble with vowels of other languages and just as American readers may sometimes fail to find the vowel echoes in the poems of their British contemporaries, whose pronunciation is often different from that of American English. And in the third place, as with alliteration, the definitions of and opinions about assonance have been as uncertain as they have been varied. But while the term has been employed for almost every kind of echo, whether of consonant, of vowel, or even of phrase and word, today the definition is more or less settled.[18]

Assonance is the repetition of the sound of a vowel or diphthong, but not of a following adjacent consonant or consonant cluster, in stressed syllables near enough to each other for the echo to be discernible to the ear. Assonance may involve three or more syllables and be very striking, as in Byron's

> The castled crag of Drachenfels
> Frowns o'er the wide and winding Rhine,

where three stressed syllables in one line contain [æ] and three in the other have [aɪ].[19] Or more commonly it can involve only two syllables and be so subtle that it is hardly noticeable, as in Stephen Spender's "More beautiful and soft than any moth." One can of course speak of polysyllabic assonance, where both the vowel of the stressed syllable and the vowel of the following unstressed syllable, or syllables, of one word are found in a nearby word, as in Dylan Thomas's use of "infancy" and "mystery" in place of rhymes in "Poem in October." And it is also possible to have feminine assonance, where only the vowels of final unstressed syllables are the same in sound, as with Karl Shapiro's "Arlington"–"capitol" ("The Potomac"). Such echoes are rare, however, even in twentieth-century poems, and feminine assonances, by themselves, are both difficult to use and relatively ineffectual.

But while the definition seems settled, there is by no means universal agreement as to the value or historical importance of assonance. In fact, the reading of poetry has suffered notably because a myth, negative in nature, has long obscured the vowel echoes that should have been sounding clearly. The myth can be exposed in a number of widely unrelated studies of sound effects in poetry.

First, there are the popular encyclopedias—the *Britannica*, the *Americana*, Funk and Wagnalls—which still treat assonance almost exclusively as a substitute for rhyme in Old French and other Romance poetries and still insist not only that "in the Romance languages the ear prefers the correspondence of vowels while in the Teutonic languages the preference is given to consonants" but also that "assonance as a conscious art . . . is scarcely recognized as legitimate in English literature."[20] Such statements, even though limited to "end assonance," are indeed misleading: They ignore internal assonance, and they say in effect that vowel echoes by themselves are relatively unimportant in English.

Second, Coventry Patmore, quoted with approval in W. H. Gardner's highly regarded book on Hopkins, believed that "if rhyme . . . is the great means in modern languages of marking essential metrical pauses, alliteration is a very effective mode of conferring emphasis on the accent, which is the primary foundation of metre."[21] Here the implication is, by omission, that phonic echoes other than of initial consonants are not so important in emphasizing stress.

Third, a recent provocative study, while analyzing the complex end echoes in the poetry of Dylan Thomas, offers the theory that before Thomas

> assonance had never been much used . . . in English verse, and for good reason. A poet who relies upon the vowel to support his rhyme schemes builds upon linguistic sand; for vowels, especially in English, depend much less than consonants upon spelling, varying in pronunciation greatly and in inconsistent ways from one place and time to another. In comparison, the consonant is an immutable rock. A poet who works with assonance must therefore abandon most of

the dubious security of the letter and compose instead with his own voice and for his own ear.[22]

Not only does this opinion agree that assonance has been relatively unimportant; it offers an explanation for the unimportance.

The fact is that assonance, at least as much as alliteration, has been a conscious acoustic device in poetry of all countries. It has been pointed out in Greek and Latin. Certain readers, James R. Lowell, for one, have noticed that Homer "was fond of playing" with vowel echoes, and Hopkins found Euripides especially to be "a great master of this vowelling." There is no doubt that Virgil has much assonance as we now define the term. In fact, Dryden quoted this line from the *Aeneid* in order to praise its author's "musical ear":

Quo f*a*ta tr*a*hunt retr*a*huntque, sequ*a*mur.[23]

Here Virgil stressed the *a* sound four times against a kind of background—what Hopkins would have called "counterpoint"—provided by the three unstressed *u* sounds. Lucretius's vowel repetitions are as frequent, if not so apparent, as his alliterations. He has, in fact, numerous lines with two and three stressed vowels alike, such as this one from *De Rerum Natura* (3.794) where the [k] alliteration should be no more prominent than the echo of the two closely related grades of *o:*

Quod quoniam nostro quoque constat corpore certum.

In old French and other Romance languages, including Provençal, instead of employing full end rhyme the poet normally echoed the vowel of the final stressed syllables, although the lines often end with unstressed syllables that are sometimes themselves the same, sometimes different, and often a primary vowel is not exactly like its fellows. The best known of many possible illustrations is probably

La Chanson de Roland, written before 1100. Here every *laisse*, or stanzaic section, attempts to echo the vowel or diphthong of the final stressed syllables no matter how many lines are involved. But the echo is not always perfect. Furthermore, the weak syllables that frequently end the lines are as nearly identical as the poet could make them. For example, in the Digby Ms., perhaps the best to work with, *laisse* 253, one of the shortest, has the end words *chevalchet – damage – reguardet – vertudable – halte – dessaffret–halne–altres*, each of which has *a* in the last stressed syllable even though the *a* of *reguardet* may not have the same quality as the other *a*'s. And of the unstressed final syllables two end in *et*. What has not been pointed out enough is that in old Romance languages the poetry employing such end assonance often echoed vowels internally also, just as later poetry does: *Rollancz–chataine, Rollant–remaigne*, etc.[24]

And internal assonance has continued to be a most prominent acoustical element in French poetry. Tristan, an ornamental précieux poet of the early seventeenth century, for example, might have his two end rhymes but also include five assonances in these four lines of "Les Amours":

> Ossem*en*s entassez, et vous, pierres parl*an*tes
> Qui c*on*servez les n*om*s à la Postérité,
> Représent*an*s la v*ie* et sa frag*i*lité
> Pour c*en*surer l'orgueil des *â*mes insol*en*tes.

Racine, a quieter poet, preferred vowel echoes to alliteration, as in this line from *Iphigénie* 5.4:

> L'Aul*i*de aura vom*i* leur flotte cr*i*minelle.

And by common consent the romanticists and later French poets were supremely conscious of all the devices of sound, as evidenced by a line from Hugo's "Le petit roi de Galice,"

Muleti*ers* qui pouss*ez* de vall*ée* en vall*ée*,

where [e] occurs in every stressed syllable; or by another of Hugo's lines, this one from *Oceano nox*,

Que ch*an*te un m*en*di*an*t à l'*an*gle d'un vieux pont,

where [ã] comes four times in rhythmic peaks. It has, in fact, been argued that, even more than with English, many "rhymes" in French are not rhymes but assonances since no consonant is sounded after the vowel: "*verre d'eau* ne rime pas avec *tombeau*, ni *pain* avec *main* . . . ; ce ne sont là que des assonances."[25]

Other modern literatures have abundant vowel echoes, German being only one. Goethe, a most sophisticated poet, relied heavily on them for his ear appeal. There are, for example, six different assonances in the famous eight lines in which Faust announces his version of the contract with Mephistopheles, including this one of three syllables:

Es s*ei* die Z*ei*t für mich vorb*ei*!

And Heine, praised by Tennyson for his "musical" quality, opened "Am Meer" with three short-line stanzas two of which contain three obvious internal assonances each:

Wir s*a*ssen am Fischerh*au*se
Und sch*au*ten n*a*ch der S*ee*;
Die *A*bendn*e*bel k*a*men
Und stiegen in die Höh.
. . . .
Wir sprachen von Sturm und Schiffbruch,
Vom S*ee*mann, und wie er l*e*bt,
Und zw*i*schen H*i*mmel und W*a*sser
Und *A*ngst und Freude schwebt.

Among German poets of another rank, Brentano has written whole poems in which nearly every line has a polysyllabic assonance, as in this stanza:[26]

Aus des Bildes stillen Blicken
Schwer vom blanken Nachend wallend
Macht ein kunterbunt Gemunkel
Will es Gott, so komm ich morgens
Und sie pflückt gebücht in Züchten.

It is by no means obvious, then, that Germanic poets prefer consonant to vowel repetitions. Furthermore, since so many nations, ancient and modern, have known the charms of vowel echoes, there is need apparently to question the popular notion that in English verse "assonance is not used as deliberately and consciously as alliteration."[27]

For most great poems written since 1500 in Britain and the United States, the reverse is perhaps true: Assonance may have been more widely and more effectively employed than alliteration has been. In Shakespeare's most famous sonnets, for example,[28] internal vowel echoes come more often than do initial consonant echoes. Sonnet 73 has

Death's second self, that seals up all in rest,

often noted as an example of Shakespeare's alliteration, but the line also has [ɛ] stressed at least four times, and in *Hamlet* (1.4) line 17 seems to have the same sound five times:

This heavy-headed revel east[29] and west.

Sonnet 15 has [e] stressed four times in two lines,

Where wasteful Time debateth with Decay,
To change your day of youth to sullied night,

while in *Venus and Adonis* three lines together (496–98) have eleven [aɪ]'s, or [əɪ]'s, in important syllables, five of them in one line:

Do *I* delight to die, or life desire.

Or there is Swift's octosyllabic couplet in "The Progress of Beauty,"

> So rotting Celia stroles the Street
> When sober Folks are all abed,

in which the alliterations of *s* and *st* strike the eye but whose two vowel echoes surely are as pleasing to the ear. Or one can take a modern British poem such as Thomas Hardy's widely anthologized "Convergence of the Twain," which is notorious for its alliteration, and note that while its consonant repetitions are indeed very apparent its assonance is not only more frequent but perhaps even more effective, as these two stanzas clearly demonstrate:

> Well: while was fashioning
> This creature of cleaving wing
> The Imminent Will that stirs and urges everything
>
> Prepared a sinister mate
> For her—so gaily great—
> A Shape of Ice, for the time far and dissociate.

In these six lines there are three alliterations but there are eighteen important syllables that echo five different vowels. Of course it is true that because the English language has fewer vowels and diphthongs than it has consonants there will be more accidental assonance than accidental alliteration, but perhaps no reader of poems would wish to argue that any one of Hardy's three initial consonant echoes seems more intentional than any one of his five internal vowel repetitions. Assonance, then, is not only subtle and yet pleasing to the ear; it is a very popular sound effect with poets in spite of the fact that so little has been said about it. Even less has been written about consonance.

Consonance is the repetition of the sound of a final consonant or consonant cluster in stressed syllables near enough to each other for the echo to affect the ear. Of the three definitions of important phonic echoes this one is the most controversial, but perhaps it is the most needed. As with *alliteration* and *assonance*, *consonance* has had a variety of meanings. It has been employed for the repetition of any sound, whether vowel or consonant. Most frequently it has meant a repetition of a consonant or of "consonant patterns" anywhere in a line of poetry,[30] a definition which makes the word as vague and as unsatisfactory as "tone patterns," an expression sometimes used for a poet's vowel effects. Some prosodists even avoid the word altogether, apparently because its meaning is so uncertain.

One rather widely used definition insists that consonance "differs from alliteration by the repetition of two or more identical consonant sounds, for example, li*v*e, lea*v*e; groa*n*ed, grou*nd*,"[31] but without the vowel echo. And indeed a number of twentieth-century poets have occasionally played with this kind of double repetition. Hopkins, Wilfred Owen, and Dylan Thomas may be most notorious for its use, but they had a precedent in older poetry. Pulci's *Morgante Maggiore* (st. 23), for example, has lines like these:

La casa cosa parea bretta e brutta,
Vinta del vento; e la natta e la notte
Stilla le stelle ch'a tetto era tutta.[32]

Hopkins seldom repeated both initial and final consonants so consistently, preferring to mix his double echoes with other kinds, but there are clusters of such sounds in some of his poems, as in part of a line from "The Woodlark," "The blood-gush blade-gash." Owen opens successive lines of one poem with couplets such as *Leaves–Lives*, *Birds–Bards*, *Bees–Boys*; and in at least two poems Auden repeats both initial and final stressed consonants in place of end rhyme. One is the widely anthologized "reader to rider" poem; the other concludes the lines of the first two stanzas with *began–flush–flash–gun;* and *pass–relief–laugh–peace.*[33] So while such double repetitions occur seldom in the history of poetry, they do occur often enough that terms have been invented to describe the phenomenon, among them *bracket alliteration* and *bracket conso-nance*. Neither term is, of course, logical since in each example given the syllables both alliterate and consonate; a similar term, *consonant bracketing*, is probably better, but it refers also to double repetitions that are medial, or mixed with other, unechoed, consonants—*splice–loose*, *bream–grooms*, *intent–twist*. For many reasons, there-fore, it would seem that *consonance* is most legitimately to be applied to the echo of final consonants only, a device so popular with poets that it needs a name. And such a use of the term seems now to be growing widespread.[34]

A great many poets have known the ear appeal of conso-nance, and some have even preferred it to alliteration as being more subtle. Lucretius for example echoes the final [r] in line 229 of *De Rerum Natura* (4):

> Ce*r*nere adora*r*i licet et senti*r*e sona*r*e.

And Heine sounds final [t] in each stressed syllable of this line from *Belsatzar*:

> Und blind*l*ings reiss*t* der Mu*t* ihn for*t*,

although a fast reader might miss the second one. Even French, which fails to pronounce many final consonants, echoes others, among them [r] and [s] in this line from Boileau's *Art poétique* (2):

> Changer Narci*ss*e en fleu*r*, couvri*r* Daphné d'écor*ce*.

With final [k] Browning emphasizes the anapaestic stresses in a line of "How They Brought the Good News from Ghent to Aix":

> Rebu*ck*led the chee*k*-strap, chained sla*ck*er the bit.

And Emily Dickinson, like Dylan Thomas after her, often preferred the device to end rhyme, as in "I like to see it lap the miles," where there is no end rhyme but in which two end words of each stanza consonate—*up–step*, *peer–pare*,

while–hill, and *star–door*. And so while the intentional
echo of final stressed consonants is less common than alliteration or assonance, it is nevertheless a perennial favorite
for poets concerned with sounds.

Although each of the three sound effects—alliteration,
assonance, and consonance—is individually important to
poets, with many fine poets no one of them is necessarily
employed by itself; that is, they work together, and with
other effects, for the total achievement at which the poet
aims. Two examples will show how all three of the echoes
can come in a very short passage. The first is from T. S.
Eliot:

> She entertai*n*[s] Sir Ferdina*n*[d]
> **Kl***ein*. Who **cl**ipped the l*i*on's w*i*ngs
> And flea'*d* his rump and par'*d* his **p**aws.

Here the alliteration of [p] and of the cluster [kl] are easily
marked, but the three lines also have two assonances and
two consonances, one being the three [n]'s, the other being
two balanced [d]'s. The second example is the beautiful
final line of Dante's *Divina Commedia*, with its [m] alliteration, its [o] assonance, and its consonance of [l]:

> l'am*o*r que **m**ove il s*o*le e l'a*l*tre ste*l*le.

It is also true that the three echoes are not always easy to
segregate and discuss with total certainty. Assonance
causes most trouble because the sound of a vowel in one
century is often quite different for another century, or even
for another section of a country. As a result, what has been
said about imperfect or bad rhymes in British poetry before
1800[35] has not always been in accord with what has been
deduced from orthography and from the rhymes themselves. For example, Shakespeare, Spenser, and Dryden
pronounced *feast* and *east* to rhyme with *west* and *rest*.
And during much of the period from 1660 to 1780 *oi* in *soil*
rhymed with the *I* in *Nile*, being pronounced [əɪ], or [ʌɪ],

rather than [aɪ]; *eat*, alone and at the ends of words, was frequently pronounced something like [ɛt] and rhymed with *set*; the noun *wind* was actually pronounced to rhyme with *find*; and *o* in words like *strong*, *song*, *Cromwell* was, until at least the eighteenth century, often pronounced something like the *u*, [ʊ], in modern American or southern British *full*, while both *move* and *love*, which rhymed with *strove* and *grove* and *above* in the sixteenth and seventeenth centuries and even in the poems of Pope, Gay, and Prior, also had a vowel apparently close to that of *full*, as did *wood*, *food*, and, for many people like Spenser and Dryden and Pope, *blood*. Furthermore, even where a modern American or Englishman cannot be sure exactly how Chaucer or Shakespeare or Dryden or Pope pronounced a vowel, we can frequently agree that it was obviously pronounced one way in two or more nearby words, that some kind of echo took place then and that an echo still takes place. For example, the diphthong *ou* in Dryden's

Pr*ou*d of his p*ow*'r, and b*ou*ndless in his will (*Medal* 134)

was almost surely not pronounced as most Americans and Englishmen would say it now, just as the *ou* would be one sound for a speaker from the Piedmont section of Virginia today and another for a speaker from Texas. Nevertheless, Dryden intended a three-syllable echo and any reader of Dryden can find it. The recognition of assonance, however, can place little dependence on sight: To find it best in Dryden one must be aware of British pronunciation in the seventeenth century, just as to find it best in Dylan Thomas an American cannot trust his own vowel sounds.[36]

On the whole, alliteration is the easiest of the phonal echoes to recognize, not only because the eye often helps to pick it out but because for a given language the sound of a consonant normally changes little over a period of time or from dialect to dialect. Yet even here there is a problem traditionally encountered. Does a single consonant alliter-

ate with the same consonant at the beginning of a consonant cluster, *b* with the first sound of *br*, for example, as in
Campion's "Cherry-Ripe,"

> Her brows like bended bows do stand?

Do the *b*'s alliterate in "brighten at the blaze," from
Goldsmith's *The Traveller* (194)? Or must the consonant
clusters be identical, as in the same poem (99–100),

> But let us try these truths with closer eyes,
> And trace them through the prospect as it lies?

The normal answer has been that English poets from the
time of *Beowulf* have preferred that the whole cluster echo
if possible but that the echo of *f* in *friend* and *foe*, or of *b* in
brows and *bended*, though perhaps somewhat less pleasing, is still so effective that it is to be considered alliteration.
The most important exceptions occur with *sh*, pronounced
as one sound [š], and with certain initial clusters beginning
with *s–st*, for example. Such a cluster has nearly always
been said to alliterate only with an identical cluster, just as
sh alliterates only with *sh*. In other words, the three initial
s's do not alliterate in this line from *The Traveller* (104),

> That shades the steep, and sighs at every blast;

and in the last line of "Sweeney Among the Nightingales,"

> To stain the stiff dishonored shroud,

the *st*'s alliterate but not the *sh*.

Consonance, even as defined here, is for several reasons
more of a problem than is alliteration. Again consonant
clusters cause most trouble. There would perhaps be no
problem with this line from James Thomson's *Winter* (105),

> It boils and wheels and foams and thunders thro',

in which, although the clusters are not identical—two
being [lz] and one [mz]—the echo of [z] is so striking that

every ear should hear a three-syllable consonance. Sometimes, however, the eye and the ear will not agree in identifying the final sound in a group of consonants in stressed syllables. There may be universal agreement about the final [n] of "She entertai*n*[s] Sir Ferdina*n*[d] / Klei*n*" but perhaps some hesitation over this line from Gray's "The Descent of Odin,"

> Right against the eastern gate,

where there are probably two final *t*'s and no final *st*'s, since the *t* of *against* may not be sounded and *eastern* is perhaps broken between the *s* and the *t*. The ideal echo of a single final consonant is no doubt encountered in Gray's "moo*d*y ma*d*ness"[37] (*Eton College* 79) or in George Crabbe's *Village* (1.51),

> Where other care*s* than tho*se* the Mu*se* relates.

And the ideal echo of a final cluster may perhaps be that in William Collins's "Ode to Fear" (46–47),

> Thou who such weary lengths ha*st* pa*st*,
> Where wilt thou re*st*, mad Nymph, at la*st*,

where in the slow, weary couplet the sound of *st* ends four stressed syllables.

It has been suggested that, as with harmonious alliteration, consonance should include the echo of sounds that are closely related but not exact, among them *b,p; k,g; v,f; d,t; z,s; m,n*. But such a broad use of the term can lead to even broader uses—the inclusion of unstressed echoes, for example, a matter of some importance for twentieth-century poetry—and then to vagueness in analyses. The outstanding exception may be the case of final stressed nasal sounds that are not identical, as in Edward Young's "dim Dawn" (*Night Thoughts* 1.122), where the conjunction of *m* and *n* is undoubtedly pleasing, or in James Thomson's *Winter* (223),

The keener Tempests come: and fuming dun,

where every stressed syllable ends in a nasal sound, and all may be working together to suggest the noise of the tempest.

The universal hesitation over the question of where a strong syllable ends and a following weak one begins[37] points to two pertinent facts about consonant echoes—that alliteration and consonance are sometimes closely related and that there must be a certain number of consonant repetitions in poetry which cannot be segregated and called by one of these terms. Kenneth Burke and, especially, David Masson may be the most important—if extreme—analysts of what they have called the "musicality" of verse that derives from the recurrence of consonants, as well as of "consonant cognates," regardless of their importance or their position in the words. In an attempt to explain consonantal effects in the poetry of Coleridge not explainable by alliteration, Burke, for example, has selected and named a number of exotic kinds of phonic similarities. "Bathed by the mist," he says, has two "concealed alliterations"— *b–b–m* (including the *m* because it is a "cognate" of *b*), and *thd–th–t* (*t*, *d*, and *th* all belonging to the family of linguals and therefore acoustically alike). Other phenomena he has discovered are given such names as *consonantal acrostic*, *tonal chiasmus*, *augmentation*, *diminution*, and *collitteration*. Of these phenomena two at least seem to be of some value in explaining the beauties of poetic language. Burke's *augmentation* is found in "That slid into my soul," where the *sl* of *slid* is expanded into the *s–l* of *soul*, as in music, he says, when a theme has been established in quarter notes and then is treated in half notes. *Diminution*, the reverse of *augmentation*, occurs in "But silently, by slow degrees," where the *s–l* becomes *sl*. Both augmentation and diminution can sometimes be seen at work, consciously or unconsciously, in poems of all centuries. Burke, who disregards rhythm, stress, or syllable division, leaves the impression that he thinks vowels to be of relatively little importance to poets, while his theories about consonants are normally directed at unique combinations of sound.[38] David Masson, one of the most respected of theorists dealing with sophisticated interpretations of the sounds in poetic language, employing certain of Burke's terms and inventing others—*circumsyllabic sequence*, *chiasmatic bracketing*, *sub-alliteration*, etc.—has sometimes gone even beyond Burke in his analyses.[39] Although, unlike Burke, he spends some time with the "tonal" quality of vowels, the consonant and consonant cognate phenomena he has been most interested in, as with Burke, seem to have been used far less by poets than have the devices described here by the terms *alliteration* and *consonance*.

A less unique example of consonant recurrence that cannot be completely explained by these two terms, however, may be found in the fourth stanza of James Thomson's *Castle of Indolence*. In the nine lines of that stanza the sound [l] occurs twenty-four times, far more than in any nearby stanza, with twenty-two of the twenty-four coming in stressed syllables. Of the twenty-two, sixteen are initial or final and can be said to alliterate, or consonate, or rhyme. The other six are tucked away medially in such words as *bleat* and cannot be described as being a part of alliteration or consonance. It is possible, however, that Thomson was employing all of the soft liquid sounds to help create his pleasant rural image, which goes from *purling rills* to *sleep*, even though a few of the *l*'s participate in no echo that has a name.

But while poets like Thomson are sometimes fond of running a suggestive sound unit through a sonnet, or a stanza, or even a whole poem, the great norm is not only to vary the phonal repetitions and to deploy them for ornament but to place them in those positions of stress and prominence that permit us to call them alliteration, assonance, consonance, or rhyme. The typical use of such echoes in heavily ornamented poetry may be discovered in these first two stanzas of Sir Walter Ralegh's "The Nymph's Reply to the Shepherd":

Time drives the flocks from field to fold,
When rivers rage and rocks grow cold,
And Philomel becometh dumb;
The rest complains of cares to come.

The flowers do fade, and wanton fields
To wayward winter reckning yields.
A honey tongue, a heart of gall,
Is Fancy's spring, but sorrow's fall.

Here, in addition to the four end rhymes, which have not been marked, and the one internal rhyme (*flocks–rocks*), there are seven internal assonances and thirteen initial or final stressed[40] consonant echoes, including five three-syllable alliterations. In other words, in only eight short lines remarkable for compactness, for balance of phrases, for a variety of imagery, Ralegh has in *stressed syllables* involved over sixty vowels, consonants, or consonant clusters in assonance, alliteration, consonance, or rhyme. Furthermore, it would indeed be difficult to find other significant repetitions of phones, or phonic "cognates," in the passage, two exceptions coming in what Burke would call the *fl*, *f–l* augmentation in the first line of each stanza. Not only, then, are *assonance* and *rhyme* the key terms for vowel echoes in poetry, but the words *alliteration*, *consonance*, and *rhyme* can explain most of the intended, or noticeable, effects that poets produce with consonants.

These effects, of course, include far more than the simple ear appeal, the pleasant sound, that derives from the various kinds of repetition found in a poem such as "The Nymph's Reply." The most important of the complex uses for phonic echoes has been in the relating of sound to the "sense," the emotion, the "meaning," of the poem. Ono-

matopoeia, though often restricted to single words—
scrape, *gurgle*, *buzz*—is the popular term for such a relationship. In its broader use[41] onomatopoeia applies to a
more extended, more continuous, sound representation,
what Pope and Dr. Johnson called "representative meter,"
what Tennyson referred to as "the marriage of sense with
sound," what today is often spoken of as sound symbolism
in language, or as sound metaphor.

And today this broad meaning of onomatopoeia is being
pursued vigorously by certain students of language and
certain critics of poetry. One group, growing in size but
perhaps still extreme, quotes Rilke, Verlaine, Hopkins,
and Yeats to show that "all sounds . . . call down among us
certain disembodied powers, whose footsteps over our
hearts we call emotions,"[42] and then by tracing those
footsteps tries to reveal the disembodied powers found in
the sounds of poetry. David Masson, for example, has not
only pointed out some eighteen ways English sound patterns can be manipulated for effect but he has also, and at
length, treated what he calls the acoustic, kinaesthetic, and
lexical "sources for the evocative power of the sounds of
words."[43] Yet another approach is that of Dell H. Hymes
and James Lynch, who have analyzed "the phoneme occurrences of whole poems" or found the dominant sound in
a sonnet in order to discover how these particular phones,
these dominant vowels or consonants, contribute to the
poem's "prose and poetic statement."[44] No doubt the most
extreme exponent of universal sound symbolism has been
Maurice Grammont, whose theory of *harmonie imitative* is
that the great poets "*almost always* sought to establish a
certain rapport between the sounds of the words they were
using and the ideas they were expressing. . . . One can
depict an idea by sounds. . . . One can even translate a
visual image and an audible image."[45]

Although the success of Grammont's method has, even
according to his most hostile critics, been "tout à fait re-

marquable,"[46] one of these critics, noting that Grammont's theories of *harmonie imitative* led him to believe that all sounds are reproducible by language, voices the popular objection that in such a system almost any phone is, under one set of conditions, supposed to indicate one sound, even emotion, but that, under another set of conditions, it can be said to indicate an entirely different sound or emotion.[47] In his life of Pope, Dr. Johnson stated the complaint in another way:

> This notion of representative metre, and the desire of discovering frequent adaptations of the sound to the sense, have produced, in my opinion, many wild conceits and imaginary beauties. All that can furnish this representation are the sounds of the words considered singly, and the time in which they are pronounced. Every language has some words framed to exhibit the noises which they express, as *thump, rattle, growl, hiss*. These, however, are but few, and the poet cannot make them more, nor can they be of any use but when sound is to be mentioned. . . . Motion, however, may be in some sort exemplified; and yet it may be suspected that even in such resemblances the mind governs the ear, and the sounds are estimated by the meaning.[48]

While for many linguists and creative writers Grammont and Masson may be too "advanced," universal sound symbolism, at least in a moderate way and in spite of Dr. Johnson, has always been more or less attempted, even defended, by poets themselves, many of whom have argued that imitative "harmony" in poetry is much like imitative harmony in music.[49] Lucretius, in fact, attempted in *De Rerum Natura* the sounds of musical instruments themselves (4.546):

> Et reboat raucum regio cita barbara bombum,

and water sliding over slippery rocks (5.950):

> Lubrica proluvie larga lavere umida saxa.

Not only are there words here that, individually, are to be called onomatopoeic such as *raucum* and *bombum*, but vowel and consonant echoes that are clearly intended to emphasize the nexus of sound and sense. In the second line, for example, at least four of the words are individually onomatopoeic in Dr. Johnson's sense, but the six words have initial [l] in four stressed syllables, [u] in three, and [ɑ] in at least two—every important syllable takes part in an alliteration or an assonance or both. Thus, the strong echoes, even more than the weak repetition in -*ca*, -*ga*, and -*xa*, force the ear to hold on to key sounds in important suggestive words.

Of course, all attempts at sound symbolism are not so obvious as those of Lucretius, and certain students of linguistics and certain literary critics have in general had a difficult time convincing readers of poetry that certain sounds tend to suggest certain meanings; that there are, in fact, sound universals in every language, sometimes the same universal being found in a number of related languages; and that poets have employed and can employ sounds for effects other than those that merely please the ear. One of the points of contact made by aestheticians and students of language is that concerning the nature of rhyme. After W. K. Wimsatt, and then Wellek and Warren, took the theories of Zhirmunsky and Lanz and went beyond them to analyze the many artful uses of rhyme by Pope, students of language and literary critics alike, even the most conservative, have accepted the analyses—at least to a certain extent—and, perhaps as a consequence, have been more willing to listen to each other since. "Rhyme," Wellek and Warren say,

> is an extremely complex phenomenon. It has its mere euphonious function as a representation (or near represen-tation) of sounds. . . . But . . . Aesthetically far more im-portant is its metrical function signaling the conclusion of a

line of verse, or as the organizer . . . of stanzaic patterns. But, most importantly, rhyme has meaning and is thus deeply involved in the whole character of a work of poetry. Words are brought together by rhyme, linked up or contrasted. . . . In a brilliant paper W. K. Wimsatt has studied these effects in Pope and Byron, who aim at the shock of confronting "Queens" and "screens," "elope" and "Pope," or "mahogany" and "philogyny."[50]

Among those who are primarily students of language Roman Jakobson and Samuel R. Levin are only two who have adopted and added to the theories of Wimsatt.[51] Jakobson, for example, especially likes Wimsatt's *paranomasias* in rhymes, as when Pope makes *Tibalds* more ridiculous by rhyming the word with *ribbalds*. But Jakobson also dwells on the use of homoeoteleuton, which, strictly speaking, is not rhyme but rather the repetition of end syllables, as with *congratulations–decorations*, and emphasizes the "semantic propinquity" involved in rhyming lexical units such as *dove–love*, *light–bright*, *place–space*, *name–fame*.[52] The psychology of all this can be summed up in the statement that "the acoustic fact of rhyme stimulates a heightened awareness of the words in which the rhyme occurs"; that is to say, the rhymes can be used to emphasize serious similarities or dissimilarities, to effect ironies by association, to induce smiles or strengthen impressions, in short to affect the reader's cognition whether consciously or unconsciously.

But if by common consent a poet may achieve such results by the use of internal or end rhyme, that is by repeating the vowel and the following consonant at the ends of stressed syllables, similar results should be possible if smaller units of sound are echoed in stressed syllables, especially if the echoes—at least those called alliteration, assonance, and consonance—are and have been more popular with poets than rhyme has been. For example, while rhymes are now known to organize stanzaic patterns, emphasize terminal words, and parallel like or unlike ideas, alliteration has long been regarded as an onomatopoeic device and as a means of stressing the rhythmic peaks in a line of poetry.[53] And we now know that assonance and consonance can also do far more than merely sound pleasant to the ear or simply accentuate stresses in rhythmical units.[54] One illustration will show some possibilities. In the same couplet (*Epistle to Dr. Arbuthnot* 25–26) admired by Wimsatt and Jakobson, in which Pope rhymes his own name with *elope*,

> Poor Cornus sees his frantic wife elope,
> And curses Wit, and Poetry, and Pope,

there are two important cognitive effects achieved by *internal* acoustics. One is the vertical alliteration of [k] and consonance of [r] that make more ridiculous the cursing, horn-wearing Cornus; the other is the neat paranomasia involved in alliterating and assonating *Poetry* and *Pope*, the two phonic echoes making the man himself identical almost with the art. But single sound units have yet other possibilities, it has been claimed.

The most important of these can be considered best by starting with the term *phonestheme*, a word apparently invented by J. R. Firth in 1930 and now popularly employed to mean "a phoneme or cluster of phonemes shared by a group of words which also have in common some element of meaning or function."[55] Although most students of language seem to consider such a theory to be very tentative, a number of them do agree on the existence of phonesthemes, one kind of language universal, even though nearly every such student warns against excesses.[56] That is to say, while certain words are always onomatopoeic, a given phone, or morpheme, or combination of phones does not always force a given cognitive reaction, and so phonesthemes to be effective must be aided by lexical associations.

Most of the phonesthemes so far discovered by simple count or by psychological tests are initial or final consonants or consonant clusters in stressed syllables—those consonants, in other words, that can alliterate or consonate—although much theorizing has also been done about the effect of vowel sounds. One of the most convincing cases made for any phonestheme is that for the sound *-ash*, which can of course be involved in rhymes. By one count, of the forty-eight possible forms involving *-ash* in stressed syllables, twenty-four exist and twenty-one of these signify "'headlong,' 'hit,' or the result of hitting," as in *splash*, *bash*, *dash*, *lash*, even *cash* and *rash*.[57] Jespersen, on the other hand, makes one category of *-sh* [š] and *-ch* [č] and. believes that stressed syllables with such endings occur frequently in "anti-words," such as *hush* and *bitch*. The most acceptable theory for a possible phonestheme involving initial consonants may be that for the cluster *st-*, which surprisingly often suggests "firmness" or "arrest," not only in English but in other Germanic languages, as in *stand*, *stoop*, *stable*, *stout*, *still*, *strong*, *stone*, *statue*, even *stupid*, and many other words, but not of course in *stink* or *stroll*. Other consonant phonesthemes argued for include *gl-* for visual phenomena, *tw-* for twisting motions, *sk-* for swift movement, and *fl-* and *sl-* for movements not characterized by loud sounds. Theories, not very convincing, have also been advanced for initial [b], [f], and [w], a favorite alliterating phone with Tennyson.

More convincing are those theories that point to [s] or [z], to [n] or [m] or any nasal sound, and to [d] and [l], whether, in each case, initial or final. It has often been felt, not just by a few recent students of language, that [s] and [z] have helped indicate whistling, buzzing, singing, and other related noises, for example, the "swishing of water," one critic suggests,[58] as in Surrey's line,

Calm is the sea, the waves work le*ss* and le*ss*,

where obviously the effect of the echo of final [s] depends on the suggestion given in the early words of the line. Similarly, nasal sounds are supposed to help create any one of numerous effects—song or harmony, the blowing of wind, whining or mourning—as in Herbert's line from "Ephes. 4.30. Grieve no . . . ,"

Oh take thy lute, and tune it to a strain;

or these final lines from Milton's "At a Solemn Musick,"

O may we soon again renew that Song,
And keep in tune with Heav'n, till God ere long
To his celestial consort us unite
To live with him, and sing in endless morn of light.

As a possible phonestheme [d] has perhaps not attracted the attention it deserves, even though well known writers have always seemed to think that its sound helps accentuate the emotions that go with dread, dullness, darkness, or death. Poe, for example, who believed that even the first word must contribute to the "effect," that is, the atmosphere, began a tale of death and horror with "During the whole of a dull, dark and soundless day"; and Wilfred Owen, after establishing a sad mood, ended an "Anthem For Doomed Youth" with "And each slow dusk a drawing-down of blinds." The sound of [l] has also been of great use to poets, and in various ways, one student of semantic universals arguing that "it is particularly well fitted to produce an impression of softness,"[59] as in Keats's lines from *Endymion* (1.157–58),

Wil[d] thyme and valley-lilies whiter still
Than Leda's love, and cresses from the rill,

which, one indeed notes, have five final and three initial [l]'s, all in stressed syllables. What may be noted too is that the lines also have two assonances involving five syllables and that while the effect may be soft, the lateral consonant, the liquid [l], helps to describe pleasant sounds and sights in nature, another favorite use for the phone.

While consonants and consonant combinations have drawn more attention from advocates of sound universals in language, there are certain vowels that have also received attention—from some language specialists and apparently from many poets—as helping to increase, even stimulate, certain cognitive reactions. Avoiding the extreme theories, one can suggest possibilities in the front vowels [i], [ɪ], [ɛ], the back vowels [u] and [ʊ] and their companion [ʌ], the mid-back [o], and the diphthong [aɪ]. From Jespersen to Ullman, Masson, and Bolinger, a number of phoneticists are agreed that the vowels around [ɪ] tend to reflect lightness and smallness, as in German *licht* and English *little*, while those close to [ʊ] are said to be darker in significance. For melancholy, [o] is "natural," and not just in Poe's famous theory about "nevermore" in *The Raven*, or in the first two lines of his *Lenore*, which have six [o]'s, as in the opening words, "Ah, broken is the golden bowl!"; and not just in the sound-conscious Tennyson's song of "The Dying Swan," whose voice "With a music strange and manifold, / Flow'd forth on a carol free and bold," or better still his "Ballad of Oriana," which has nineteen [o]'s in the first fifty-six stressed syllables. Although it has often been pointed out that changes in vowel sounds through the centuries have affected the value, the quality, of phonesthemes, certain vowels seem to hold their evocative power even as they change. That seems to be true for the diphthong [aɪ], which occurs so often in words having to do with brightness, eyes, light, sight but which in Shakespeare's time had a sound something like [əɪ]. Again one must remember how often [aɪ] does not reflect light unless the lexical associations help. Perhaps the vowel phonestheme most useful and most commonly accepted by phoneticians and poets alike is the [ʌ] of American *blood*, not quite the same as the British [ʌ], which is pronounced farther back in the mouth (see n. 36). David Masson shows how Wilfred Owen's "great discovery in assonance is the short 'u' to present the sensuous and spiritual desert of war . . . the dead disillusionment of 1917–18."[60] And in a poem by Owen such as "Dulce et Decorum Est," [ʌ] does indeed dominate the sounds and help increase the feeling of ugliness and disgust, as in the lines,

> If you could hear, at every jolt, the bl*oo*d
> Come gargling from the froth-corr*u*pted l*u*ngs
> Bitten as the c*u*d
> Of vile, incurable sores on innocent t*o*ngues.

But well before Owen's discovery other poets had employed the vowel in the same way, and Jespersen had pointed out that it helped represent "dark states of mind": *dumps, sulky, grunt;* or dislike, scorn, disgust, contempt: *blunder, bump, bungle, clumsy;* or dissatisfaction: *grumble, mumble, grunt.*[61] With the practice of poets before us, then, with the experiments and statistics of certain critics and certain students of linguistics, we now know far more about rhyme and phonic echoes, about phonesthemes and other kinds of sound universals, about sound symbolism and metaphor, than Dr. Johnson ever dreamed of.

But again the warning: If we divide sound universals into two classes—words, such as *swish*, that are always onomatopoeic; and all other language sounds that are merely associated with an emotional or intellectual response—those of the second class must have cognitive, lexical reinforcement from the context and are most effective when echoed. John Crowe Ransom's famous attempt to annihilate sound symbolism is as unfair as Dr. Johnson's even more famous kick of the rock to destroy Bishop Berkeley's idealism; for when Ransom urged that the sounds in Tennyson's line, "And murmuring of innumerable bees," can accompany entirely different meanings, as in the nonsense parody, "and murdering of innumerable beeves," Ran-

som's first important word established a tone so entirely
different from that found in *murmuring* that the universal
warning about lexical support has not been obeyed. What is
becoming more and more apparent, in spite of Ransom and
Dr. Johnson, is that sound symbolism, when treated cauti-
ously and related to the poet's total effect, is an undeniable
fact and that "the uses of this principle in poetry are innumerable, nor are they . . . confined to the imitation of noises.
Sounds may also evoke light and colour, as well as states of
mind and moral qualities."[62]

To show that such claims are not unfounded, that poets
through the centuries have known or sensed much of what
scholars are now revealing as fact about sound symbolism,
one can test a short passage from Shakespeare, who has
many onomatopoeic words that can be collected from the
sonnets, plays, and narrative poems, but who—more
notably—has whole passages in which the sounds combine
to help with the total effect. One of the best such passages
may be the bat-beetle lines in *Macbeth* (3.2.40–44):

> ere the bat hath flown
> His cloister'd flight, ere to black Hecate's summons
> The shard-borne beetle with his drowsy hums
> Hath rung night's yawning peal, there shall be done
> A deed of dreadful note.

Here are the sound-plus-sense words such as *peal, rung,
hums, drowsy, yawning,* and here also are slow, hard
words—"shard-born beetle"—but, what is not always
noticed, here also are rich alliteration, assonance, and consonance. There are at least three alliterations—*b* (in four
syllables), *fl,* and *d;* there are at least three assonances—
"b*a*t"–"bl*a*ck," "cl*oi*ster'd fl*i*ght," "s*u*mmons"–"h*u*ms"
"d*o*ne"–"r*u*ng"; and there are four consonances—
"ba*t*"–"fligh*t*," "bla*ck* He*c*ate," "yaw*n*ing"–"do*ne*,"
and "dee*d*"–"drea*d*ful." These repetitions not only include the phonesthemes [n] (two final, as well as five other

final nasals), [d] (two final, four initial), and [ʌ], or [ʊ], (four times) but involve at least sixteen of perhaps twenty stressed syllables and combine with other sounds and with the rhythm to give us one of the most onomatopoeic passages in Shakespeare's plays. Onomatopoeia, "imitative harmony," representative meter, universal sound symbolism—all these, then, are terms not just for single words such as *bleat* and *suck* but for whole lines, even groups of lines, which repeat key sounds, normally the echoes being designated as alliteration, assonance, and consonance. This is the best, the most effective, use of poetic language.

For the sound of that language, the "music of the words," does take us far beyond the words themselves. It would indeed, as Roman Jakobson has said, be a gross oversimplification to consider any individual phone, syllable, word, or group of words "merely from the standpoint of sound."[63] If among these individual sounds, rhyme in the hands of a fine poet like Pope is more than an attractive noise, and if poets employ alliteration, assonance, and consonance sometimes as much as, often more than, they do rhyme, then it is important to know that these three devices can also be something more than mere recurrent figures of sound, that in fact they can have not only an acoustic appeal but also a cognitive and an emotional appeal: they can be persuasive, emphatic, functional. No group of poets has been more aware of the possibilities of these various appeals than were Dryden, Pope, and their contemporaries; but while their use of phonic echoes was highly original, most advanced, and enduringly influential, it was at the same time heavily dependent on traditions well established by 1660.

The Tradition that Dryden Was Given

"We learn that sound as well as sense persuades"—Waller.

The poets who influenced Dryden and his followers included, of course, important ancients—Homer, Lucretius, Horace, and Virgil—but by 1660 the native tradition was well established. In that tradition the lyric, narrative, dramatic, and philosophical poems of Dryden, Pope, and their peers seem to owe most to major writers such as Spenser, Shakespeare, and Milton, and to minor figures like Waller and Denham. That is true not only for such questions as subject, theme, and image but also for a study of the sounds of poetic language. By the time of Elizabeth Gascoigne was urging poets to employ "English" monosyllables rather than "foreign" polysyllables, Campion was comparing poetry with music, and all their contemporaries were adapting well-tested rhymes and verse forms or making use of rhyme, which had been popular since Lawman's *Brut*, or alliteration, which had been important with the author of *Beowulf* and the poets of the alliterative revival. But what has not been pointed out is that the Elizabethans also had inherited assonance and consonance and were employing phonal repetitions in varied ways.

Chaucer, steeped in Italian and French poetry, as well as that of his own country, and master of all the devices of rhetoric, is only the best of the older poets who handed down these repetitions and helped make them functional.[64] His alliteration has been studied; Paull F. Baum, for example, pointing out how it binds couplets together,[65] as with the three *f*'s in lines 188–89 of the *Parlement of Foules*:

That swymmen ful of smale fishes lighte,
With fynnes rede and skales sylver brighte.

But Chaucer, like other poets of his day, had an ear for

vowel echoes too, the same couplet stressing six [I]'s. And, like his contemporaries, he could use consonance, as in *Troilus and Criseyde* (4.254):

> Which that his herte twi*ste* and fa*ste* thre*ste*,

or all three kinds of phonal repetitions in one couplet of the General Prologue (279–80),

> This worthy man ful w*e*l his w*it* bis*ette*
> Ther w*i*ste no w*ight* that he was in de*tte*,

where eight of the nine stressed syllables are emphasized even more because they participate in such repetitions. Chaucer not only reinforced his rhythm with echoes; he stressed the caesura in[66]

> His hors were goode, but he was not gay,   (GP 74)

> Have ye no mannes h*e*rte, and han a b*e*rd?   (NPT 2920)

And he balanced nouns, adjectives, or verbs with vowel or consonant echoes, as in

> Lest any wight dev*y*nen or dev*y*se,   (*T&C* 3.458)

> Bitwixen *A*tthenes and *A*mazones;   (KT 880)

he tied adjectives to noun, with alliteration but especially with assonance—"browes blake," "Straunge strem," "*a*bbot *a*ble," "wh*i*stlynge w*y*nd," "n*o*ble p*o*st," "*a*ller c*a*ppe"; and he echoed the vowel or consonant in the final two stressed syllables of a line: the General Prologue has over fifty examples of terminal assonance alone—"this t*a*le p*a*ce," "it s*ee*med m*e*"—a kind of repetition that would become very popular for the end-stopped couplet after 1660. In fact, when we consider Chaucer's realistic, colloquial bent, it may be that his phonic echoes—his assonance even more than his alliteration and consonance—are far richer than one would expect, even from such an advanced craftsman. Poets like him provided the tradition that knew how to use vowel and consonant echoes for ornament, onomatopoeia, or rhetorical and structural effects, a tradition very strong by the time of Spenser, the first English poet to have an obvious direct influence on the way Dryden, Pope, Thomson and their contemporaries employed the sounds of words.

Long ago Spenser was given the title of "poet's poet" because, in great part, of his use of language.[67] In that respect *The Shepheardes Calender* and *The Faerie Queene* represent two stages in his development and two quite different traditions. In spite of his great admiration for Chaucer, a poet who depended far less than he on devices of sound, Spenser's early poems are closer to the more primitive alliterative tradition of *Sir Gawain* and, say, George Gascoigne. Although a great deal has been said about Spenser's alliteration in *The Faerie Queene*,[68] it is much heavier, startlingly heavy, in *The Shepheardes Calender*. A typical pair of lines in "June," for example, will go thus:

> The grassye ground with daintye daysies dight,
> The bramble bush, where byrds of every kinde . . . .

But while in his youthful *Shepheardes Calender* Spenser was keeping the alliterative tradition alive, he was at the same time showing that he had already discovered other kinds of echoes in the poets who were his masters. Eight lines from "June" demonstrate his early versatility:

> But friendly Faeries, met with many Graces,
> And lightfote Nymphs, can chace the lingring night
> With heydeguyes and trimly trodden traces,
> Whilst systers nyne, which dwell on Parnasse hight,
> Doe make them musick for their more delight;
> And Pan himselfe, to kisse their christall faces,
> Will Pype and daunce, when Phoebe shineth bright:
> Such pierlesse pleasures have we in these places.

Here, of about forty stressed syllables, at least thirty participate in eight different alliterations, six different assonances, and three consonances—eight of the sixteen phonic echoes being polysyllabic. Furthermore, the stanza has five adjective-noun phrases bound together with echoes, a caesural balanced assonance in the fourth line, and a complex cross sound balance of one adjective-noun with another in "lightfote Nymphs . . . lingring night." The three-syllable repetition of final [s] is not untypical, for while Spenser has relatively little consonance, he knew how to use it, as in another line from "June,"

> From other shades hath wea*nd* my wa*nd*ring my*nde*.

The only untypical fact about the stanza is that it has so much assonance, even though the early Spenser could often almost forget the consonant echoes in an ear-pleasing couplet, in "Januarye," for example, where eight syllables stress two vowels only:

> Both p*y*pe and Muse shall s*o*re the wh*i*le ab*y*e.
> So br*o*ke his *oa*ten p*y*pe, and downe did l*y*e.

In *The Shepheardes Calender* Spenser was also showing that he could often make the sounds go well with the sense, especially with feelings of melancholy. Sad "November" laments with the [d] phonestheme:

> For dea*de* is **D**ido, dea*d*, alas! and **d**rent,

and through a whole line carries the sound of *Waile* by alliterating its [w] and assonating its [e]:

> **W**a*i*le ye this **w**o*full* w*a*ste of N*a*tures warke;

while the equally sad "Januarye" in one slow couplet artfully echoes the phonesthemes in *wanne, forlorne, mourning,* and *pyning* by repeating seven final [n]'s in stressed syllables and three different internal vowels, all in addition to the expected alliteration:

Thou weake, I wanne; thou leane, I quite forlorne:
With mourning pyne I; and with pyning mourne.

Although the alliterative *Shepheardes Calender* was a model for all the better known eighteenth-century poets, the author of *The Faerie Queene*, older and far more widely influential, was not so prone to repeat vowels and consonants. When one analyst complains of a "tendency to the unnatural and artificial" [69] in the alliteration of the following lines (1.2.17),

No foote to foe. The flashing fier flies,
As from a forge,

he not only has selected a unique group of sounds from *The Faerie Queene;* [70] he has overlooked the assonance of [o] and [ǝɪ,aɪ] in the passage chosen. Examination of even a rather richly ornamented part of *The Faerie Queene* will show that the later poem, though lavish by most standards, has far fewer phonic echoes than do Spenser's pastorals. In the sixteen stanzas of *Mutabilitie* describing the four seasons and the twelve months, although the initial consonant echoes exceed the vowel echoes, only twelve are three-syllable and none involves more than three syllables, a sharp contrast with the hundreds of polysyllabic alliterations in *The Shepheardes Calender*. Typical is the fact that certain stanzas in this group, those on April and winter, are heavy with alliteration while each of certain others, on September and December, has only one in all its nine lines. Furthermore, the absence of final consonant echoes in those stanzas is also typical. Nevertheless, *Mutabilitie* does have a few fine, obviously intended, examples of consonance, as in these balanced nouns (7.52):

So many turning cranks these have, so many crookes.

One of the best of the few examples in *The Faerie Queene* occurs in an onomatopoeic line (1.1.14) with four final [l] sounds:

Most loathsom, fi*l*thie, fou*le*, and fu*ll* of vi*le* disdaine.

The Faerie Queene and, one can add, the sonnet sequence *Amoretti*—the older Spenser—are, then, as far from the alliterative tradition in one direction as they are from Chaucer in the other. In their still abundant but more varied sound effects they approach the sophistication of Shakespeare.

Chaucer let his Parson speak slightingly of the "Rum, ram, ruf" of alliteration and in *Midsummer Night's Dream* (5.1.147–48) Shakespeare let Peter Quince burlesque alliterative excesses with such lines as

> Whereat, with blade, with bloody blameful blade,
> He bravely broach'd his boiling bloody breast.

But the young Shakespeare, like the young Spenser, tended to employ many phonic echoes himself. The most alliteration-laden passage of *Lucrece* is probably this beautifully ingenious stanza with seven different images in seven lines to make one point:

> 'Tis double d*ea*th to drow*n* in k*en* of sh*o*re;
> He t*en* t*ime*s p*ine*s that p*ine*s beh*o*lding food;
> To s*ee* the salve doth m*a*ke the wound *ache* m*o*re;
> Great Gr*ie*f gr*ie*ves m*o*st at that would do it good .
> D*ee*p w*oe*s r*o*ll forward like a gentle flood,
>   Who, being stopp'd, the bounding banks o'erflows:
>   Grief dallied with no law nor limit knows.   (1114–20)

There is much alliteration here indeed—eight different examples involving over twenty stressed syllables. Nevertheless, these echoes are far from being so blatant as those in *The Shepheardes Calender*. Furthermore, this stanza is not quite typical of even the young Shakespeare. One from *Venus and Adonis* will provide another extreme, six lines of a wonderful, image-filled, Elizabethan contrast of Love and Lust, the key words providing the dominant sounds:

> Love comforteth like sunshine after rain,
> But Lust's effect is tempest after sun;
> Love's gentle spring doth always fresh remain,
> Lust's winter comes ere summer half be done
>   Love surfeits not, Lust like a glutton dies;
>   Love is all truth, Lust full of forged lies.   (798–804)

Here the vowel of *Love* and *Lust* occurs sixteen times in the six lines to go with the four [ɛ]'s in the second and third lines. Almost as effective, perhaps, may be the twelve final nasal sounds in the first four lines, where the analogies are all taken from nature. But except for the [l] of the key words and "lies," there is only one example of alliteration, the [f] of the last line. The alliterative stanza from *Lucrece*, on the other hand, has five assonances, four polysyllabic, scattered among the many alliterations.

There are other important facts to notice about the echoes in these passages. First, in the stanza from *Lucrece* there are four adjectives tied to their nouns with alliteration. Second, Shakespeare, like his contemporaries and predecessors, occasionally liked to parallel his echoes for emphasis. In the *Lucrece* stanza the nouns *law* and *limit* of the last line provide a modest example, while the chief illustration is in the frequent antitheses of *Love* and *Lust* in the *Venus* stanza. In this couplet from *Lucrece* (797–98),

> Mingling my talk with tears, my grief with groans,
> Poor wasting monuments of lasting moans,

the first line parallels the repetition of [t] with the repetition of [gr]; in the second the adjectives consonate while their nouns alliterate, all in perfect rhetorical balance. In another couplet from *Lucrece* (419–20),

> Her azure veins, her alabaster skin,
> Her coral lips, her snow-white dimpled chin,

the structurally balanced adjectives in the first line assonate the [æ]—in fact with a double echo in *alabaster*—while in the second line not only do the parallel nouns assonate but an adjective is bound to its noun with assonance. And, like Chaucer, but more often, the young Shakespeare also bound successive lines with assonance. Here, for example, in *Venus and Adonis* (365–66, 605–6) he twice echoed the [I] in five syllables of a couplet:

> This beauteous combat, wi*l*ful and unw*ill*ing,
> Show'd like two si*l*ver doves that si*t* a-bi*ll*ing.

> The warm effects which she in h*i*m finds m*i*ssing,
> She seeks to k*i*ndle with cont*i*nual k*i*ssing.

Such structural uses of vowel and consonant echoes, however, are far from being so prominent in Shakespeare's poems as they were to be in those of the Restoration and eighteenth century.

But Shakespeare's most noticeable acoustic effects are for onomatopoeia, for the more one reads Shakespeare the more masterful he appears to be in wedding sound to sense. Even in the early *Lucrece* and *Venus and Adonis* one finds that mastery. Gloom, dread, sadness—such emotions invite, even seem to create, onomatopoeia in poetry, and in the couplet quoted from *Lucrece* there are examples of how Shakespeare could emphasize these emotions with phonal repetitions—"grief with groans," "Great grief grieves." The [d], always effective for darkness, for "death's dateless night," whether alliterated or consonated, opens the stanza taken from the tragic *Lucrece:* "'Tis **d**ouble **d**eath to **d**rown." Later in the same poem the crime is said to have taken place "in the **d**rea**d**ful **dead** of **d**ark midnight."

Also melancholy, if not so jarring, is the phonestheme [o], which is most effective when employed in slow, monosyllabic phrases: just as "Great grief grieves most" is greater grief because of the hestitating stressed monosyllables, so in the next line "Deep woes roll forward" combines slow, successive stresses with the repetition of [o].

This vowel is also the dominating echo in Sonnet 30, "The sad account of fore-bemoaned moan."

Likewise Shakespeare seemed to have discovered that the diphthong [aɪ], or [əɪ], helps in creating images of fire, light, and brightness. The light could be weak but increasing, as in *Venus and Adonis* (338):

> Even as a dying coal revives with wind,

or weak and fading (*Lucrece* 1378–79),

> And dying eyes gleam forth their ashy lights,
> Like Dying coals burnt out in tedious nights.

It could be a star (*Venus and Adonis* 814–15),

> Look, how a bright star shooteth from the sky,
> So glides he in the night from Venus' eye;

or it could be flashing lightning (*Venus and Adonis* 348),

> It flash'd forth fire, as lightning from the sky.

This phonestheme is employed with great success in the popular Sonnet 18, wherein the poet compares his love to a bright summer's day when "sometime too hot the eye of heaven shines." But the pursuit of such sound-for-sense echoes is endless, especially in *Venus and Adonis*, *Lucrece*, and the sonnets.

When we turn to the greater, to the dramatic but still lyric Shakespeare, we find somewhat fewer phonal repetitions; but if we consider that here the poetry is designed to be spoken, even though still not the normal speech of men, the smaller proportion is to be expected. There are, of course, purple passages that abound in sound effects, especially in the earlier plays such as *A Midsummer Night's Dream* and *Romeo and Juliet*, for example:

> The grey-ey'd morn smiles on the frowning night,
> Chequering the eastern clouds with streaks of light,
> And flecked darkness like a drunkard reels

From for*th* **d**ay's pa*th* and T*i*tan's f*i*ery wheels:
Now, ere the su*n* advance his bur*n*ing *eye,*
The **d**ay to cheer and n*i*ght's **d**ank **d**ew to **d**ry,
I must up-fill this osier c*a*ge of ours
With b*a*leful weeds and precious-juiced flowers.
(R&J 2.3.1–8)

These rhymed couplets echo phones as much as any lines in Shakespeare's plays. Besides the nine [əɪ,aɪ]'s in stressed syllables to help with the sunshine, there are other assonances as well as alliterations—one with four syllables—and some striking consonance, notably the four [k]'s in the third line.

In the later plays only an occasional line or short passage will repeat so many single sounds, as when Macbeth says to Lady Macbeth's doctor,

My **m**i*nd* she has **m**a*t*ed and am*az*'d my *si*gh*t,*

where even the *my*'s, perhaps less heavily stressed, cooperate in the echoes, or when Hamlet's father tells him how Claudius "in the **p**or*ches* of mine ea*r* did **p**o*ur*" the poison, a line whose consonant-vowel echoes vibrated in the ears of Stephen throughout that long day in Joyce's Dublin. In general, the great tragedies of 1600 and after save such echoes for sudden or subtle effects, as in Ophelia's warning retort to Laertes' caution about Hamlet:

Do not, as some ungracious pastors do,
Show m*e* the st*ee*p and thorny way to heaven,
Whiles, like a puff'd and r*e*ckless libertine,
Hims*e*lf the **p**rimrose **p**ath of d*a*lliance treads,
And r*e*cks not his own rede.   (1.3.47–51)

Here, while using but a single phonic echo of importance, she creates three beautiful images in three lines, but then she concludes with four such echoes in two lines, rising to heights that make the words ring in the memory.

Although there are fewer sound balances in the plays

than in the early poems, the later Shakespeare continued to make his phonic repetitions fit his sense. For example, he liked unobtrusively to emphasize *sleep* by echoing that word's vowel:

> How sweet the moonlight sleeps upon this bank!
>
> (*MV* 5.1.54)
>
> After life's fitful fever he sleeps well,   (*Macb* 3.2.23)
>
> Come, my queen, take hands with me,
> And rock the ground whereon these sleepers be.
>
> (*MND* 4.1.89–90)

He could be soft and smooth with initial [s], as in *Richard II* (2.1.46),

> This precious stone set in the silver sea;

or, as with the bat-beetle lines in *Macbeth*, he could be slow and roughly sharp with monosyllables that alliterate, assonate, and consonate:

> now could I drink hot blood
> And do such bitter business as the day
> Would quake to look on.   (*Ham* 3.2.408–10)

Many such onomatopoeic passages in the plays provided Shakespeare with the opportunity to let his vowel and consonant repetitions do more than simply add color and decoration. It was this dramatic blank verse, with its many phonic echoes, that was to be the great model for Dryden, Otway, Rowe, and other dramatists to follow.

Another blank verse tradition leading into the eighteenth century, especially to Thomson, Young, and Congreve, is that of John Milton, the only important non-dramatic poet before 1720 to employ unrhymed decasyllabics. His chief incentive to use them was apparently classical and not Elizabethan—neither Homer nor Virgil had rhyme in his epic—for he called the verse of *Paradise Lost* "the English heroic line without rhyme," an expression which was not altogether redundant since Dryden at the time was writing "heroic" drama in rhymed couplets. The Miltonic line has often been analyzed,[71] and Ants Oras has done a provocative comparison of the style of *Paradise Lost* with that of *The Faerie Queene*, an analysis which has some intriguing conclusions for a study of phonic echoes.[72] One of his most important conclusions is that Milton worked at a mounting, crescendolike effect with vowel and consonant repetition.

And that seems to be true. Although Milton has been shown to have a high percentage of final consonant clusters,[73] he was not prone to echo them. And while he could often write a whole series of lines without any kind of echo, he occasionally employed heavy alliteration,

> Moping melancholy,
> And moon-struck madness,   (*PL* 11.484–85)

or heavy assonance and alliteration, as in

> The dismal Situ[w]ation waste and wild.   (*PL* 1.60)

Occasionally the sudden concentration is for onomatopoeia, as in

> Brusht with the hiss of rustling wings,   (*PL* 1.768)

which sets the mood with the sound-sense word *Brusht* and then echoes the final [s] in *hiss* and *rus[t]ling* as well as the [ʌ,ʊ] of *Brusht*, all to aid in the image of the ugly, buzzing devils in Pandemonium. Milton is perhaps even better with fire, as in the passage,

> Of fiery Darts in flaming volleys flew,
> And flying, vaulted either Host with fire,
>
>   (*PL* 6.213–14)

which not only carries the initial consonants of *fire* and *flame* in five words but—four times—has the vowel phonestheme of *fire*. Another short fire passage in *Paradise Lost* (2.594–95),

> the parching air
> Burns frore, and cold performs th'effect of fire,

used a slow tempo, four initial [f]'s, an [o] assonance, and
two consonances to give Dr. Johnson's Dick Minim cold
shivers in a hot-house (*Idler* 60).

In spite of these bursts of echoes, however, a study of
the sound effects in *Paradise Lost* shows not only that
long stretches of that poem—Satan's first speech, for example—have proportionately few phonic recurrences but
that Milton used neither alliteration nor assonance so much
as either Spenser of Shakespeare.[74] So while certain features of his heroic line were much admired and imitated in
the eighteenth century—its organlike qualities, its long
periods, its reflective, philosophical nature—and while the
octosyllabics of *L'Allegro* and *Il Penseroso* were widely
employed, Milton's internal sound effects may have had
only a limited influence in his day or later. For its rich use of
phonic echoes, then, eighteenth-century blank verse goes
rather to Shakespeare and to the heroic couplet, which has
its tradition too.

The end-stopped nature of the closed, or heroic, couplet
is only one of its characteristics.[75] Mark Van Doren, in his
often reprinted study of Dryden, points out many others,
among them

> a tendency towards polysyllables within the line, a tendency
> towards emphatic words at the ends of lines, and a frequent
> use of balance with pronounced caesura. The end-stop, and
> the modification of sentence-structure to suit the length of
> measure, made for pointedness if not for brevity, and pro-
> vided in the couplet a ratiocinative unit which served admir-
> ably as the basis for declarative or argumentative poems.
> The polysyllables made for speed and flexibility, and en-
> couraged a latinized, abstract vocabulary. The insistence
> upon important words for the closing of lines meant that the
> sense was not likely to trail off or be left hanging. And the

use of balance promoted that air of spruce finality with which every reader of Augustan verse has long been familiar.[76]

The heroic couplet, then, is noted not only for its emphasis, balance, and finality but for its variety. Furthermore, it is undoubtedly one of the most distinctive of verse forms, and in the hands of its masters it was a challenging and intricate medium. One of its chief and most challenging intricacies, neglected by Van Doren and others who have studied it, was its use of internal sound effects. But here, as with their other talents, Dryden and Pope did not achieve great artistry without models. Among their acknowledged teachers were two poets who during that period just before and after the Restoration wrote the closed couplet when it was becoming a polished form. Their names were Edmund Waller (1606–87) and Sir John Denham (1615–69), both of whom were inordinately praised by Dryden and his successors as two of the "fathers" of English poetry.[77]

For a hundred years it was fashionable to quote Waller, as the Restoration and eighteenth-century drama will show. He was "sweet." He was "smooth." "On a Girdle" and "Go Lovely Rose" are only two of his most popular short lyrics, vers de société, the forms of which he varied. But he normally wrote his longer poems in the decasyllabic couplet, for example, the topographical, reflective "On St. James's Park" and the burlesque "Battle of the Summer-Islands." Although Waller's couplet poems do not contain so many internal phonic echoes as do those of later poets, they do depend heavily for their effects on assonance and alliteration, and, as with the blank verse of Shakespeare and Milton, his echoes frequently come in clusters, as in "On St. James's Park,"

> On which reflecting in his mighty mind,
> No private passion does indulgence find,

where there are three different alliterations and two assonances, one of which carries through four vowels and binds the lines closer together.

Dryden spoke of the pleasure and profit he received from hearing and reading the *turns* of Waller and Denham.[78] By a *turn*, one scholar tells us, Dryden meant the repetition of an important word or phrase, as in

Those made not poets, but the poets those,

from Denham's "Cooper's Hill."[79] Another scholar illustrates *turn* with a play on words from Waller's "St. James's Park" which describes the coy ladies with their fishing rods who catch more than fish and so are

At once victorious with their lines and *eyes*.[80]

In one of the two turns, a chiasmus, the reverse repetition of *poets* and *those*, is a standard eighteenth-century kind of parallelism, but like his immediate followers Denham also assonated the important words. In the illustration from Waller, the balanced nouns that provide the play on words also echo a vowel sound.

Although such parallel phonic echoes were to become a feature of the couplet, with Waller they are not yet so prominent, nor are his couplets "rigidly balanced"[81] even though there are many such simple parallelisms in "St. James's Park" as

For mending Laws, and for restoring Trade,

Of rising Kingdoms and of falling States,

and such examples of chiasmus as

They bathe in Summer, and in Winter slide.

All of these lines are rhetorically balanced but none of them has an echo that reinforces the rhetoric. Waller's "sweet," "smooth" couplets then do not, in comparison with the couplets of Dryden and Pope and Goldsmith, employ so many sound effects to emphasize parallel words. Nor do they abound in internal echoes, although they do provide clusters of effective sounds, turns such as

> For composition with th'unconquer'd fish,
>
> ("Battle" 3.70)

and

> That tunes my lute, and winds the strings so high.
>
> ("Battle" 1.69)

Where Waller was called graceful, sweet, smooth, or soft, Sir John Denham was always referred to as strong, weighty, manly.[82] And while Waller was the fashionable poet, Denham's "Cooper's Hill" was the most influential of topographical, reflective poems. For 150 years no lines were better known, more often parodied, than the four (189–92) which liken the flow of the Thames to the lines of the ideal poem. Although Denham is not normally considered so fine a poet as Waller, he went beyond his friend and mentor in the varied use of vowel and consonant echoes, thereby approaching closer to the practice of the great writers of the couplet. That he consciously strove to echo phones internally can be seen by comparing the earliest edition of "Cooper's Hill" (1642) with that published in 1668, the year before he died.[83]

The final version is smooth and polished and repeats many phones in stressed syllables. But while the original also employs such sound effects, there is a great difference: Although it has almost as many consonant echoes, it has far fewer assonances. The first version, to provide the most striking evidence only, makes use of some eleven polysyllabic assonances, all of which—in spite of Denham's drastic revisions—were kept, such as this zeugma (334),

> When Kings give liberty, and Subjects love;

but the final version has eleven others,[84] among them some of the poet's best, for example, one describing the lordly stag (297):

> He straight revokes his bold resolve, and more.

Furthermore, Denham almost invariably retained his most sounding turns, including the last line of the poem, which has two assonances. Among the acoustically appealing lines added in revision are 229-30:

> This scene had some bold Greek, or British Bard,
> Beheld of old, what stories had we heard.

Because so many lines in the poem offer evidence of attempts at improvement, in sound as well as in sense, it is not surprising that Pope, another careful craftsman, praised Denham for his reworking of "Cooper's Hill."[85]

And that the young Pope studied Denham's revisions is a certainty when we look at one of those revisions. The 1642 "Cooper's Hill" has this couplet,

> And though his clearer sand no golden veynes
> Like Tagus and Pactolus streams containes,

which became in the final form a much more pleasing turn (165-66),

> Though with those streams he no resemblance hold,*
> Whose foam is Amber, and their Gravel Gold.

The original lines have a number of echoes—an alliteration, a consonance, and the repetitions of [o] and the *a* of *amber* and *Gravel;* the revised couplet has both the assonance in *amber–gravel* and the [o] stressed four times, but it also exchanges the [t] for a [g] alliteration and the nasalized final [z] for the three-syllable, even better, con-

---

*The vowel of *streams* and that of *resemblance* may have been very close to each other for Denham, as they were for his contemporary Dryden, who often rhymed *streams* with *stems* and *condemns* (see chapter 2). If so, the first line has an assonance too.

sonance of [m]. One of Pope's earliest poems, *Spring*, has
this couplet (61–62):

O'er golden sands let rich Pactolus flow,
And trees weep amber on the banks of Po.

He had taken *Pactolus* from Denham's discarded simile
and *amber* from the final version and written his own
ear-appealing lines.[86]

But Denham was able to teach later poets more about the
importance of phonic repetitions than simply to add them in
revision. Although he seemed to find little need for matching sound to sense, he employed sound balance much more
than Waller and earlier poets had done. In "Cooper's Hill"
he balanced nouns in such phrases as "shade and shelter,"
"Their feasts, their revels," "Pleasure with Praise,"
"Luxury, or Lust," or in lines like these:

When Kings give liberty, and Subjects love,   (334)

Aspiring mountain, or descending cloud.   (18)

He balanced verbs, as in line 308 completely reworked for
the later editions:

Which wanting Sea to ride, or wind to fly.

He especially liked to emphasize the caesura with assonance:

Though prodigal of life, disdains to die,   (315)

When he to boast, or to disperse his stores,   (181)

But such a Rise, as doth at once invite;   (45)

but he also stressed it with consonance, as in each of these
successive lines (222–23):

The common fate of all that's high or great
Low at his foot a spacious plain is plac't.

The second line of that couplet illustrates one of the most
characteristic of Denham's sound effects and one of the

most influential, his use of phonic echoes in the last stressed syllables of a line. This kind of terminal repetition, found as far back as Chaucer, would become a more significant characteristic of the end-stopped heroic couplet than it had been for any kind of poetic line used before 1660. In "Cooper's Hill" there are fifty-eight lines with such repetitions, almost one in every six. Again Denham preferred assonance: of the fifty-eight terminal echoes, twenty-eight are assonances, as in "s*a*ct the l*a*nd," "P*o*ets th*o*se," and "t*i*me, or f*i*re." Eighteen are alliterations, as in "*r*etir'd content" or "*d*isdains to *d*ie." But there are also eighteen with consonance—a very high proportion when we remember that in the entire poem there are twice as many initial as final consonant repetitions—among the terminal consonances being "Fa*te* to mee*t*," "pu*re* and clea*r*," and "cha*st* so ju*st*."

All students of eighteenth-century poetry would agree that Denham's poems are a landmark in the development of the heroic couplet, especially in its increasing use of balance and antithesis. One of the best evidences is to be found in "On the Earl of Strafford's Tryal and Deathe." The two versions of this poem Denham wrote twenty years apart, publishing the first in 1641, the other not until 1668. The first version has twenty lines; the second discarded the last four and replaced them with fourteen. As with "Cooper's Hill" there are various reasons for the revisions, one in each case being political. Nevertheless, the fourteen new lines are smoother, more nearly "correct" in Walsh's and Pope's sense of the word, and do have better movement and balance.[87] But the new lines also show a remarkable development in the use of acoustic effects. The last four lines have the only good turns in the earlier poem, including "Our nation's glory and our nation's hate," which was borrowed from Waller,[88] Denham changing Waller's word *crime* to *hate* in order to provide a terminal assonance. The fourteen lines that replaced the four, however, are replete with echoes, including some excellent examples of sound balance to go with rhetorical balance, among them these couplets:

> Now private pity strove with publick hate,
> Reason with rage and Eloquence with Fate:
> Now they could him, if he could them forgive;*
> He's not too guilty, but too wise to live;
> ....
> This Fate he could have scap'd, but would not lose
> Honour for Life, but rather nobly chose.

It is not just that there are many echoes here, although that is an important fact about the development of the end-stopped couplet; it is how they are made to help the cognitive content of the lines, something even more important: In the six lines quoted, an adjective is tied to its noun with alliteration, an adverb to its adjective with assonance; "Reason" and "Rage," "pity" and "hate," "rage" and "Fate" are rhetorically balanced nouns that have sound balance also—one pair alliterates, one consonates, one assonates; there are two terminal echoes; and there are three caesural sound balances. Altogether the seven added couplets have seventeen different internal echoes, most of which provide some kind of assistance to the cognitive or emotional message.

Denham's poetic equipment—his intelligence, his sensitivity, his originality, his images, his sounds—has not been of the type to raise him to any high rank in the history of literature, but his growing concern with the possibilities in consonant and vowel repetitions must be important in any history of eighteenth-century poetry, especially for those aware of the myth that with increased emphasis on balance and the caesura and with the gradual discarding of triplets after Dryden "heroic verse became very monotonous."[89] Byron had no patience with that myth, and in the

*For the [ɪ], or [ɛ], of *him* and *them*, see n. 36.

twentieth century Yvor Winters rejects it thus: "What, then, makes the couplet so flexible? The answer can be given briefly: its seeming inflexibility."[90] In *An Essay on Criticism* (86–87) Pope described the best poetry of his day with a wonderful image of the fiery yet controlled horse:

> The winged courser, like a generous horse,
> Shows most true mettle when you check his course.

But Pope was also giving us words to describe the straining beauties inherent in the best of closed couplets, which he knew were not monotonous; for after such teachers as Shakespeare, Spenser, Waller, and Denham,

> Dryden taught to join
> The varying verse, the full, resounding line,
> The long majestic March, and Energy divine.
>
> (*To Augustus* 267–69)

In the hands of its masters, heroic verse was varied. The caesura could shift, the trochee, spondee, and pyrrhic could be substituted for the iamb, a dozen kinds of parallelism could be deployed, sound could fit sense subtly, Anglo-Saxon could balance Latin vocabularies, or the time could be speeded up with tumbling polysyllables or slowed down with harsh initial or final consonants, with monosyllables, even with marks of punctuation. Of all the ways the Restoration and eighteenth century had of varying their verse, no one was more important than the calculated use of vowel and consonant echoes; and after 1660 such echoes affected all the other artifices the poets had for handling their tension-packed, mettlesome Pegasus.

2

John Dryden's
Heavenly Harmony

"Poetry requires ornament"—Dryden[1]

Part of the critical neglect of Dryden's luxuriant acoustic effects can be attributed, as with other poets, to his own failure to discuss them. Yet he probably said more about the sounds of poetry in general than had any well-known poet before him. It was, in fact, one of his favorite subjects.[2] After invention and variety of thought, he said early in his career, a poet's third "happiness" is "elocution, or the art of clothing and adorning that thought so found and varied, in apt, significant, and sounding words."[3] Late in his career he listed the artist's three chief requirements as *invention*, *design*, and *expression, expression* being "that in a poem which colouring is in a picture . . . that which charms the reader, and beautifies the design."[4] But while he always put this coloring last and with Horace constantly attacked *nugaeque canorae*, "tuneful trifles," Dryden believed the beauty of language to be the first poetic beauty to "arise and strike the sight."[5]

For this ear appeal of poetry he apparently coined a term which became a favorite in the eighteenth century, *harmony of numbers*. To him, to Pope, and to Johnson *numbers* meant the rhythm of the line. Although Dryden wrote songs in trochaic, anapaestic, even dactylic meter, for heroic poetry the *numbers* had to be iambic feet or, as he preferred it, ten syllables,[6] for he over and over emphasized the importance of irregularity in time and stress and once, at least, pointed out with apparent pride that he had "not everywhere observed the equality of numbers" in

his own verse because, he said, "I would not have my sense
a slave to syllables."[7] But *harmony of numbers* meant
more than *rhythmus:* it meant "musical numbers."[8] It
included everything having to do with the artful collocation
of ear appealing words—with slow or fast movement, with
the proper choice of monosyllables, polysyllables, harsh
words, or soft words, with variety of sound in every way:
Ovid, he complained, in spite of much "sweetness" has
"little variety of numbers and sound."[9] *Harmony of numbers* also meant, as with Pope, "elegant turns on the words,
which render the numbers extremely sweet and pleasing."[10] It meant, finally, as a critic of Hopkins saw,[11] all
those "textural qualities" which contribute to Dryden's
elocution, all "those phonal devices like alliteration, assonance, consonantal patterns and vocalic scales, by means
of which subsidiary rhythms are set up within the larger
metrical structure and the semantic rhythm is often considerably strengthened."

For learning how to achieve harmony of numbers, Dryden recommended several masters and acknowledged his
own debts. Early in his career Shakespeare had influenced
his style, as is evident from a reading of *All for Love* (1677)
as well as from Dryden's admission in the preface to that
play. But for "sweetness" in his native language, the older
Dryden spoke often of Spenser, whose turns were the best
in British verse, even better than those of Waller and Denham, because he had studied Virgil.[12] It was Virgil, then,
who for Dryden's entire career was the greatest master of
sound in language. His "chief talent . . . was propriety of
thoughts and ornament of words"; his expression, "his
colouring, was incomparably" better even than Homer's;
and he had an "almost inexhaustible" stock of "figurative,
elegant, and sounding words." This was Virgil's "most
eminent" grace, and it is for this quality that from *Annus
Mirabilis* (1667) to the end of his life Dryden insisted
proudly, "I have always endeavoured to copy him."[13]

That Dryden succeeded in making his "numbers" attractive to the ear is attested not only by the judgment of his eighteenth-century admirers but by the opinions of poets and critics who have written after the Victorian bias against "neoclassicism" has been almost laid to rest. Dr. Johnson followed Pope in esteeming Dryden's "flowing and sonorous words," his variety in pauses and cadence, his smooth meter.[14] Perhaps Johnson's most striking opinion about him—at least for the twentieth century—is this: "From his prose, however, Dryden derives only his accidental and secondary praise; the veneration with which his name is pronounced by every cultivator of English literature, is paid to him as he refined the language, improved the sentiments, and tuned the numbers of English poetry."[15] Among twentieth-century admirers of Dryden's well-tuned numbers, perhaps the best known are W. H. Auden and T. S. Eliot,[16] but one who stands out is another poet-critic, Mark Van Doren. Not only has he written the study of Dryden most often reprinted but in his autobiography he admits, in as strong terms as Dryden used for Virgil, that he "would never forget" the feeling Dryden gave him for "melodic structure": "And since I had come to admire his music, that music was to be the chief determining influence upon the poems I myself would write. . . . Whenever I have revised a poem I have done so with sound in mind and the movement of sound. I have made statements, as Dryden did, but also I have endeavored to make music . . . music must be there and must be heard."[17] The opinions of poets from Pope to Van Doren are important evidence that Dryden's "numbers" are "harmonious," but those opinions can only lead us to the best evidence—Dryden's verse itself. Certain of his acoustic qualities have been pointed out, but almost nothing has been said about the phonic echoes[18] which he employed as no one before him had ever used them. In the first place, because he knew that "poetry requires ornament,"[19] by far his most important use for sound effects was to provide plentiful and varied phonic echoes simply to please the ear. Of these echoes his alliteration has been most noticed.

The eighteenth-century prosodists said little about alliteration and that little was usually disparaging.[20] The most conservative of them, Edward Bysshe, for example, even attacked Dryden's alliteration as excessive. And indeed there are so many of his lines which echo stressed initial consonants that, when taken out of context, they make him seem close to poets like Gascoigne and the Spenser of the *Shephearde's Calender*. Dryden actually has hundreds of lines with three-syllable alliteration, every single consonant sound being represented from [b] and [d] to [t] and [w], as in these lines from the *Georgics:*[21]

> Then burs and brambles, an unbidden crew, (1.227)
>
> Some, when the kids their dams too deeply drain, (3.610)
>
> From thence return, attended with my train, (3.37)
>
> Who, mixing wicked weeds with words impure. (2.179)

Furthermore, many consonant clusters are to be found alliterating in three syllables; for example, the third *Georgic* has two lines with three [gr]'s each:

> Is joyless of the grove, and spurns the growing grass,
> (336)
>
> On greensward ground—a cool and grateful taste. (507)

If to these many different three-syllable alliterations we add echoes of clusters, such as [pl] and [fl] in line 4 of the third *Georgic*, we find more than thirty different consonants and consonant clusters alliterating in his poetry:

> Arcadia's flow'ry plains, and pleasing floods.

Occasionally he has four-syllable alliteration:

> And sees the secret source of subterranean floods.
> (*Georg* 4.522)

A father's right, and fear of future fame.   (*Ab&Ac* 420)

And very often he has two different alliterations in one line:

Let gentle George in triumph tread the stage, (*MacF* 151)

Pursues the sun in summer, brisk and bold.   (*H&P* 1723)

Although such double and polysyllabic consonant echoes
are indeed noticeable, especially when removed from their
proper surroundings, Dryden worked at keeping them
muted and well spaced. Furthermore, by far most of his
alliteration is of two syllables only, varied and subtle, for he
believed with Horace, Boileau, and Pope that "it is the
greatest perfection of art to keep itself undiscovered."[22]
The chief way he found of muting and varying his alliteration was to mix it with assonance.

Although he had no name for the device, at least twice
Dryden came close to discussing assonance.[23] In the preface to one of his operas, *Albion and Albanius* (1685), while
offering a kind of apology for having to use English he
became almost ecstatic about the quantity of vowels in
Italian that made it the "softest, sweetest, the most harmonious" of all languages ancient or modern. A decade
later, after having translated Virgil, he decided that Italian,
in fact, had a "redundancy of vowels"and was too soft.
Latin, on the other hand, having the "vowels and consonants . . . mixed in proportion to each other," was the most
nearly perfect language for the ear-appealing poet. Then,
after lamenting the disproportionate number of consonants
in his own language, he advised the English poet "to manage his few vowels to the best advantage, that they may go
the farther. He must also know the nature of the vowels,
which are more sonorous and which more soft and sweet."
And Dryden did manage his vowels in an infinite variety of
acoustical ways.

As with his alliteration he has hundreds of lines that
stress the same vowel three times, among them,

[o]   Drawn from the moldy rolls of Noah's ark,
                                        (*Ab&Ac* 302)

[e]   Or taste, or flavor, of the Lesbian grape,
                                        (*Georg* 2.129)

[æ]   Brought back his galley shatter'd with the shock,
                                        (*Aeneis* 5.356)

[aʊ] The wary plowman, on the mountain's brow,
                                        (*Georg* 1.159)

[ɪ]   She half commits, who sins but in her will,
                                        (*H&P* 340)

[ʊ,ʌ] With thirty sucking young encompass'd round.
                                        (*Aeneis* 3.503)

Perhaps the diphthong [aɪ], or [əɪ], was Dryden's favorite for polysyllabic vowel echoes, as in lines 616–17 of the first *Georgic* where it is found in six stressed syllables:

> And a pure heav'n resigns to quiet night,
> No rising winds or falling storms are nigh.

He has an astounding number of lines with two different assonances:

[ɛ], [e]   We fled amaz'd; their destin'd way they take,
                                        (*Aeneis* 2.280)

[ɛ], [o]   Expell'd and exil'd, left the Trojan shore.
                                        (*Aeneis* 1.3)

And he even has dozens that stress one vowel four times, for example,

[ɛ]   Which every sect will wrest a several way,
                                        (*Rel L* 309)

[e]   The various labors of that fatal day. (*Aeneis* 12.726)

Such variety and copiousness indicate how important Dryden believed assonance to be as an "ornament" to poetry.

Finally, more than any of his predecessors Dryden was

aware of the possibilities of consonance. With him it could often be polysyllabic:

[l]   Empty the woo*ll*y rock, and fi*ll* the ree*l*, (*Georg* 4.493)

[t]   The traitor heard, and fel*t* the poin*t* within his hear*t*.
(*Aeneis* 11.1252)

[p]   And, as young stri*p*lings whi*p* the to*p* for sport,
(*Aeneis* 7.528)

[n]   Sere*n*ely sho*n*e the stars, the moo*n* was bright.
(*Aeneis* 7.10)

Or he could echo two different final consonants or consonant clusters in one line:

A poi*n*ted fli*n*ty ro*ck*, all bare and bla*ck*.   (*Aeneis* 8.307)

And because he has so much alliteration also, a number of Dryden's consonances are combined with initial echoes to produce "bracketing," as with *words–weeds*, *Bear–boar*, *pass–peaceful*, *gaudy–giddy*, *ordain–drown*, *hooded–head*, *bays–boughs*, *sacred–succor*. After Dryden and at least until Emily Dickinson, Pope was the only first-rate poet to use so much consonance of all kinds.

No poet is better evidence than Dryden, however, that it is most artificial to select lines in which only alliteration, assonance, or consonance is to be found. As with other poets, the three effects combine to help create the desired, the necessary, pleasing "harmony." In this striking line from *Absalom and Achitophel*, for example,

And *p*o*p*ularly *p*r*o*secu*te* the Pl*ot*,   (490)

although the alliteration is most noticeable to many readers because the eye catches the initial [p] so quickly, the same three syllables that contain the [p] also have a vowel close to that of modern American "bought"; and, in addition, the last two heavy syllables have the [t] consonance. And in these two beautiful lines (21–22) from the second *Georgic*,

Hence rise the bran*ch*ing bee*ch* and v*o*cal *oak*,
Where J*o*ve of *o*ld ora*c*ulously sp*oke*,

not only are there the alliteration of [b] and the five stressed [o]'s, but there are two very effective consonances, one of [k],[24] the other of [č].

Such artful "managing" of consonants and vowels did not come without effort. Dr. Johnson said that "Dryden very early formed his versification."[25] But while he may very early have been smoother than, say, Donne, which is perhaps what Johnson meant, Dryden formed his style only after years of training and experimenting. He did, in fact, have three styles for the heroic couplet: that of the 1660s and 1670s, the period of the rhymed heroic plays and his other dramas; that of the satirical, religious, and argumentative poems, the middle period; and that of the great translations, the final period. If we compare the poems of any one era with those of the other two, a signal difference is that Dryden did not always employ his acoustic effects with the same profusion nor deploy them for the same ends.

The earliest verse shows that he was not yet conscious of the many ways poets have of pleasing the ear and fitting sound to sense. It is hardly fair to speak of his juvenile "Upon the Death of Lord Hastings" (1650), which has perhaps no intended internal phonic echo in all 108 lines; but it is quite fair to analyze the much more mature and ambitious *Astrea Redux* (1660), which has about one alliteration and one assonance to every four-line stanza, with so few examples of consonance that one would assume Dryden had not yet discovered its possibilities as a poetic device. During the next two decades he was writing his plays and learning much. These plays, whether rhymed heroic or blank verse, have songs, purple passages, rhetorical bursts of passion, long verse arguments—all of which challenged the poet to compose pleasing phonic echoes and to adapt those echoes to his meanings and his emotions. As a result this period is significant in the development of Dryden as a poet learning to keep "sound in mind."

The Conquest of Granada (1670), surely Dryden's most anthologized and most maligned heroic drama, is splendid evidence that the young poet was attempting to manage both consonants and vowels. Alliteration one would no doubt expect from any good poet in his late thirties,

> Betwixt a private person and a prince,
>> (*Conq.*, Pt. I 2.1.117)

although one might not expect it so neatly arranged, either there or in

> Discord the day, and death does rule the night. (Pt. I 3.1.250)

But the profuse, yet unobtrusive, assonance in the *Conquest* may be surprising:

> Her voice is like a siren's of the land;
> And bloody hearts lie panting in her hand,   (Pt. I 3.1.72–73)

especially when it is combined with other echoes or balanced so well:

> We take the profit, and pay them with praise. (Pt. I 2.1.274)

And there is enough consonance in *The Conquest* to make one think that before he was forty Dryden's ear was beginning to hear that echo too, as these successive lines may indicate:

> Did your disdain exten[d] to all mankin[d].
> But give me leave to grieve, and to complain.
>> (Pt. I 2.1.88–89)

The songs in *The Conquest*, as well as in his other plays, employ vowel and consonant echoes especially to emphasize the accented syllables and bind together the lines of an iambic couplet:

> By nature and by love, this lonely shade*
> Was for revenge of suff'ring lovers made;
>
> (Pt. 1 3.1.214–15)

even in anapaestic lines they make the stresses more noticeable:

> Alas! I discover too much of my love,
> ....
> She makes me each day a new martyrdom prove.
>
> (Pt. 1 4.2.143, 145)

Written seven years later than *The Conquest of Granada*, Dryden's *All for Love* (1677) can be compared with its model in blank verse style, *Antony and Cleopatra*, and one will discover that Dryden was by that time consistently employing even more phonic echoes than Shakespeare had used. Enobarbus's purple passage describing the siren of the Nile (2.196ff.), and beginning "The barge she sat in like a burnish'd throne / Burn'd on the water," has at least one such echo to every two of its twenty-eight lines; in Dryden the description is Antony's and has even more in the twenty lines beginning, "Her galley down the silver Cydnus rowed." And throughout Dryden's greatest play he employed a wealth of consonant and vowel echoes, among the many these:

> My uncombed locks, matted like mistletoe,
> Hang o'er my hoary face; a murm'ring brook
> Runs at my foot. (1.1.238–40)

> He joins not in your joys, nor minds your triumphs;
> But, with contracted brows, looks frowning on. (3.1.30–31)

> So would I feed a while my famished eyes
> Before we part; for I have far to go. (4.1.214–15)

With Shakespeare, Spenser, and especially Virgil as his

---

* For the probable assonance of [ʊ,ʌ] in *love* and *lonely*, see chapter 1, n. 36.

teachers, then, and with thousands of couplets and blank verse lines behind him, by the time he reached his second period and wrote *Mac Flecknoe* (1678?), Dryden had become a careful craftsman. Not only had he instructed himself in such matters as cadence, the caesura, and monosyllabic lines; along the way he had learned about consonance, and henceforth he was to average at least one assonance and one alliteration to three lines of verse.

Even in his later poems, however, there are short passages in which Dryden did not choose to play these three instruments very loudly, but at other times they come through with great force. Especially are they to be heard at the beginning or end of a poem, in descriptions of nature, a battle, or a person, in the more onomatopoeic passages, or in some other key lines. Such a practice conformed to his theory that "the most beautiful parts of the picture and the poem must be the most finished, the colours and words the most chosen."[26] The first ten couplets of *Absalom and Achitophel* (1681), for example, without counting the rhymes, have at least thirty-five phonic repetitions, some polysyllabic, the opening lines being typical:

> In pious times, ere priestcraft did begin,
> Before Polygamy was made a sin,
> When man on many multiplied his kind.

And in a particularly damning part of the famous sketch of Achitophel there are more than two striking internal echoes per line (173–83), including

> In friendship false, implacable in hate;
> Resolv'd to ruin or to rule the State.

> With public zeal to cancel private crimes.
> How safe is treason, and how sacred ill.

This heavy dependence on acoustic effects is typical not only of *Absalom and Achitophel* but of all the argumentative satirical poems of the middle period. They are an even more prominent feature of the final period, represented best by the translation of Virgil's works.

Dryden believed that the first *Georgic* was the most "sublime" of all the poems by Virgil, and, he added with pride, "if ever I have copied his majestic style, 'tis here."[27] That translation, truly one of his most pleasing to the ear, yet hardly more so than his *Aeneis*, can be compared with *Annus Mirabilis* to see how very much the later Dryden worked with phonic echoes. His fourth *Georgic*, on bee culture, he modestly pretended to be less successful than the translation of his young friend Addison—"After his *Bees*, my latter swarm is scarcely worth the hiving."[28] In 170 lines selected at random[29] from his "swarm" and carefully analyzed, there are to be found some 80 assonances, almost as many alliterations, and about half that number of consonances, including such clearly intended ones as "ca*st* of sca*tt*er'd du*st*," "drea*d*ful . . . dea*d*ly," "cla*mm*y gu*m*," and "li*q*uid ne*c*tar." The average is more than one internal phonic echo to a line. On the other hand, while 170 of the most pleasing lines in the early *Annus Mirabilis*, the description of the sea battle with the Dutch,[30] will yield many vowel and consonant echoes, it still has far fewer than any late poem—some 45 assonances, slightly more alliterations, and perhaps 15 consonances, none very effective.

Furthermore, in Dryden's mature style internal vowel repetitions nearly always occur more often than either initial or final consonant echoes. Extreme examples of proportionately heavy assonance can be found in the first 100 lines of *The Medal*, which have 40 stressed vowel echoes to go with 25 alliterations. On the other hand, there is one remarkable exception: The poem which in old age the poet addressed to his cousin John Driden (1700), undoubtedly his most echo-laden complete work, has perhaps 75 assonances in the 209 lines—9 of 3 syllables—but it has over 100 alliterations—also 9 of which are 3 syllables. The more he practiced poetry, then, the more Dryden practiced his preachment that "poetry should have ornament."

Much of the time, however, he went beyond mere decoration, important as that was to him, and employed his sound devices either to emphasize the cognitive content of his poems or for onomatopoeia. In the epigrammatic style of his middle period—that of his satires and religious arguments—he was scrupulously careful to parallel ideas, words, phrases, whole lines, even whole sections; and in these poems he was just as careful to make his sounds aid his rhetorical balance. No poet before him, from Chaucer to Denham, argued so well or so much in verse,[31] and no poet before him could so subtly relate sound to argument. There are many ways he had of doing it.

First, he related sound to argument with parallel words. When he placed two important nouns in a line, as he often did, one just before the caesura, the other at the end of the line, he liked to select nouns that contained the same initial, medial, or final sound. Here are lines where the nouns alliterate:

> Of Ahaz' dial, and of Joshua's day,　　　(*H&P* 1832)
>
> Are burthens for a camel, not a king;　　　(*Ab&Ac* 952)

here they assonate:

> For who would read thy life that reads thy rhymes?
> 　　　　　　　　　　　　　　　(*Ab&Ac*, pt. 2 505)
>
> As fittest for discourse, and nearest prose;　　(*Rel L* 454)

here they consonate:

> Of truth in dreams, from melancholy fumes,　(*H&P* 1806)
>
> Th' immortal part assum'd immortal state.　　(*H&P* 12)

The parallel stressed syllables, of course, do not always come in the most strategic spots in the line, and sometimes they echo more than one sound:

> Is well to chancels and to chimneys known, (*H&P* 1725)
> The laws of nations and of nature too.   (*H&P* 244)

If the balanced nouns do not repeat sounds, their adjectives may:

> How safe is treason, and how sacred ill,   (*Ab&Ac* 182)
> But scatter'd limbs of mangl'd poets lay.   (*MacF* 99)

Or the adjectives as well as the nouns may echo one or more sounds:

> Whose dawning day in every distant age,   (*Ab&Ac* 236)
> The people's rage, the persecuting State,   (*H&P* 1940)
> Jotham of piercing wit, and pregnant thought. (*Ab&Ac* 882)

The important parallel words are very often verbs:

> We loath our manna, and we long for quails, (*Medal* 131)
> Or canst thou lower dive, or higher climb?   (*Rel L* 77)
> Foment the war, but not support the king.   (*Ab&Ac* 284)

Or they may be verbals:

> Resolv'd to ruin or to rule the state,   (*Ab&Ac* 174)
> Railing and praising were his usual themes, (*Ab&Ac* 555)
> To kill the father and recall the son.   (*Medal* 100)

Or the verbals as well as their objects can balance sounds:

> To please the fools, and puzzle all the wise. (*Ab&Ac* 115)

Or, for an extreme example, in a line where Dryden could not stifle his urge to pun, four words beginning with [f] provide two puns, one pun balancing another, each alliterating and assonating, and the words of one pun cross consonating with the words of the other:

> Fierce to her foes, yet fears her force to try. (*H&P* 452)

Another type of auditory emphasis, this one traditional, is found in Dryden's many adjective-noun combinations. In *Mac Flecknoe* we find "**false f**riends," "**father F**lecknoe," "**famish'd Ph**aleg," and "**penny p**amphlet"—all alliterations at least; in *Religio Laici*, "Th' Egyptian B*i*shop," "Un*i*ve*r*sal ch*u*rch," "*s*av*i*ng f*ai*th," "*e*v*e*ry s*e*ct," "th' or*i*ginal scr*i*pture," "M*a*ker's f*a*ce," "*i*gnorance inv*i*ncible," and "trad*i*tion wr*i*tten"—all assonances; and in *Absalom and Achitophel*, "dou*bt*ful ti*t*le," "ge*n*eral gai*n*," "exte*nd*ed wa*nd*," and "o*d*ious ai*d*"—all consonances. Although other types of sound emphasis are more typically to be associated with his argumentative and satiric verse, this one was Dryden's favorite throughout his career.[32] It can, in fact, often be found twice in one of his lines, as here in the *Aeneis* (1.883) where each of two noun-epithet groups assonates:

The Gr*e*cian ch*i*efs, and your ill*u*strious bl*oo*d;

or in these two successive lines from the same poem (12.265–66) where each of three such combinations alliterates:

And thus with **p**ious **p**ray'rs the gods ador'd:
"All-**s**eeing **s**un, and thou, Ausonion soil. . . ."

Related to this acoustical wedding of adjective and noun are two other kinds of emphasis. One joins adverb to verb with an echo: "sere*ne*ly sho*ne*" and "**str**ongly they **str**ike" (*Aeneis* 7.10; *Georgics* 4.254). The other creates an adverb or adjective by joining "like" to a noun that echoes a sound in "like": "v*i*per-l*i*ke" (*Ab&Ac* 1013), "leech-like," and "Cyclop-l*i*ke" (*Medal* 149, 227). Dryden may have noticed this kind of word creating in Shakespeare, whose ghost in *Hamlet* describes Claudius thus:

Most lazar-l*i*ke, with v*i*le and loathsome crust.   (1.5.72)

Far more than Chaucer, even more than Denham, Dryden repeated stressed phones at the ends of lines. In fact, he employed this kind of terminal emphasis so much that he made it standard in the eighteenth century. Not infrequently the same kind of echo, even of a final consonant, occurs in each line of one of his couplets:

> And, by the same blind benefi*t* of fa*te*
> The Devil and the Jebusi*te* did ha*te*.   (*Ab&Ac* 537–38)

These terminal echoes are just as numerous in Dryden's last, more lyrical, poems as in the political or religious poems of the middle period, where such emphases might be thought of as being especially effective. Here in the *Aeneis* each of the rhyming words of a couplet repeats the vowel of the preceding accented syllable:

> He, who the scepter of all *A*sia sw*ay*'d,
> Whom monarchs like domestic sl*a*ves ob*ey*'d. (2.760–61)

And often his repetitions involve the last three important syllables:

> Nor southward to the rainy regions run,   (*Georg* 3.437)

> Within their walls the Tr*o*jan h*o*st incl*o*se, (*Aeneis* 10.179)

> But since like slaves his be*d* they di*d* ascen*d*,
> No true succession coul*d* their see*d* atten*d*. (*Ab&Ac* 15–16)

If the rhyming words of the heroic couplet are so important as by universal agreement they are,[33] their importance could be emphasized even more by such terminal sound effects. And, of course, these terminal echoes can go with numerous other functional sound effects:

> Then l*et* him mark the sheep, or wh*et* the shining share.
>   (*Georg* 1.354)

Here, besides the terminal alliteration, there are the balanced verb-verbal rhymes of *let–whet* and the caesural alliteration of *sheep–share*, altogether four functional phonic echoes in one line.

One can hardly deny the effectiveness of Dryden's use of sounds as an aid to his intellectual message. The device may be employed to support an argument, as when in *The Hind and the Panther* (899) he explains of the early apostles,

> To spread their faith, they spread their labors too.

Here *faith* and *labors* are balanced by means of rhetoric (each is an object), by position in the line, and by assonance. Or, in a century that knew all the devices of classical rhetoric, Dryden could manipulate his sounds to emphasize the key words in a rhetorical device. Most of the time—in fact, hundreds of times with Dryden—the device was some sort of simple parison, as in the *faith–labors* line, or as in each line of this couplet from the translation of Lucretius's *De Rerum Natura* (184–85),

> All filth without, and all a fire within,
> Tir'd with the toil, unsated with the sin.

In the first line the alliteration of *filth* and *fire* stresses a perfect parison; but the second line has a more nearly unique kind of parallelism—the adjective–prepositional object combination *tir'd–toil* echoes both the vowel sound and the initial [t] while the balancing combination *unsated–sin* echoes the initial [s], the echo in the first part of the line and the echo in the second part balancing as neatly as the two structurally parallel units.

Less popular than parison, but still more popular in Dryden's and Pope's day than in any other, were zeugma and chiasmus. The most nearly perfect use of sound in one of Dryden's zeugmas can be illustrated by this line from "Anne Killegrew" (70) where the two subjects assonate:

> Her wit was more than man, her innocence a child!

Examples of balanced sounds in chiasmus are more frequent in Dryden and probably more pleasing, as in this line,
where the two important verbs consonate:

> They writ but seldom, but they daily taught. (*H&P* 915)

Both the second and the third lines of *The Hind and the
Panther* employ chiasmus, and each has some kind of
sound balance also:

> Fed on the lawns, and in the forest rang'd;
> Without unspotted, innocent within.

In the first line the objects of the prepositions assonate; in
the second, each of the balanced, but reversed, adverb-
adjective pairs consonates while one pair also echoes the
stressed vowel.

Such balancing of sound effects to reinforce the argument is most noticeable in Dryden's satiric verse. There the
antithetical juxtaposition of the noble and the ignoble, a
phenomenon inherent in the mock-heroic style, gave him
many opportunities to employ sound echoes to emphasize
his ironies. In *Absalom and Achitophel*, for example, more
than once the then Anglican poet placed *devil* in the same
line as *Jebusites*—his name for the Roman Catholics—the
ironic relationship being strengthened by the assonance of
[ɛ].* In Part 2 of the same poem he selected the name
Hebron for Scotland partly because it both alliterates and
assonates with *hell*, as in this couplet (352–53) where a son
of Hebron is as bad as a son of hell:

> Let Hebron, nay, let hell produce a man
> So made for mischief as Ben-Jochanan.

A still more common type of irony, this an antithesis, is
illustrated by line 342 from *Absalom and Achitophel*,

---

*Or is it [ɪ]? See chapter 1, n. 36, for the closeness of [ɪ] and [ɛ] in the
seventeenth century, according, for example, to both Wyld and
Kökeritz. *Devil* often rhymed with *civil*.

But what was right in them were crime in me,

the antithetical words being chosen for their assonance. No doubt Dryden's favorite ironic juxtapositions, as with other satirists, were *heaven* and *hell* and *friends* and *foes*. But he had ways of keeping these images from being trite, as he did in line 466 of *Absalom and Achitophel* where the sharp antithesis of *friends* and *foes* is stressed by two phonic repetitions but where each noun is accompanied by an adjective that is chosen not only because it is ironic but because it both assonates and alliterates with the other adjective:

To plots, from seeming friends, and secret foes.

The effect of these acoustic parallels must be related to, surely as important as, the effect of such ironic rhymes as *decay–obey, dispute–absolute, pretense–sense*, all in *Mac Flecknoe*. Although Swift, Gay, Garth, Thomson, Young, Dr. Johnson, and other eighteenth-century writers have a wealth of phonic echoes, Dryden and Pope were the only important poets of their period to force these echoes so frequently to aid in balance and thereby achieve even greater emphasis in argument and satire.

Both the aesthetic effects of managing sounds simply for sound's sake and the intellectual effect of managing them for emphasis and parallelism are closely related to the third of the ways in which Dryden manipulated his vowel and consonant echoes, that is, for extending onomatopoeia, for sound symbolism. Early in life he had noted that in Virgil's verse "the very sound of his words have often somewhat that is connatural to the subject,"[34] and no poet tried harder to follow his master in that respect than Dryden did. One can, of course, find many striking examples of onomatopoeia in his religious and satiric poems, but the great translations of his later career—his Lucretius, his Ovid, his Theocritus, and especially his Virgil—provided him more opportunities to display his virtuosity not only in selecting a single word whose sound might suggest its meaning but, more important, in arranging sequences of words in which a number of sounds together help evoke a mood or create an emotion.

Dryden was able to obtain such results with each of the three devices being considered. With initial [k] he could produce the harsh noise of battle, as in

> To run where clashing arms and clamor calls,(*Aeneis* 2.455)

or in the couplet

> New clamors and new clangors now arise,
> The sound of trumpets mix'd with fighting cries,
>
> (*Aeneis* 2.421–22)

which is an attempt to capture some of the sound symbols achieved by Virgil's Latin (2.314):

> exoritur clamorque virum clangorque tubarum.[35]

Or the same alliteration can help with the frightful noise aboard ship in a storm:

> The cables crack; the sailors' fearful cries;
>
> (*Aeneis* 1.128)

or with the noises made by crows,

> The crow with clam'rous cries the shower demands,
>
> (*Georg* 1.532)

and ravens,

> And croaking notes proclaim the settled fair.
>
> (*Georg* 1.558)

Dryden could give us savage animals in the forest by making every stressed syllable in a line both alliterate and consonate:

> The grunts of bristled boars, and groans of bears.
>
> (*Aeneis* 7.20)

A different kind of animal sound comes in two lines,

> The hoofs of horses, with a ra*tt*ling sound,
> Bea*t* shor*t* and thi*ck*, and sha*ke* the ro*tt*en ground,
>
> (*Aeneis* 11.1267–8)

which translate one of Virgil's most famous sound-sense patterns,

> quadripedante putrem cursu quatit ungula campum;
>
> (11.875)

but where Dryden depended chiefly on alliteration of [h], [r], [š], on two final [k]'s and four final [t]'s, on a neat balancing of the onomatopoeic *rattling* with *rotten*, and on monosyllabic words in the second line, in Virgil's line the effect of speed comes more from the dactyls, and, one of many analysts suggests, the short syllables render "a kind of troubled confusion" while "the *u* sounds [produce] a dark, dull, thudding noise." [36] By running final [s] along one line, Dryden may have succeeded even better with the hissing of snakes than he had with the galloping of horses,

> So fier*ce* the hi*ss*ings of her speckled snake*s*,
>
> (*Aeneis* 7.458)

a line that may be an improvement, in sound-sense relations at least, over the words Virgil had used,

> tot pullulat atra colubris;   (7.329)

or again,

> Her curling snake*s* with hi*ss*ings fill the pla*ce*.
>
> (*Aeneis* 7.626)

Dryden's most obviously intended use of consonance for onomatopoeia, however, perhaps the best example from all British poetry, occurs in the fourth *Georgic*, the beautiful account of apiculture, where in line 801 he reproduced the sound of bees by ending every accented syllable with [z]:

> A buzzing noise of bees his ears alarms.

Dryden's sound symbolism helps with scenes and moods other than those having to do with war, storm-tossed ships, or the animal world. In a line from the first *Georgic* (115),

> And sleepy poppies harmful harvests yield,

harvests is tied to its adjective by an alliteration of [h] as well as by an assonance of the *r*-colored vowel, but the unique consonance of [p] that binds *poppies* to its adjective results in an effective onomatopoeia moving through two words. In a couplet in the same *Georgic* (491–92),

> Soft whispers run along the leavy woods,
> And mountains whistle to the murm'ring floods,

there are three words which Dr. Johnson, or anyone else, would say are sound-sense words, but two of them, *whispers* and *whistle,* aid each other because they begin with the same four phones while *murm'ring* is partially echoed in *mountains*, all these echoes, and others, helping to produce one of Dryden's most onomatopoeic couplets. Again from the first *Georgic*, the lines 104–5,

> or lest the barren sand,
> Should suck the moisture from the thirsty land,

contain a well-known sound-sense word *suck*, which alliterates with *sand*, but the dominating echo of many echos is that relating *moisture* to *thirsty* and found earlier in *tes*[*t*].

Long before the term was invented, Dryden echoed phonesthemes in order to create extended sound metaphors, nearly always providing the lexical support that a phonestheme should have. Besides the -*s* and -*z* for such noises as hissing and buzzing, he frequently alliterated *fl*-, an initial consonant cluster often said to begin words denoting movement not characterized by loud sounds,[37] as in the first *Georgic* (262 and 416–18),

Lest, crack'd with summer heats, the flooring flies,

To persecute from far the flying d*oe*—
Then, when the fle*ecy* sk*ies* new cl*o*the the w*oo*d,
And c*a*ke*s* of r*u*stling *ice* come r*o*lling down the fl*oo*d,

where the phonestheme is carried through three lines and goes with other echoes, especially the three [k]'s and the -*s* of *fleecy, cakes,* and "rus[t]ling ice," to help create a complex sound-sense passage. Although the same -*fl* occurs only once in "To *fl*oat the meadows, or to *f*ence the *f*ie*l*d" (*Georgics* 1.364), its effect is enhanced by the *f-* in *fence* and the *f–l* in *field,* an example of Burke's augmentation.[38] Another initial consonant phonestheme, the *gl-* cluster that is said to go naturally with visual phenomena,[39] can be found in lines that set the scene for the best use of the sound, as in Dryden's description of a sunset in the first *Georgic* (605).

If fiery red his **gl***o*w*ing* **gl***o*be descends,

where the [o] assonance makes the sun glow even more.

Of all the initial consonant phonesthemes that have been pointed out to us in recent years, almost surely Dryden's favorite—at least in his mature verse—was the cluster *st-*, which in English and all Germanic languages comes so often in words implying firmness, stability, arrest.[40] He liked it in short images,

And **st***em* the **st***ream* to meet the pro*m*is'd rain,*
(*Georg* 1.532)

where the sound is aided by other echoes, the consonance of [m], for example. Or he combined *st-* with another phonestheme and a variety of vowel repetitions, here in one line,

* For the vowel in *stem–stream* see chapter 1, n. 36. Dryden rhymed these two words often, as well as rhyming *stream–condemn.*

Strongly they strike, huge flakes of flame expire,
>   (*Georg* 4.254)

here in two heavily ornamented lines,

Or sharpen stakes, or head the forks, or twine
The sallow twigs to tie the straggling vine,
>   (*Georg* 1.357–58)

where the second phonestheme, *tw*- for twisting phenomena,[41] is just as prominent; or he could extend it
along a hexameter line,

Like him, with mighty strides, they stalk from steep to steep,
>   (*Aeneis* 3.846)

or through two successive couplets,

So the boat's brawny crew the current stem,
And slow advancing, struggle with the stream;
But if they slack their hands, or cease to strive,
Then down the flood with headlong haste they drive,
>   (*Georg* 1.290–93)

where the *st*- stands out for the slow striving and stemming
image before it gives way to a final line that tumbles along
swiftly when the crew gives up the struggle and is taken
over by the swift current.

But Dryden could echo his vowels for onomatopoeia too.
As a good poet he knew that the soft front vowels are best
for the light and airy sights and sounds in nature, and so he
let accented [i] dominate not only lines 5–7 in the first
Georgic,

The birth and genius of the frugal bee,
I sing, Maecenas, and I sing to thee.
Ye deities, who fields and plains protect,

but lines 204–6 in the second,

Perpetual spring our happy climate sees:
Twice breed the cattle, and twice bear the trees;
And summer suns recede by slow degrees,

where the softness of the vowel is aided by the softness of the initial [s]. The translations of Virgil's pastorals are, as one would expect, teeming with front vowels pronounced something like [i], [ɪ], or [ɛ], line 82 from the third, for example,

> The trees are cloth'd with leaves, the fields with grass,*

and this couplet (66–67) from the seventh,

> Ye mossy springs, inviting easy sleep,†
> Ye trees, whose leafy shades those mossy fountains keep.

As with other poets Dryden found that the word *sleep* invites an [i] assonance as quickly as do the green leaves of trees:

> His dream Aeneas and his sleep forsook,‡ (*Aeneis* 8.92)

and

> That Queen, whose feast the factious rabble keep,§
> Expos'd obscenely naked and asleep. (*H&P* 1304–5)

If [ɪ], perhaps its nearby companion [i], is a phonestheme that under certain conditions suggests little, tiny, delicate, dainty things or notions, as some students of language have said,[42] Dryden seems to have been unaware of the fact. There are, of course, lines in his poems that use the phone for such images. For example, in *The Hind and the Panther* [ɪ] dominates a well-known line with an ironic image of smallness:

*For *leaves*, one of Wyld's e^1 words, which probably had [i] with Dryden, see chapter 1, n. 36; *fields* surely had [i] (see Wyld, *Rhymes*, p. 103).

†The word *ease*, one of Wyld's e^2 words, rhymed most often with such words as *praise* in the seventeenth century, perhaps having Kökeritz's [ɛ:].

‡The word *dream* probably did not have the [i] of *Aeneas* and *sleep*, since it is one of Wyld's e^2 words that went to [e] or [ɛ:] by Dryden's day.

§The word *feast* had [ɛ] both with Dryden and Pope; therefore, no assonance with *Queen*—only the alliteration with "factious," which assonates with its noun "rabble."

> Much malice mingled with a little wit;   (1295)

and in the second *Georgic* the same [ı] goes with children and kissing:

> His little children climbing for a kiss.   (760)

But for Dryden such front vowels seem most suggestive for outdoor scenes, as in lines 61 and 65 from Virgil's second *Pastoral*:

> White lilies in full canisters they bring,
> The short narcissus and fair daffodil.

The closed [o] and the vowels [ʊ] and [ʌ], for example, are more effective in other circumstances.

Just as Shakespeare had stressed fourteen [o]'s in his Sonnet 30, "The sad account of fore-bemoaned moan," and Poe was to select that vowel as the key sound in his sad *Raven*, Dryden seemed to agree that the [o] is melancholy under certain conditions. In *All for Love* (5.1.74–75) he let it dominate Serapion's lament when tragedy is certain:

> Time has unroll'd her glories to the last
> And now closed up the volume.

Or in the *Aeneis* (2.853) he combined it with [r], with initial [m], and with final [z] to suggest sounds of agony:

> And mourns with mortal groans th'approaching fate.

Although [o] (perhaps [ɔ]) may have several uses as a phonestheme, Dryden assonated it much more often in the *Aeneis* than, for example, in the *Georgics*, which have few occasions for the expression of sorrow. In the *Aeneis* the echo seems to have come readily with such words as *woe*, *ghost*, and *soul*, as in these lines:

> And thrice invoke the soul of Polydore,   (3.94)
>
> A glorious name, among the ghosts below,   (4.939)
>
> Whose holy soul the stroke of Fortune fled.   (11.241)

Readers have often commented on the [o] as a sound-sense vowel, and now we are learning the importance of the vowel in *dunce*.[43] Dryden, like Pope after him, found this sound most useful as an echo in passages, invariably ironic, describing people or things distasteful. In *All for Love* defeated Antony, railing at the fleeing Egyptian force, the "bastard of the Nile," endows him "with all his m*o*ther's m*u*d / Cr*u*sted about his soul." And in the translation of Juvenal's Sixth Satire, the bitterest attack on women ever penned, there are fourteen stressed occurrences of this vowel in eight lines (14–21), six of which are emphasized even more by coming in the rhyming words. Perhaps Dryden's best use of this phonestheme is in his wonderfully onomatopoeic passage on Shadwell in *Absalom and Achitophel*, part 2. This description of Og (457–59), whose name Dryden rhymed with *rogue* (and *rogue* with *clog*), begins with a triplet featuring at least five vowels close to [ʊ,ʌ] in sound:

> Now stop your noses, readers, all and s*o*me,
> For here's a t*u*n of midnight work to c*o*me,
> *O*g, from a treason-tavern rolling h*o*me.

Although Shadwell's name in *Mac Flecknoe* did not attract much assonance, since there Dryden preferred to create his effect with "Sh——," that poem still makes use of [ʊ,ʌ] and vowels close to it. Here, for example, it comes four times in a line that also has an alliteration and a polysyllabic consonance:

> **F**u**ll** on the **fi**l**ial** d*u*l**l**ness: **l**ong he st*oo*d.[44]   (136)

Another vowel phonestheme, apparently less noticed in poetry, is that of the diphthong [aɪ] (probably [əɪ] for Dryden) spelled *i* or *oi* in the seventeenth and early eighteenth centuries. Although this sound has several possibilities and while it was Dryden's favorite for assonance, even more than poets before him he made it assist in creating the effect of light. This couplet, for example, has five [aɪ,əɪ]'s to help give the notion of sunrise:

> Now came the day desir'd. The skies were bright
> With rosy luster of the rising light.   (*Aeneis* 5.138–39)

And the same vowel occurs in five stressed syllables in these two lines:[45]

> The brands are toss'd on high; the winds conspire
> To drive along the deluge of the fire. (*Aeneis* 12.952–53)

Dryden's most famous light image, reflected in many poems after him, comes in the often admired opening lines of *Religio Laici* where he argues that

> Dim as the borrow'd beams of moon and stars
> To lonely, weary, wand'ring travelers,
> Is Reason to the soul.

The light image expanded in the next eight lines is made more vivid by ten [aɪ,əɪ]'s, which, except for the end rhymes, are the only echoing vowels. If Dryden needed to borrow this phonestheme, he could have taken it, as well as the notion of the mournful [o], from Shakespeare or Spenser.

There are, of course, ways of being onomatopoeic without necessarily employing echoes, just as there are other means of appealing to the ear with language. Dryden, for example, talked of the ruggedness of monosyllabic lines "clogg'd with consonants"[46] and of the beauties of *r* no matter where it comes in the word.[47] But even in his designedly slow, harsh lines, Dryden often increased the feeling of ruggedness by a careful choice of echoes, for example, in his description of a boar at bay,

> He whets his tusks, and turns, and dares the war,
> (*Aeneis* 10.1004)

in which the consonance of [s] and [z] and the alliteration of [t] are prominent among the superabundance of consonants in a monosyllabic line that is made even slower by the punctuation. Ornament, "color," then, can for Dryden help "harmonize" any kind of "numbers" from the roughest to the smoothest.

In spite of Dr. Johnson, Dryden is now hailed as a chief pioneer in the simpler prose style developed in his day. And one of the most common of conclusions is that the Senecan or "curt" prose of the first half of the seventeenth century—rather than the Ciceronian—led to the eighteenth-century plain style in "all the arts," to a style appropriate for a period in which *thought* became so important, when "*in both poetry and prose*" there was "an emphasis on simplicity, clarity, intelligibility, propriety, naturalness, refinement, ease."[48] But such generalizations have completely neglected the colorful eighteenth-century language of poetry. It is here where Dryden was even more of a pioneer. And so Johnson was right in claiming that he "tuned the numbers of English poetry." He was, in fact the chief master for poetic style in a period when style was controlled so well that it was deceivingly simple. And one of his chief influences would lie in the ways he varied his sounds: first, by echoing his vowels and consonants he provided that "coloring," which in poetry, he believed, "is the first beauty to strike the eye"; second, by a clever selection of nouns, adjectives, verbs, and verbals which repeated sounds, he was able to stress an antithesis or a syntactical similarity; and, finally, believing that certain sounds evoke certain feelings, aware at least unconsciously of any number of phonesthemes, he echoed vowels and consonants not only to produce noises that are harsh or soft, gay or mournful, beautiful or ugly, but even to assist in the evocation of visual images. With Virgil as his guide, with Shakespeare and Spenser before him and Blake and Byron after him Dryden "managed" his few vowels and abundant consonants for such an astounding variety of colorful effects that his chief disciple, recognizing the extreme importance of ear appeal to poets and paraphrasing lines from one of Dryden's wonderfully onomatopoeic odes to music,[49] was able to say enthusiastically in *An Essay on Criticism*,

> The power of music all our hearts allow
> And what Timotheus was, is Dryden now.

3

"Music Resembles Poetry":
The Auditory Appeal
of Pope's Meter

"Music her soft, assuasive voice applies"
(St. Cecilia's Day)

The versification of Alexander Pope has in recent years received much attention. His rhetorical devices, his variety, the speed of his verses, his theories of the pastoral have all been studied. Those who have spoken of his ornaments of sound have concentrated on rhyme, alliteration, and onomatopoeia. W. K. Wimsatt, for example, argues that "rhyme is the apex of the rhetorical phenomena which characterize Pope's verse," while Jacob Adler believes that Pope went against contemporaneous critical taste in his "highly visible use of alliteration" and reminds us that as Pope matured he placed much more emphasis on the relationship between sound and sense, "a rule he always praised and usually followed."[1] But his assonance, more important even than his alliteration, has been almost completely neglected,[2] while his consonance has not been noticed at all. Furthermore, it can now be demonstrated how conscientiously Pope worked with his manuscripts in order to achieve a greater auditory appeal.

One important fact to note at the beginning of a study of any aspect of Pope's versification is that although he edited Shakespeare, translated Homer, and imitated Horace, Virgil, and Boileau, his prosodic theories and performance are most heavily indebted to John Dryden. The few pages which the two poets wrote on their craft are strikingly alike.[3] In the first place they both praised Virgil and Homer for "harmony of numbers" and for "sonorousness." Second, both admired Spenser's eclogues, Dryden even more than Pope, whose four pastorals were competing with *The Shepheardes Calender*. Third, Pope's theory of "representative meter" is reminiscent of Dryden's belief that "we must not only choose our words for elegance, but for sound," and of Dryden's admiration for Virgil because "the very sound of his words have often somewhat that is connatural to the subject"; Pope, however, went further—in theory, at least—when he asserted that the sounds of words are "undoubtedly of wonderful force in printing the image on the reader." Fourth, Pope's famous belief that the monosyllabic line is for melancholy, slowness, or labor is obviously inspired by Dryden's much longer analysis of monosyllables in poetry. And finally, Pope's pleas for "elegant turns on the words, which render the numbers extremely sweet and pleasing" and for "numbers . . . the smoothest, most easy and flowing imaginable" echo Dryden's pleas—in the same phrases sometimes— that poets should place words for "the sweetness of the sound," should know which vowels "are more sonorous and which more soft and sweet," and should imitate Virgil's elegance of expression, his harmony of numbers, and his "figurative, elegant, and sounding words." But while Pope's theories of prosody are much like those of his mentor Dryden, a more significant parallel can be made if we compare their poetic performances, a fact that is especially true of their use of phonic echoes.

Because he had Dryden as a model, Pope learned the artistic uses of such echoes very early. Although his first poems were designed more to please the ear and his late ones—the *Moral Essays*, the *Essay on Man*, the *Dunciad*—to be less lyrical and more heavily argumentative or satirical, Dr. Johnson's opinion that he "formed his style early" is much more appropriate for Pope than it is for

Dryden. Pope's four pastorals (1709) were youthful training pieces that imitated Spenser, Virgil, and, more particularly, Dryden's translations of Theocritus's idylls and
Virgil's eclogues, but whether they "were written at the age
of sixteen," as Pope claimed, or nearer to the age of twenty-
one when he published them, these pastorals may be as
acoustically affective as Pope always thought. At any rate
they have a much higher proportion of assonance and
alliteration than is to be found in any of Dryden's youthful
pieces. Even *An Essay on Criticism* (1711), both early and
argumentative rather than "sweet," has a high proportion
of stressed phonal repetitions. And while *An Essay on Man*
and others of the verse essays are less ornamental, at the
end of his career Pope in the *Dunciad* was employing more
sound effects than perhaps any other major poet in English.
The normally subdued use of these devices would no doubt
be a chief reason for Tennyson to admire Pope, for Byron to
praise him above all other poets, and for Dr. Johnson to say
that "he had colours of language always before him, ready
to decorate his matter with every grace of elegant expression. . . . By perusing the works of Dryden, he discovered
the most perfect fabrick of English verse, and habituated
himself to that only which he found the best."[4]

Like Dryden, Pope's first purpose in employing sound
recurrences was to make poetry "sweet and pleasing."
From Dr. Johnson to Maynard Mack critics have ap-
plauded the imagery in this passage from "The Elegy to
the Memory of an Unfortunate Lady":[5]

> Most souls, 'tis true, but peep out once an age,
> Dull sullen pris'ners in the body's cage:
> Dim lights of life, that burn a length of years,
> Useless, unseen, as lamps in sepulchres;
> Like Eastern Kings a lazy state they keep,
> And close confin'd to their own palace, sleep.   (17–22)

Undoubtedly the images here are attractive, but also

significant is the fact that the six lines contain four alliterations, one of four syllables, but also at least five assonances, including those in the spondees that begin the first two lines. And nearly every favorite or important passage in Pope will have many such internal echoes, all contributing to an ear appeal that would force even the hostile Wordsworth to admit that "he bewitched the nation by his melody." For example, the opening of the first pastoral, "Spring" (1709), has ten assonances and seven alliterations in the first fifteen lines, while the dying-pheasant passage in *Windsor Forest* (1712), highly praised for its imagery, may owe its attractiveness as much to the beauty of its sounds:

> Shor*t* is his J*oy*! he *f*eels the *f*iery Wound,
> Fl*utt*ers in **Bl***oo*d, and panting **b**eats the Ground.
> Ah! what av*a*il his glossie, v*a*rying Dyes,
> His P*ur*ple Crest, and Scarlet-c*i*rcled *Eye*s,
> The vivid Gree*n* his sh*in*ing **Pl**ume*s* unfold;
> His **p***ai*nted Wing*s*, and Breast that *f*l*a*me*s* with Gold?
>
> (113–18)

Even in a so-called prose poem such as *An Essay on Man* the exordium and peroration are heavily charged with phonic echoes. To please the reader's ear Pope varied these repetitions as ingeniously as he did his rhythms, his rhymes, and his tone. The point can be made easily by beginning with the least popular of the three sound effects being considered.

Many poets have either not known the advantages of consonance or found it hard to employ artistically. Long before he was thirty, however, Pope had learned that consonance could add pleasure to the ear and variety to the tone. For example, in one of Strephon's most attractive couplets in "Spring," eight stressed syllables end with some kind of nasal sound,

> Si*ng* the*n*, and Da*m*on shall atte*n*[d] the Strai*n*,
> While yo*n* slow Oxen tur*n* the furrow'd Plai*n*.   (29–30)

Although less obviously concerned with auditory appeal,
An Essay on Criticism has much consonance, some of it
polysyllabic and prominent, as in this line, where all five
stressed syllables are involved in final echoes:

> Ah ne'e*r* so di*re* a Thi*rst* of Glo*ry* boa*st*,   (522)

while each line of this couplet in the same poem has a
consonance which was surely intended,

> A Mu*se* by the*se* is like a mistress u*s'd*,
> This hour she's idoli*z'd*, the next abu*s'd*.   (432–33)

In *The Dunciad*, his last important poem, Pope perhaps
used consonance most effectively. There it can be thick and
obvious with final [k], as in

> Thi*ck* and more thi*ck* the bla*ck* blo*ck*ade extends, (4.191)

or [z]

> A gentler exerci*se* to clo*se* the game*s*,   (2.366)

or [t],

> As taugh*t* by Venus, Paris learn*t* the ar*t*;   (2.217)

or it can go almost unnoticed, as with "pert flat eyes," "in
long wigs, in bags," and "gripes his fist the faster" (2.43,21,
210). It is true then that although Pope may have found less
use for consonance than for other echoes, in all British
poetry, at least before 1900, only Dryden has so much of it.

But while he has so many final consonant echoes, and
while everyone has noticed his alliteration, it is Pope's
assonance that is most important to the sound of his poetry.
As with Dryden one can find hundreds of Pope's decasyllabic lines in each of which there will be three stressed
syllables containing the same vowel. *The Rape of the Lock*
has over thirty such prolonged echoes. Here, for example,
are two lines in a row from that poem each of which has [I]
in three stressed syllables:

Th*i*n gl*i*tt'ring Textures of the f*i*lmy Dew;
D*i*pt in the r*i*chest T*i*ncture of the Skies.   (2.64–65)

Occasionally Pope wrote a line that has the same vowel four times in stressed syllables, and the "First Satire of the Second Book of Horace" even has an eleven-syllable line, harsh and heavy, with six important vowels alike:

With G*u*n, Dr*u*m, Tr*u*mpet, Bl*u*nderb*u*ss & Th*u*nder? (26)

Pope's great admirer Byron was to imitate this hard line in *Don Juan* (7.78):

B*o*mbs, dr*u*ms, g*u*ns, b*a*stions, b*a*tteries, bayonets,
   b*u*llets;
Hard words, which stick in the soft muses' gullets.

Such lengthened or complicated echoes call attention to themselves, as no doubt the poet wanted them to, but assonance involving just two syllables is much more frequent and much less obtrusive. With Pope, however, it very often accompanies another vowel echo.[6] In fact, all five stressed syllables of one line may assonate two vowels, as in *The Dunciad* (1.234):

Where v*i*le Mund*u*ngus tr*u*cks for v*i*ler rhymes;

or ten stressed syllables in one couplet can echo five vowels or diphthongs to go with three alliterations and a polysyllabic consonance in seven of the same syllables, as in *An Essay on Man* (3.157–58):

The shr*i*ne with g*o*re unst*ai*ne*d*, with g*o*ld undr*e*st,
Unbr*i*be*d*, unbl*oo*dy, st*oo*d the bl*a*meless pr*ie*st.

Pope of course has many polysyllabic, or otherwise complex, alliterations and consonances, and he learned well how to combine one, or both, of the devices with his assonance, as in each of these examples from four entirely different kinds of poems:

Thin Trees arise that shun each others Shades,   (WF 22)

Tho' Wit and Art conspire to move your Mind,
                              (Ess on Crit 531)

The hungry Judges soon the Sentence sign,   (Rape 3.21)

A second see, by meeker manners known,   (Dun 3.143)

Instant, when dipt, away they wing their flight. (Dun 3.27)

To demonstrate that Pope employed more sound echoes, especially assonance, than well-known poets of other periods, one can compare him with, say, John Donne, a favorite exercise for two reasons: first, Donne has a notoriously rough rhythm while Pope is considered one of the smoothest of poets; second, Pope rewrote two of Donne's "Satires," smoothing them out and employing his own characteristic style. Seymour Chatman's provocative comparison of the two sets of satires[7] draws certain conclusions which are perhaps not surprising. For example, Donne has far more run-on lines, even run-on couplets, and Pope has far fewer trochaic and other substitutions in his predominantly iambic meter. But some of Chatman's conclusions are less expected. First, Donne's rougher rhythm has about "twice as many occurrences of alliteration of two syllables in immediate succession as Pope," who made his alliteration "cooperate with the meter," that is, come on alternate, stressed syllables. Second, Pope's alliteration is not only more prominent but much more prone to serve a structural purpose, to be more than mere decoration, as in his many epithet-noun combinations, which are both characteristic of him and "carefully done."

There are other intriguing facts about the sounds in these two sets of satires. First, in his Satire II, seventy-three of Pope's lines have obvious internal vowel or consonant echoes whereas only forty of Donne's do. Second, in Donne's two satires there is an average of only one assonance to seven lines, while in Pope's versions there is one

assonance to three lines. Third, eleven lines in Pope's
Satire II have polysyllabic echoes; there are only two in
Donne's original. Fourth, Pope's version of the same poem
has eighteen lines with two or more different echoes;
Donne's has only eight. Pope was the smoother poet then,
but he was also far more concerned with echoing phones
internally.

Not only can one compare the styles of Pope and Donne
to show that Pope repeated phones more; but also, to
demonstrate that these auditory appeals were often conscious on Pope's part, one can compare an early with a late
version of one of his own poems.[8] Although George Sherburn concluded that when the poet corrected his lines "the
effect is not decorative but functional,"[9] a comparison of
any one of Pope's manuscript poems with its later, published, counterpart reveals a persistent concern with sound
effects, both decorative and functional. For example, there
are the 1712 holograph and the 1713 published version of
Windsor Forest. In its final form this early poem has not
only much alliteration but far more assonance than is found
in the holograph. What is most important, however, is to
discover that time after time the lines in the earlier version
were altered in order to achieve some kind of internal echo.

Some of these changes affect the consonants. In this line,
which already had an *s* alliteration, Pope simply substituted one adjective for another—*suppliant* for *haughty*—
thereby changing the image completely, but in doing so he
added an initial [s] that effected a polysyllabic alliteration:

> There Kings shall sue, and haughty States be seen.
>
> (1712.377)
>
> There Kings shall sue, and suppliant States be seen.
>
> (1713.383)

Although the published poem is slightly longer than the
original, in the following example Pope compressed two
lines into one, in the process parting with three echoes

involving eight sounds but ending with two involving five:

> Sudden, before some unsuspecting Town;
> The Young, the Old, one Instant makes our Prize,
>
> $\qquad$ (1712.112–13)
>
> Sudden they seize th'amaz'd, defenceless Prize.[10]
>
> $\qquad$ (1713.109)

More impressive yet is the almost complete reworking that is evident in another line, which in 1712 had only a terminal [z] consonance but which in 1713 carefully retained the consonance—even though one [z] word was replaced by another—and added not only an alliteration but an assonance:

> But far more blest who Study joins with Ease! (1712.239)
>
> Successive Study, Exercise, and Ease. $\qquad$ (1713.240)

And it was to assonance that Pope in his revisions gave most attention. Here,

> To trace the Circle of the tim'rous Hare, $\qquad$ (1712.126)
>
> And trace the Mazes of the circling Hare, $\qquad$ (1713.122)

Pope discarded *tim'rous* and his [t] alliteration, moved *circle* to *circling* in order to keep his image, and added *Mazes* to make an [e] assonance. In another line,

> A dreadful Series of successive Wars, $\qquad$ (1712.307)
>
> A dreadful Series of Intestine Wars, $\qquad$ (1713.325)

in correcting the redundancy of *Series* and *successive* he had to lose his alliteration of [s], but he was able to find a new adjective that would let him keep the vowel echo in the balancing adjectives. Another line without assonance,

> His Kindred Stars he watches in the Skies, $\qquad$ (1712.240)

became two, the second of which accents the [I] three times,

Bids his free Soul expatiate in the Skies,
Amid her Kindred Stars familiar roam.　　(1713.254–55)

Again a line with three [o]'s,

Not fabled Poe a nobler Journey goes,　　(1712.219)

kept two [o]'s but added an echo of [e] as well as a consonance:

Nor Po so swells the fabling Poet's Lays.　　(1713.227)

In spite of his interest in consonant repetitions, then, the revisions of *Windsor Forest* prove that even at an early age Pope was also very concerned about what Dryden had called "managing" his "few vowels." A study of the first 170 lines of that poem reveals that in the interval of time between its two texts he altered about one-third of the lines. In the process he discarded 5 alliterations and added 9 for a gain of 4, but while losing 7 vowel echoes he added 21, thereby gaining 14 assonances in only a part of a poem already well ornamented.

The same exercise conducted for other poems by Pope will produce the same results. Here, for example, is a couplet from the 1709 manuscript of *An Essay on Criticism* (84–85),

That Art is best, which most resembles Her;
Which still presides, yet never does Appear,

which has no really successful assonance. This couplet became in the 1711 published poem (74–75),

Art from that Fund each just Supply provides,
Works without Show, and without Pomp presides.

For the second line of the new couplet Pope achieved a neat chiasmus, but for the first he was able to "manage" two vowel echoes. Years later Pope was still revising his poems to add ornament. Part of one couplet very near the beginning of his *Iliad* originally read,

> For Chryses sought by presents to regain
> His captive daughter.

Here because the two [k]'s and the two [ɔ]'s were so far apart that the ear was hardly affected, Pope inserted between them another [k] and another [ɔ] that started the echoes going,

> For **Chryses** so*u*ght with *co*stly *gi*fts to *g*ain
> His **c**aptive d*au*ghter,

thereby ending with two polysllabic echoes and, at the same time, picking up an alliteration of [g].[11]

As with Dryden, however, Pope's internal echoes very often did more than merely please the ear; they were also intellectually and emotionally functional, serving, for example, for binding and for emphasis. Much has, in fact, been said about how with Pope alliteration was a favorite aid for cementing an adjective to its noun.[12] On the other hand, he did not favor consonance for such binding, as Dryden did. Furthermore, the few examples of adjective-noun consonance in *Arbuthnot* include "Reli*g*ious Ra*ge*," which may have been intended for an eye, or imperfect, alliteration, since Pope, when tying his epithets to their nouns, was much more prone than Dryden to be satisfied with unstressed echoes. In the second *Dunciad*, for example, he has "the proud Parnassian sneer" (5), "dark dexterity" (278), "ferocious feature" (328), where in each case one of the initial consonants is in a weak syllable. But in spite of what has been said about Pope's use of alliteration for noun-adjective linkage, he preferred assonance in this position, as in the following combinations taken from *Arbuthnot*—"Heroic prose" (109), "pidling Tibalds" (164), "Castalian state" (230), "Amphibious Thing" (326). And if the noun-adjective assonance was not forthcoming, Pope might work in two adjectives with the same vowel—"Civil and Religious" (394). Dryden had often found it possible to use such linkage to make an adjective or adverb of *like* and some noun. Pope was not so fortunate in inventing that particular kind of echo, in the second *Dunciad* being content with "cow-like" and "ox-like," even though the "ox-like" assonates with its noun *eyes* (164). But in one line of that book he managed his vowels in "Milo-like" (284).

Just as frequently as his chief master, Pope was able to emphasize with sound echoes the rhetorical balance of two verbs, two nouns, two adjectives, two noun-adjective combinations. He did it chiefly with assonance:

> P*a*nts on her Neck, and f*a*ns her parting Hair, (*WF* 196)
>
> Or r*u*mpled P*e*tticoats, or t*u*mbled B*e*ds, (*Rape* 4.72)
>
> The b*u*zzing B*ee*s about their d*u*sky Qu*ee*n, (*Dun* 4.80)
>
> Sp*o*rus at C*ou*rt, or J*a*phet in a J*a*yl. (*Arbuth* 363)

He did it with consonants, as in *Arbuthnot*:

> A maudlin **P**oetess, a ryming **P**eer, (16)
>
> A **p**ainted Mistress, or a **p**urling Stream, (150)
>
> Now trip**s** a Lady, and now strut**s** a Lord, (329)
>
> Ex**pl**ore the Thought, ex**pl**ain the asking Eye. (412)

He did it with both vowels and consonants:

> Fr*ui*ts of dull Hea*t*, and S*oo*terkins of Wi*t*, (*Dun* 1.126)
>
> Inten*t* to r*ea*son, or poli*te* to pl*ea*se,* (*Es on Man* 4.382)
>
> H*i*st'ry her **P**ot, Div*i*nity his **P**ipe, (*Dun* 3.196)
>
> Corr*e*ctly c*o*ld, and r*e*gularly l*o*w, (*Es on Crit* 240)
>
> All j*oin* to **g**uard what each des*i*res to **g**ai*n*.
>
> (*Es on Man* 3.278)

---

*Whether *reason* and *please*, each one OF and belonging to Wyld's *e*² group, had [e], [ɛː], or the "new-fangled" [i] is not certain, nor does the rhyme word, *ease*, help, since it is also an *e*² word. Whatever the vowel sound, however, the two words assonate.

That Pope consciously strove for such sound balance within his lines can be seen if we again resort to comparing the published form of a poem with a more primitive one. In *Windsor Forest*, for example, a line that originally read,

> The Bow'ry Mazes and the glimm'ring Glades,
>
> (1712.230)

became

> The Bow'ry Mazes and surrounding Greens.   (1713.262)

Here Pope gave up a noun-adjective alliteration as well as the assonance and consonance of his structurally balanced nouns, but he ended by working out an assonance of parallel adjectives and retaining the [z] consonance in parallel nouns even though one noun, *Glades*, was exchanged for another, *Greens*. The best of a number of possible illustrations of his concern for balancing sounds begins with these lines (38–39) in the 1709 manuscript of *An Essay on Criticism*,

> Some hate as Rivals all that write; and others
> But envy Wits, as Eunuchs envy Lovers,

which ended up in the published edition as

> Each burns alike, who can, or cannot write,
> Or with a Rival's, or an Eunuch's spite.   (1713.30–31)

The alliteration and assonance in *Rivals* and *write* in the original couplet became two balanced [aɪ, əɪ]'s in each line, one just before the caesura, one at the end of the line, a kind of parallelism much favored by Denham and Dryden.

Pope was also as prone as Denham and Dryden to doubly emphasize the rhyming sounds of a couplet by echoing one or more phones in the final stressed syllables of a line. In part 2 of *An Essay on Criticism* there are twenty-one such terminal assonances, as in the first two lines, which close with "conspire to blind" and "misguide the Mind." In that

same part 2 there are twelve examples of terminal alliteration and thirteen of terminal consonance, while in *The
Rape of the Lock* each of nine of the first twenty-six lines
echoes a phone in the final stressed syllables. A memory-
provoking feature of one of the most memorable similes in
The Dunciad (1.183–84) is that each of the two lines closes
with an echoing [o]:

> As clocks to weight their nimble m*o*tion *o*we,
> The wheels above urg'd by the l*o*ad bel*o*w.

One of the best examples of Pope's revisions for this kind of
emphasis is found near the end of the eighth *Iliad* where

> And *st*ars unnu*m*ber'd tre*m*bling beams be*st*ow

was later changed to

> And stars unnumber'd gi*l*[d] the gl*ow*ing p*o*le.   (692)

The published line did not repeat the [st] phonestheme or
the final [m], but it gained a [g] alliteration, an [l] consonance, the *g–l*, *gl* diminution, and, especially, the terminal
[o] assonance.

All such sound emphases, Pope obviously believed,
were aids to argument. In this line from *An Essay on Man*,

> When rock'd the m*ou*ntains, and when **groa*n'd**the **gr***ound*,
> (3.250),

not only was he attempting to effect onomatopoeia with the
initial and final echoes in *groan'd* and *ground*, but he was
also achieving a cognitive effect by selecting nouns—
mountains and *ground*—which balance both syntactically
and by echoing the accented vowel. Such simple parisons
with sound balance were as popular with Pope as with
Dryden.

But more than any poet before him, Pope liked the less
simple rhetorical forms of zeugma and chiasmus. And it is
astounding how clever he was at matching sounds in the

rhetorically matching words. Here the prepositional objects in a zeugma alliterate:

> He pay'd some Bards with Port, and some with Praise.
> (Arbuth 242)

Here the verbs assonate:

> The Seas shall waste; the Skies in Smoke decay.
> (Messiah 105)

Here the nouns as well as the verbs consonate:

> What Walls can guard me, or what Shades can hide?
> (Arbuth 7)

Here the verb objects both alliterate and assonate:

> Boyer the State, and Law the Stage gave o'er. (Dun 2.413)

Here the verbals alliterate and consonate:

> Have I no Friend to serve, no Soul to save?[13] (Arbuth 274)

Pope was just as clever with chiasmus, especially when adjectives began and ended the line:

> Fresh as the Morn, and as the Season fair, (Spring 20)
> Gross as her sire, and as her mother grave.[14] (Dun 1.14)

One of the best of double sound balances in a chiasmus is in line 37 of *Windsor Forest*,

> See Pan with Flocks, with Fruits Pomona crown'd,

where the repetition of weak initial *P* in "Pomona" is not so effective as the [n] consonance in the same nouns. And in this very interesting chiasmus from *An Essay on Man* with the caesura exactly in the middle of the monosyllabic line,

> Seas roll to waft me, suns to light me rise, (1.139)

each of the five words in the first half has its parallel in the second half; two pairs of words, both unimportant, are exact repetitions, the two verbs alliterate, the two infinitives consonate, and the two nouns both consonate and alliterate—all in addition to the terminal assonance and the consonance of the first and last words of the line.

This kind of structural balance is perhaps most effective in the satiric verse, where over and over Pope forced his sounds to strengthen his ironies. One of the most characteristic of such ironic parallelisms in the *Moral Epistles*, the *Imitations of Horace*, and *The Dunciad* has to do with names of people being attacked. In *The Dunciad* especially the examples of alliterating names of Pope's bêtes noires are abundant. In the second part of that satire alone he employed such combinations as the following, each combination occurring in one line only: *Ridpath–Roper, Morgan–Mandeville, Toland–Tindal, Warren–Wilkins, Joseph–John, Cook–Concanen, Breval–Bond–Besaleel.* Less frequently he assonated the names: *Cibber–Tibbald* (1.286), *Bladen–Hays* (4.560). Much more often the ironic sound parallels are not names. In *The Dunciad*, for example, we are exalted in the first half of a line with "Intrigu'd with glory," only to be devastated immediately by "and with spirit whor'd" (4.315). *Glory* and *whor'd*, two antithetical ideas, have not only corresponding positions but the same vowel. Even better is the line,

> Cibberian forehead, or Cimmerian gloom.   (*Dun* 4.532)

Here the desired relationship between the head of the king of dunces and the dismal abode of dead spirits is emphasized not only by the parallel placing of adjectives but also by selecting adjectives that assonate and consonate. No poet has ever employed his sounds more often than Pope did to achieve greater emphasis in argument and satire.

And few poets have been more onomatopoeic. Dr. Johnson's famous passage on the relation of sound to sense was inspired by Pope's verse, but Pope went far beyond

Johnson's limited definition of representative meter and attempted to make whole series of sounds help present emotions or ideas. For example, while Dr. Johnson would no doubt have agreed that *lisp* is onomatopoeic, Pope was liable to echo that word's sound in an accompanying word, as he did with "Practis'd to Lisp" (*Rape* 4.33). What has not been pointed out enough is that his onomatopoeia depends heavily on alliteration, assonance, and consonance. For example, while Dr. Johnson would also have agreed that *murmur* and *flutter* are sound-sense words, Pope could carry the initial [m] and the final [r] of one word and the final [t] of the other's stressed syllable all along the line, thus prolonging the effect:

No **mo**r**e** the Streams their **Mu**r**murs** shall forbea**r**,

(*Winter* 57)

And li**tt**le Hear**t**[s] to flu**t**ter a**t** a Beau.   (*Rape* 1.90)

In a nearby couplet in the *Rape* (1.65–66), in fact, final [t] comes five times to give auditory support both to "flutter" and "Coquette":

The ligh**t** Coque**tt**e[s] in Sylphs alof**t** repair,
And spor**t** and flu**t**ter in the Fields of Air.

Less notable about the couplet, perhaps, are the bracketing in *light–loft* and Burke's augmentation in the *fl-*, *f–l* sequence. Pope's final [t] may work even better with an image of the effeminate Italian opera as, mincing onto the stage,

She tripp'*d* and laugh'*d*, too pre**t**ty much to stand,

(*Dun* 4.50)

the key word *tripp'd* coming early and attracting an echo in two other words, all of which aid lexically and acoustically in producing the ridiculous picture.

Pope's use of the phonesthemes so far pointed out by twentieth-century scholars is instructive. Unlike Dryden he has almost no initial *tw*'s, and although he employed a number of *gl*- and *st*- words, he seldom alliterated them, even in the *Pastorals* and *Windsor Forest*, where one might expect, say, the *gl*- for visual phenomena.[15] In *The Dunciad*, however, initial *st*- is sometimes found repeated because of the need for such images as standing, stuttering, stultifying, stupefying. There, for example, Pope made fun of the contemporaneous stage for burning barns and cornfields to attract audiences:

> Thy stage shall stand, ensure it but from Fire;   (3.312)

he attacked Oxford University for censuring real philosophy:

> Each staunch Polemic, stubborn as a rock,
> Each fierce Logician, still expelling Locke;   (4.195–6)

and he described "Mother Osborne" as "stupefied to stone" (2.312). There are only three examples of *st*- alliteration in all of the *Rape*, each of them with its proper cognitive support, however, the best perhaps being

> Steel cou'd the Labour of the Gods destroy,
> And strike to Dust th'Imperial Tow'rs of Troy. (3.173–74)

But the relatively few *st*- phonesthemes, even in the *Dunciad*, the *Moral Essays*, and the *Imitations of Horace*, seem to show that Pope was not well aware of the possibilities of this particular alliteration.

His preferred consonant phonesthemes, then, were not clusters but phones. In the *Dunciad*, for example, the [l] of *trill*, a sound-sense word, comes three times in one couplet (4.57–58) that also employs other echoes, notably the vowel phonestheme [ʊ,ʌ], to annihilate both church and stage:

> One Tri*ll* shall harmonize joy, grief, and rage,
> Wake the d*ull* Church, and l*ull* the ranting Stage.

Or the [l] can help with laziness, luxury, and listlessness:

> Then look'd, and saw a lazy, lolling sort,
> . . . .
> Of ever-listless Loit'rers.   (*Dun* 4.337, 339)

And it is an important sound in dozens of punning rhymes, among them *whirl–Curll*, *skull–dull*, and *dull–full* (*Dun* 3.163–64, 25–26, 171–72).

The much more jarring phonestheme [d], whether initial or final, served Pope throughout *Winter*, where the shepherds lament the death of Daphne and where the last line combines a [d] alliteration with a polysyllabic consonance of [l]:

> **D**aphne farewe**ll**, and a**ll** the Wor**l**[d] a**d**ieu.

A poem such as the topographic *Windsor Forest* has little need for images of death and desolation, but one of its couplets (347–48) in particular, opening with *sullen* and closing with *blood*, is able to employ both initial and final [d] and combine it with many other echoes, including [l]:

> And *su*llen Mo*l*e, that h*i*des his **d**iving Fl*oo***d**;
> And *si*lent **D**arent, st*ai*n'**d** with **D**anish Bl*oo***d**.

But for Pope [d] became a prominent phonestheme only in the late satirical poems; in fact, any book of the *Dunciad* has as many onomatopoeic alliterations and consonances of that sound as all the rest of his poems together. "Dulness," as queen, naturally collects a court full of other *d* words. In Book I she is paralleled with *Daughter* (11–12); she "never dies" (18); she "beholds the Chaos, dark and deep" (55); she is "ductile" (64); to her, Ridpath is "as dear as Mist" (208); and one of her favorites, Eusden,

> sleeps among the **d**ull of ancient **d**ays;
> Safe, where no Critics **d**amn, no **d**uns molest,   (294–95)

surrounded not only by [d]'s but by [u, ʌ]'s. In Book II the "tribe" of Dulness is "industrious" (33); in an echo-filled couplet (233–34), she holds up to her followers as a prize

> this **D**rum, whose hoarse heroic bass
> **D**rowns the loud clarion of the braying Ass;

the scene of her games extends

> To where Fleet-**d**itch with **d**isemboguing streams
> Rolls the large tribute of **d**ead **d**ogs to Thames;   (271–72)

in the games themselves one contestant steps forward with these results:

> Next Sme**d**ley **d**iv'd; slow circles **d**impled o'er
> The quaking mu**d**, that clos'**d** and op'd no more; (291–92)

another "dives precipitately dull" (316); a third is damned in an oxymoronic simile (319–20) that includes a three-syllable assonance of [æ] as well as two initial and two final [k]'s to go with the [d]'s:

> No crab more active in the dirty dance,
> Downward to climb, and backward to advance.

Books III and IV continue with scenes that are dull, drab, dirty, and dead, as three illustrations will show. One is a "sound"-ing couplet that also employs nasals for the din and stresses [ɪ] at least five times:

> **D**ire is the conflict, **d**ismal *i*s the **d**in,
> Here shouts all **D**rury, there all L*i*ncoln's-*i*nn. (3.269–70)

In another, Dulness leads her "enamoured swain" on the grand tour where he

> Ju**d**icious **d**rank, and greatly-**d**aring **d**in'd;
> **D**ropt the **d**ull lumber of the Latin store.   (4.318–19)

And finally [d] helps to draw the curtain on the dead world:

> Lo! thy drea**d** Empire, CHAOS! is restor'**d**;
> Light **d**ies before thy uncreating wor**d**.   (4.653–54)

While [d] was important to Pope, in the *Dunciad* especially, nasals, initial or final, seem to provide the most
varied of his consonantal acoustic effects, from his recre-
ation not only of the sweet or mournful songs in the
pastorals—Damon's "strain" in *Spring* or Hylas's lament
in *Autumn*—but also of the unattractive humming, yawning, snoring, tuning of his dunces. In *Autumn* one extreme
occurs with "setting Phoebus," who "sho*ne* sere*ne*ly
bright" (13)

> When tu*ne*ful Hylas with melodious Moa*n*,
> Taught Rocks to weep and made the Mou*n*tains groa*n*.
>
> (15–16)

In the *Dunciad* are other extremes. Here the nasal hum of
dunces too wide awake is abetted by the many nasals as
well as by the phonesthemes [ʊ,ʌ] and [l], three other
echoes being purely gratuitous:

> The cla*m*'rous crowd is h*u*sh'd with m*u*gs of M*um*,
> 'Ti*ll* a*ll*, tu*n'd* equal, s*end* a ge*n*eral h*um*.   (2.385–86)

In an entirely different scene the dunces, now asleep or
sleepy, are described with the same nasals but also by
means of the same [ʊ,ʌ], and in addition there are the
polysyllabic echo of the [ɔ] in *yawn*, the striking diminution
of *s–n*, *sn* which helps to stress the irony that ties *son*[*s*] to
snore, and the punning end rhyme that "encores" the [o] of
both *snore* and *notes:*

> To the sa*me* *n*otes thy s*on*[s] shall h*um*, or sn*o*re,
> And *a*ll thy y*aw*ning d*au*ghters cry, enc*o*re.   (4.59–60)

As wonderfully mnemonic and ear pleasing as that couplet
is, there are many like it in Pope's poetry, whether sweet or
satirical, and in Epistle II of the *Moral Essays* there may be
an even better one that with an analogy describes Lady
Mary as she starts her day at the "flesh pots" in order to
end "fragrant at an evening Masque" (27–28):

So mor*n*ing I*n*sects that in m*u*ck beg*un*,
Shi*ne*, b*u*zz, and fly-blow in the setting-s*un*.

Not only are there two initial [m]'s and at least four final
[n]'s for the hum of *Insects*, but there are four [u,ʌ]'s for
the ugly *muck* and *buzz*, all to go with the typical Popeian
terminal assonance in one line and terminal alliteration in
the other.

Hiss, of course, is a favorite onomatopoeic word with
Pope, its end sound being a well known phonestheme.
Nearly always he enhanced the word's effect with other [s]
words, here the [s] being made final by the elision of *d* and *t*:

Redu*c*'d at la*s*[t] to hi*ss* in my own *d*ragon. (*Dun* 3.286)

Or the hissing goes with flames and is aided by final [z] as
well as initial [s]:

Now flame*s* the Cid, and now Perolla burn*s*;
Great Caesar roar*s*, and hisses in the fire*s*. (*Dun* 1.250–51)

Or the final [s] is for the *whistling* of minor poets as they
sing the praises of Bath or Tunbridge Wells:

Whose tuneful whi*s*[t]ling make*s* the waters pa*ss*.
(*Dun* 3.156)

Among the best of the many *hiss* passages in the *Dunciad* is
the description of one of the four "virtues" guarding Dulness (1.47–48):

Fier*ce* champion Fortitude, that know*s* no fear*s*
Of hi*ss*es, blow*s*, or want, or lo*ss* of ear*s*.

Not only does Pope here play on the words *Fierce* and
fears, but for the hissing he has two stressed syllables with
final [s] and four with final [z], all in addition to the [f]
alliteration, [o] assonance, and—if the [r] is not lost in the
preceding vowel—what David Masson calls "pure sequence" in the *f–r* of three words. But [s], especially when

final, can help produce other kinds of unattractive images, as in *The Rape of the Lock* (5.40),

> F*ans* cl*a*p, Silks ru*ss*le, and t*ou*gh Whalebo*nes* cr*a*ck,

where *clap, russle,* and *crack* are sound-sense words in a slow, rough line but where to assist in effecting the desired response Pope echoed not only the final [s] in "Silks russle" but also final [nz], initial [k], and two sets of vowels. In *Arbuthnot* there is a very similar rough line (216),

> Or pl*ai*ster'd po*s*t*s*, with Cl*a*p*s* in c*a*pitals,

in which the alliterations of [p] and [k] are obvious but where the phonestheme—the whistling final [s]—comes three times. In each line there is also a three-syllable assonance of [æ], a vowel Pope seems to have thought went well with unattractive pictures, one of the best examples in the *Dunciad* coming in his nasalized rendition of the asslike braying in the mock-heroic games:

> A*ss* intones to *A*ss,
> Harmonic tw*a*ng! of leather, horn, and br*a*ss. (2.253–54)

It may already be apparent, however, that the most unpleasant of Pope's vowels, as with so many other poets, is the one found in *ugly* and *dunce*. And it has been shown[17] how the *Dunciad*, the very title supplying the proper lexical support, so effectively echoes this phonestheme in dozens of lines such as these:

> Then n*u*mber'd with the p*u*ppies in the m*u*d,   (2.308)
>
> Behold an h*u*ndred s*o*ns, and each a D*u*nce;   (3.138)
>
> With Th*u*nder r*u*mbling from the m*u*stard bowl.   (2.226)

In this last line Pope's allusion to the London stage and its ironic way of producing thunder by rattling mustard bowls is made more ironic because he begins with the awful "Thunder rumbling" and then descends to the ill-matched

but assonating *mustard*. Then there is this couplet, which
to the five [ʊ,ʌ]'s adds two onomatopoeic words that both
alliterate and consonate:

> How here he sipp'd, how there he plunder'd snug,
> And suck'd all o'er, like an industrious Bug. (1.129–30)

Often in the *Dunciad* the vowel dominates whole sections,
as in these two groups of four successive lines. The first
group (2.405–8), which contains six [ʊ,ʌ]'s in stressed
syllables, records a mock epic simile that neatly parallels
Dutchman and *Dulness* and provides numerous accompanying vowel and consonant echoes, including polysyllabic alliterations of [s], [m], and the ever-present [d]:

> As what a Dutchman plumps into the lakes,
> One circle first, and then a second makes;
> What Dulness dropped among her sons imprest
> Like motion from one circle to the rest.

The second pair of couplets (2.415–18) has the vowel seven
times but also features five [ɛ]'s, an internal *Tongue* to go
with *hung*, and a number of alliterations and consonances,
the best of which opens with *Daniel* [Defoe], goes to *down*,
and concludes with *dead*:

> Norton, from Daniel and Ostroea sprung,
> Bless'd with his father's front, and mother's tongue,
> Hung silent down his never-blushing head;
> And all was hush'd, as Folly's self lay dead.

One of Pope's most devastating uses of the ugly [ʊ,ʌ]
comes near the end of the *Dunciad* in a couplet (4.525–26)
that begins with the proper lexical preparation in *vulgar*
and is stocked with animal images, phonic echoes, and
balanced sound-sense patterns:

> The vulgar herd turns off to roll with Hogs,
> To run with Horses, or to hunt with Dogs.

But Pope could echo vowels for beauty too. In the early

pastorals and *Windsor Forest*, for example, he assonated the soft front vowels for the pleasing sounds of nature. In "Winter" alone there are many passages that illustrate the technique. One couplet (21–22) has accented [ɪ] five times:

> Ye gentle Muses leave your Crystal Spr*i*ng,
> Let N*y*mphs and S*y*lvans Cypress Garlands br*i*ng.

And in these two quiet couplets together (79–82) there are eight stressed syllables—probably ten—each of which has the vowel sound of [i], four coming in the last line:

> In some still *Ev*'ning, when the whisp'ring Br*ee*ze
> Pants on the L*ea*ves, and dies upon the Tr*ee*s.
> To th*ee*, bright Goddess, oft a Lamb shall bl*ee*d,
> If t*ee*ming Ewes encr*ea*se my fl*ee*cy Br*ee*d.

These same vowels, it has been claimed (see chapter 1), help in English with images that are little, dainty, delicate, "teeny," that is, of course, if the proper cognitive surroundings are provided. While Dryden gives little support for the theory, Pope gives much. In the *Dunciad*, for example, although he paints ugly, dead scenes he also wishes to diminish his objects, to make them insignificant, and in the diminishing, [ɪ] is a favorite vowel. Not only are "C*i*bber" and "T*i*bald" his reigning dunces, but in the poem the chief rhyme words for *wit*, always ironic, are *sit* and *bit* whereas in *An Essay on Criticism*, where diminution is much less important, the chief rhyming words—eight of twelve times—are *fit* (appropriate) and *writ*, both very serious. Furthermore, with almost every [ɪ] name in the roll of dunces Pope has one or more assonating words that help belittle the image, as with the punning simile, "Ridpath is as dear as Mist" (1.208). But *The Rape of the Lock* provides an even better illustration of the diminished object, in this case dainty and delicate. There such important nouns as Sylph, Belinda, Nymph, Momentilla, Crispissa, Clarissa attract a hundred words like *sip, innocent, tim'rous,* *whisper*, *little*, *giddy*, *infant*, *mystic*, *silver*, and *glitt'ring*. Among the best of many "diminishing" lines are these four early ones, which to the six [i]'s add the soft [s] alliteration and, for the bell and watch, many nasals and liquid [l]'s:

> Thrice rung the Be*ll*, the S*l*ipper knock'd the Ground,
> And the press'd Watch return'd a *s*i*l*ver Sound.
> Be*l*inda st*ill* her downy P*ill*ow prest,
> Her Guardian S*y*lph prolong'd the ba*l*my Rest.   (1.17–20)

Another vowel Pope echoed for onomatopoeic effect is [o], which as Shakespeare and Dryden had done before him, he employed for melancholy or lugubriousness. Poems such as *The Dunciad* and *An Essay on Man*, then, have little need for the vowel and, indeed, echo it seldom, even in rhyme words. The last thirty lines of the *Dunciad*, for example, often admired, have no more than eight stressed syllables with [o], although that book has more examples of the vowel than does any of the other three, including several well-known ironies such as "We n*o*bly take the high Pri*o*ri R*o*ad" (4.471). The best kind of exception comes in Pope's elevated, but mock-heroic, style of Book II when Smedley dives into "The quaking mud, that cl*o*s'd, and *o*p'd n*o* m*o*re" (292). Perhaps the most extended use of the phonestheme comes in "Winter," the doleful dirge for the dead Daphne, where Pope inserted fifty-four [o]'s in accented syllables, including sixteen pairs in as many lines, all combined with much alliteration of [d] to help produce a mood of sadness.

But Pope has other sad poems that employ [o] effectively. One of them, the "Elegy to the Memory of an Unfortunate Lady," has this couplet (33–34), which opens with a word that sets the scene both lexically and acoustically:

> C*o*ld is that breast which warm'd the world bef*o*re,
> And th*o*se love-darting eyes must r*o*ll n*o* m*o*re.

Nine, in fact, of the rhyme pairs of this short poem are [o] words and the last words of all are "no more." Another mournful poem, "Eloisa to Abelard," has more, and more successful, [o] assonances than all of the long *Dunciad*. There the words *more*, *no more*, *woe*, and *soul* occur often, attracting similar sounds. Eloisa pleads with the ghost of her lover in a couplet (289–90) where four of the six long [o]'s are followed by the phonestheme [l]:

> N*o* fly me, fly me! far as P*ole* from P*ole*;
> Rise Alps between us! and wh*ole* *o*ceans r*oll*.

She begs mournfully in six lines (241–46) loaded with phonic echoes, four of the echoes being polysyllabic, one being the [w] which Spenser and Shakespeare liked for laments, and one being the [o] nine times:

> Alas n*o* m*o*re!—methinks *w*e *w*andring g*o*
> Thro' dreary wastes, and weep each other's *w*oe;
> Where round some m*o*uld'ring tow'r pale ivy creeps,
> And l*ow*-brow'd rocks hang nodding *o*'er the deeps.
> Sudden you mount! you beckon from the skies;
> Clouds interp*o*se, waves r*o*ar, and winds arise.

Near the end of her monologue (345–46) Eloisa begins a sad prophecy thus:

> Then, ages hence, when all my w*o*es are *o*'er
> When this rebellious heart shall beat n*o* m*o*re.

And at the very end six lines have seven stressed syllables with [o], including *deplore*, *behold*, *more*, *story*, and this closing couplet:

> The well-sung w*o*es will soothe my pensive gh*o*st;
> He best can paint 'em who shall feel 'em m*o*st.

Also like Shakespeare and Dryden, as well as like twentieth-century linguists such as Jespersen, Pope seems to have felt that the diphthong in *shine* and other "bright" words was "undoubtedly of wonderful force in printing the image"[18] of light "on the reader." Here, in a couplet that provides one example, the first important word *Sun's* leads to four [aɪ,əɪ]'s but also to four other [s]'s just as the other most important word *Moon's* attracts an [m] alliteration and an [nz] consonance. To show again how echo-conscious Pope was, all echoes are marked.

> So when the Su*n*'s broa*d* beam has t*i*r'*d* the s*i*ght,
> All m*i*ld asce*nds* the Moo*n*'s m*o*re s*o*ber l*i*ght.
>   (*Moral Ep* 2.253–54)

An example, much more extended, of this phonestheme is to be found in the *Messiah*, the last twenty-three lines of which, beginning "Rise, crown'd with Light," have nineteen [aɪ,əɪ]'s. The best use in Pope, however, of the diphthong is in the opening of Canto II of *The Rape of the Lock*. Here, the description of Belinda on the Thames as she "rivals" the sun has twenty [aɪ,əɪ]'s in sixteen lines, six of them occurring in the couplet,

> Br*i*ght as the Sun, her *Eye*s the Gazers str*i*ke,
> And, l*i*ke the Sun, they sh*i*ne on all al*i*ke.   (2.13–14)

Near the beginning of Book 5 of the *Iliad*, Pope carried this sound through a description of Tydides' helm and shield as Pallas bathed her hero in "celestial lightning." The manuscript of the poem shows how in these lines he worked with both imagery and sound. The last couplet gave him most trouble, as three variants indicate. First he wrote,

> The goddess with her breath the flame suppl*i*es
> Br*i*ght as the star whose f*i*res in autumn r*i*se.

Next he tried,

> Her breath div*i*ne thick streaming flames suppl*i*es,
> Br*i*ght as the star that f*i*res th'autumnal sk*i*es.

But finally he settled on, and published,

Th'unwearied blaze incessant streams supplies,
Like the red star that fires th'autumnal skies.

While making a prolonged attempt to be more "correct"
and "harmonious," Pope gave up the breath of his "god-
dess," carefully kept the simile of the autumn star, and
always insisted on having at least four [aɪ,əɪ]'s to go with
the lightning that inspired the soul of Tydides.[19]

Assonance was Pope's favorite acoustic device, and
perhaps it was even more important to him for onomatopoeia than was alliteration or consonance; but he had an
infinite variety of representative sounds. He could, for
example, give us shooting stars with a [t] consonance, even
though he might also supply auditory accompaniment with
two sets of vowel echoes, as in

Pursue the Stars that shoot athwart the Night. (*Rape* 2.82)

Or with consonance he could emphasize the [z] sound of
drowsy:

As verse, or prose, infuse the drowzy God.   (*Dun* 2.396)

But he could also fit sound to an image of sleep by the
diminution of *s–l*, *sl* in *soul* and *slumber* and by repeating
initial and final [s] as well as the vowel of *soothe*,

Which mos[t] conduce to sooth the soul in slumbers;
                                                      (*Dun* 2.369)

or the same effect could be achieved almost entirely with
vowel echoes,

Now pleasing Sleep had seal'd each mortal Eye,
Stretch'd in their Tents the Grecian Leaders lie.*
                                             (*Iliad* 2.1–2)

---

*Again one cannot be sure how Pope pronounced *pleasing*, *seal'd*, and
Leaders, since at least two of the three words probably had [e] or [ɛ:] in
the generation just before him. His favorite rhyme for *please* is *ease*, but
at least once he rhymed *ease* with *these* (*Ess. on Man* 4.21–22), as did
Dryden (see Wyld, *Rhymes*, p. 60, for the possible adopting by Pope's
time, in certain dialects, of [i] in some *ea* words in group *e*²).

Onomatopoeia, however, is not produced by phonic recurrences alone. The tempo of the line, the type of meter, the sound of individual words, even the punctuation—all can help evoke the desired response. Nor does assonance or any other sound effect by itself make a poem, as Pope knew well when in *An Essay on Criticism* he attacked the "tuneful fools" who "demand equal syllables alone" and "haunt Parnassus but to please their ear"; or when in the postscript to his *Odyssey* he warned against letting sound supersede sense; or when in his Guardian No. 40 he gleefully quoted the damning lines from Namby-Pamby Philips:

> O woful Day! O Day of Woe! quoth he,
> And woful I, who live the Day to see!

Nevertheless, we are still too hesitant in accepting the certain fact that the sense of a piece of writing cannot be separated from its sound. Just as Pope and other poets of his day depended heavily on the visual arts for their imagery, as Jean Hagstrum has proved,[20] it is also true that for them "music resembles poetry"—both arts hope to please the ear and touch the heart. And if W. K. Wimsatt, writing of Pope, the "best rhymer in English," is correct in believing that "the words of a rhyme, with their curious harmony of sound and distinction of sense, are an amalgam of the sensory and the logical, . . . the ikon in which the idea is caught,"[21] is it not just as true that vowels and consonants systematically and tastefully echoed within the line may affect the reader's unconscious and thereby help to form the image, impress the idea, and arouse the emotion? Of course, the writer's effects, as with the painter and the musician, may often be the result of inspiration rather than of calculation, but it is obvious that poets like Pope produce many of their effects deliberately. His poems attest to his concern for "sweet and pleasing" numbers, for "printing the image" with sounds, for a mnemonic and onomatopoeic use of phones; and while he has as much consonance as Dryden and more alliteration than most poets, assonance—even more than rhyme—must be considered the chief of all his echoing "voices."

4

James Thomson's
Luxuriant Language

"It . . . sometimes can be charged with filling the ear more
than the mind"—Dr. Johnson.

Few poems have been so often reprinted or so often condemned and admired as James Thomson's *The Seasons*,[1]
and one of the most controversial of that once popular
poem's characteristics is its diction. Although Dr. Johnson
admired Thomson, he spoke for a large group of readers,
including Wordsworth and Hazlitt, when in *The Lives of
the English Poets* he said of one aspect of Thomson's
diction, it "is in the highest degree florid and luxuriant. . . .
It is too exuberant and sometimes can be charged with
filling the ear more than the mind."[2] But an even greater
number of readers, if not always such honored ones, have
liked Thomson's language, from John More's (1777) praise
of the "luxuriant images," to Robert Bell's (1860) admiration for the "richness and luxuriance of phrase," to the
twentieth century's scholarly defense.[3] In spite, however,
of the perennially strong protest against Dr. Johnson's
charges about the ear-filling qualities of Thomson's poetry,
nowhere in the long and still lingering debate has anyone
spoken of the nature of the sounds in that luxuriant language.

The neglect is all the more perplexing when we remember, first, that the poet himself insisted that he chose
blank verse for *The Seasons* because it is "far more harmonious than rhyme" and, second, because he once listed
"music" ahead of image, sentiment, and thought as one of
the four chief characteristics of poetry.[4] Furthermore, it
has been shown that repetition is perhaps "the most im-

portant structural principle" in *The Seasons*,[5] and repetition is perhaps the most important characteristic of music, whether by that term we mean pure music or the pleasing sounds that words can produce. Now Thomson made less use of rhyme, anaphora, and incremental repetition than did most other eighteenth-century poets, and his metrical stresses are not so regular as those in the heroic couplet, but he did employ alliteration, assonance, and consonance with as much variety and subtlety, as frequently and consciously, as any other important writer of his day. Nowhere in Ralph Cohen's thorough tracing of Thomson criticism, however, is any one of these three terms mentioned, and yet a study of Thomson's use of such acoustic devices will reveal much about the nature of his luxuriant language.

Like Dryden and Pope he went against conservative critical theory and employed phonic echoes in abundance. Their concentration in *The Seasons* is, in fact, far greater than for a relatively unornamental poet such as Wordsworth. The first 200 lines of *Winter*, for example, have at least 100 alliterations and 110 assonances, a proportion in each case of about one to two lines, while the opening 200 lines of Wordsworth's *Prelude* have, by a generous count, only 1 assonance to 5 lines and even fewer alliterations. The contrast becomes still more significant if one notes that over 20 of Thomson's echoes, and only 5 of Wordsworth's, are polysyllabic.[6] As with other poets of his day and just before, Thomson's auditory appeal is heaviest in the purple passages, especially those describing the sights and sounds of nature, and less heavy in narrative or argumentative sections. In this image from *Spring*, for example, there are perhaps 16 stressed syllables every one of which is involved in at least one echo:[7]

> Th'exp*a*nsive *At*mosph*e*re is cr*a*mp'*d* with C*o*ld;
> But f*ull* of L*i*fe, and v*i*vif*y*ing S*oul*,
> L*i*fts the l*i*ght Clou*ds* subl*i*me, and sprea*ds* them th*i*n.
>
> (28–30)

In the 3 lines there are 4 assonances—2 of 3 syllables, 1 of 4, and the end echo in "cold" and "soul"—to go with the alliterations, two polysyllabic, of [f], [k], and [l] and the consonance of [l], [t], and [dz]. Although he does have sections with relatively few such echoes, as in the long account of the pleasures of evening reading in *Winter*, Thomson employed ornaments of sound as much as his chief models Lucretius, Virgil, Dryden, and Pope.

In order to show that these acoustic aids are typical of Thomson and at the same time more profuse than for poets with whom he is sometimes associated, we can compare a well-known passage in the poetry of John Keats with a similar one in *The Seasons*. Keats's lush *Autumn* opens,

> Season of mists and mellow fruitfulness,
>   Close bosom-friend of the maturing sun;
> Conspiring with him how to load and bless
>   With fruit the vines that roun[d] the thatch-eaves run;
> To bend with apples the moss'd cottage trees,
>   And fill all fruit with ripeness to the core;
>   To swell the gourd, and plump the hazel shells
> With a sweet kernel; to set budding more,
>   And still more, later flowers for the bees,
>   Until they think warm days will never cease,
>   For Summer has o'er-brimm[ed] their clammy cells.

Thomson's *Autumn* has many such sensuous descriptions, including one so like that in the later poem:

> In chearful error, let us tread the maze
> Of Autumn, unconfin'd; and taste, reviv'd,
> The breath of orchard big with bending fruit.*
> Obedient to the breeze, and beating ray,
> From the deep-loaded bough a mellow shower,
> Incessant melts away. The juicy pear

---

*For *breath* and, in the next line, *beating*, see Wyld, *Rhymes*, pp. 55, 59, 88–89. That Thomson almost surely had [i] in words such as *beat* see chapter 1, n. 36, with its long list of e^2 words rhyming with *ee* words, all taken from *The Castle of Indolence*.

Lies, in a soft profúsion, scatter'd round.
A várious sweetness swélls the géntle ráce.   (626–33)

The question now is not which of the two groups of images is more attractive, either lexically or acoustically, but, rather, which poet depended more on internal echoes for his effects, for his appeal to the reader's ear. Keats is to be considered a more decorative poet than, say, Wordsworth, and while this opening section of "To Autumn" is indeed ripe with language that appeals to the sight and the touch—*mists, mellow, core, moss'd, gourd, kernel, clammy*—it obviously has far fewer phonic echoes than the passage from Thomson. Of perhaps fifty-three stressed syllables in Keats's lines, only twenty-two are involved in any kind of internal alliteration, assonance, or consonance, and only three of them twice. On the other hand, of Thomson's thirty-eight stressed syllables, twenty-seven participate in such internal echoes, thirteen of them at least twice, a strikingly greater proportion. Nor is the proportion noticeably altered if one counts the end repetitions in both passages. The chief difference is not in the consonant echoes; Keats has at most five assonances, each of two syllables, while Thomson, in a shorter passage, has eleven—one of four syllables, one of three—that, in spite of the seven initial [b]'s in three lines, dominate his description.[8] Thomson's ornaments of language are indeed more luxuriant than those of Keats or Wordsworth or, for that matter, perhaps any important early nineteenth-century poet. Furthermore, we can now show that they were often conscious on his part, as conscious as they were with his friend Pope.

Because Thomson worked for twenty years at improving, altering, and expanding his major poem, we can study not only the growth of the poet's mind but also the development of his art and technique. Such a study is made easier by Otto Zippel's 1908 volume[9] containing all the many editions of *The Seasons* from the first appearance of

Winter in 1726 to the final authorized version of the four *Seasons* in 1746, two years before Thomson's death. *Winter* alone was expanded to four times its original length.

There are many kinds of changes that the poem underwent, and Thomson had many reasons for making them.[10] He altered the structure: a short passage on Scotland and a description of the aurora borealis, for example, both in the first edition of *Summer*, he moved to the 1730 *Autumn*, which was further lengthened by the transference of almost 100 lines from *Winter*. He inserted narratives to make the whole more lively and dramatic, one of them being the tale of the cottager lost in a snow storm. Like Coleridge after him he read travel books in order to find more colorful and appropriate images, among them the northern ice formations described in Martens's *Voyage into Spitzbergen and Greenland* of 1711. He added primitivistic passages about the Laplanders and the English country life and a humanitarian appeal for improved conditions in English jails. And through the years he added to or altered his consonant and vowel repetitions, even though from the beginning he emphasized what he called the "music" of language. By comparing the various editions of *The Seasons* one can find many examples of Thomson's desire to fill the ear.

Very often the changes in sound accompany changes in imagery. In *Summer* when "bounteous Power" (1728.433) became "Parent-Power" (1744.540), the poet discarded a weak image for a better one and at the same time gave up an assonance for an alliteration. Nearby, the phrase "I stand aghast" (1728.455) was changed to "I check my steps" (1744.589). In modifying what he decided was an overly strong image, Thomson lost his assonance but was able to find another to take its place. One of the best improvements in the imagery of *Summer* has to do with the description of a waterfall. In 1728 the short passage ended with "tormented" water falling

From Steep to Steep, with wild, infracted Course,
And, res[t]less, roaring to the humble Vale.   (465–66)

By 1746 the image was extended to sharpen the contrast between the turbulent fall at the beginning and the quiet vale at the end:

And falling fast from gradual Slope to Slope,
With wild infracted Course, and lessen'd Roar,
It gains a safer Bed, and steals, at last,
Along the Mazes of the quiet Vale.   (603–6)

But while Thomson was improving the image, he managed to add numerous ornaments of sound—the [f] and [l] alliterations, the three [a]'s, two more [o]'s, two [ɛ]'s, and two pairs of [e]'s—all in stressed syllables.

One of the most interesting alterations in *Summer* occurs in the tale of Damon, who in 1727 secretly watched three naked girls bathing in a cool stream. By 1744 the three girls had become only the beautiful Musidora, for whom the now gallant Damon left a note before turning his head and stealing away. The much longer account in the final version ends with four of the most echo-laden lines in *The Seasons*, those describing Musidora's feelings on finding the note:

With wild Surprize,
As if to Marble struck, devoid of Sense,
A stupid Moment motionless she stood:
So stands the Statue that enchants the World. (1336–39)

Although the five-syllable alliteration of the [st] phonestheme—carefully prepared for—stands out, Thomson also employed an [m] alliteration and three assonances involving at least eight vowels. One of the unique facts about this luxuriant language, however, is that in earlier editions the last line is found in an entirely different context (1730.1019). Thomson liked it so much that in 1744 he picked it up intact, moved it, made it fit the new story, and tied it to the other

lines with the echo that stressed the girl's stunned inability
to move.

That Thomson apparently worked hardest with assonance can be shown with certain examples from *Spring*. In
1728 he wrote,

> Whi*le* in the rosy Va*le*
> Love br*ea*th'd his *I*nfant Sighs, from Anguish fr*ee*,*
> Fragrant with Bl*i*ss, and only wept for Joy.   (276–78)

In 1730 he gave up *Fragrant* for *Replete*, thereby losing the
[fr] alliteration but adding a third stressed [i]. Then in
1744 and 1746 the final version read,

> Whi*le* in the rosy Va*le*
> Love br*ea*th'd his *I*nfant Sighs from Anguish fr*ee*,
> And full repl*ete* with Bl*i*ss; save the sw*eet* Pain.
>
>   (276–78)

Thomson had brought back the [f] alliteration, added four
other echoes, and ended with a four-syllable assonance of
[i]. Elsewhere in *Spring* a phrase without any echo, "to
deck the flowing Hair" (1728.447), was almost entirely
rewritten to provide an assonance,

> to gr*a*ce thy br*ai*ded Hair.   (1744.447)

In the 1728 *Summer* Thomson wrote,

> Of younder Gr*o*ve, of w*i*ldest, largest Gr*o*wth;
> That, h*i*gh embowering in the middle Air . . .   (404–5)

These lines, already heavy with echoes, became in 1744,

> Of yonder Gr*o*ve, of w*i*ldest largest Gr*o*wth;
> That, fo*r*ming h*i*gh in Ai*r* a woodland qu*ire* . . . (517–18)

By moving "Air" back and changing other words in the
second line, Thomson was able not only to make use of
what Dryden had called the beauties of *r* but to run the

---

*For *breath'd*, see note, p. 120.

vowel of *wildest* through three syllables. The same care for vowel echoes can be found in the texts of any *Season*.[11]

Sometimes, of course, Thomson was willing to part with a good sound in order to achieve a more important end, as he did once when he lost two assonances and a consonance in one line of *Winter* (1730.8) so he could borrow the word *ocean* from that line, move it to a nearby passage, and avoid repetition. But his revisions were much more liable to improve the echoes, or add entirely new ones. The 1744 *Summer*, for example, reworks a 1727 scene of unusual lurid darkness that slowly covers a grove of trees and then mantles the whole sky just before a crushing storm of hail descends. The earlier passage describes the cloud in four and one-half lines:

> *Thence Niter, Sulphur*, Vitriol, *on the Day*
> Stream, and *fermenting in yon baleful Cloud*,
> Extensive o'er the World, *a reddening Gloom!*
> In dreadful promptitude to spring, await
> The high Command. . . .   (741–45)

The later description, which kept the words italicized in the passage just quoted, was expanded to these eight and one-half lines:

> Thence N*i*ter, Sulphur, and the f*i*ery Sp*ume*
> Of f*a*t Bit*um*en, stea*m*ing on the D*ay*,
> With v*a*rious-tinctur'd Tr* a*ins of l*a*tent Fl*a*me,
> Pollu*te* the Sky, and in yon b*a*leful Clou*d*,
> A re*d*dening Gloom, a M*a*gazine of F*ate*,
> Ferment; till, by the Touch etherial r*ous*'d,
> The dash of Cl*ou*ds, or *i*rritating W*a*r
> Of f*i*ghting W*i*nds, while all is calm below,
> They furious spring.   (1100–1108)

This final picture is no doubt far superior in both visual and tactual imagery—*Spume, Bitumen, tinctur'd, Pollute*—but it is infinitely more ear appealing. That ear appeal is, of course, the result of a variety of effects, but outstanding among them are the thick phonic repetitions. While in the original there are perhaps one effective consonance and three assonances, one polysyllabic, in the final version there are four excellent final consonant echoes —("Spu*me*," "Bitu*m*en," "Stea*m*ing"), ("la*t*ent," "Pollu*te*"; "Fa*te*," "Fermen*t*"), and ("i*rr*itating Wa*r*"); there are seven alliterations, and there are five vowel echoes, including the five [e]'s in six successive stressed syllables beginning with "Day." It is one of Thomson's most attractive passages and was possible only because through the years he concentrated so hard on improving his work and, perhaps as much as anything else, on increasing its acoustic appeal.

It is now known that Lord Lyttelton gave Thomson some small help in improving *The Seasons*, and it was long thought that Pope's handwriting could be found in the margins of Thomson's manuscripts. But while by the middle of the nineteenth century Thomson was shown to have been independent of Pope's direct help,[12] there is no doubt that Pope's influence was exerted indirectly on his friend's major poem. The 1744 *Seasons* has more changes than can be found in any other edition; some of them echo lines written by Pope, who died that year. And the similar passages are among the most ear appealing by two of the most ear-conscious poets who wrote in English. Just as in *Windsor Forest* Pope paraphrased more than one line from Denham's *Cooper's Hill* or borrowed Dryden's "well-breath'd Beagles," Thomson was willing to take phrases from *Windsor Forest*. In 1713 Pope had rewritten an old line of the manuscript version of that poem and ended with

Nor **P**o so swells the f*a*bling **P**oet's L*a*ys.   (227)

In 1746, also completely reworking an old line, Thomson wrote,

The f*a*bling **P**oets took their g*o*lden *A*ge.   (*Spring* 325)

Not only did he borrow Pope's "fabling Poets"; he managed to work in the same [e] and [o] assonances. Even
better as an example of sound similarity in the two poets is
Thomson's mind- and ear-filling description of shooting
stars in *Winter* (127–28):

> The Stars obtuse em*it* a sh*i*vering Ray;
> Or fr*e*quent s*eem* to sh*oot* athwar*t* the Gl*oom*.

The second of these lines is remarkably like one from
Pope's *Rape of the Lock* (2.82);

> Purs*ue* the St*a*rs that sh*oot* athw*a*rt the Nigh*t*.

In each of the two lines every stressed syllable starts or
continues an echo of at least one phone. Pope has two
assonances and one three-syllable consonance of [t] to
reproduce the shooting. Thomson also has two assonances, and while he toned down the shooting by omitting
one final [t], he emphasized the image of winter gloom by
echoing the vowel of that word and, especially, by adding
the consonance of [m].

Although Thomson seems to have learned something
about sound effects from his friend Pope, there is one chief
difference between the way echoes are employed in *The
Seasons* and the way they are employed in Pope's poems:
Thomson was less able to emphasize rhetorical or structural balance by balancing sounds. The difference, of
course, stems primarily from the fact that Thomson's
run-on blank verse—without the rhyme, without such a
regular cadence, without any rule regarding the caesura—
did not lend itself to such neat cognitive effects as did the
Popeian couplet, and even his rhyming Spenserian stanzas
in *The Castle of Indolence* have relatively few of them. He
was, nevertheless, too much a product of the eighteenth
century to avoid structural balance completely, and when
he did employ it he was as prone as Dryden and Pope to let
sounds emphasize the balance. About two-thirds of the

lines in *The Seasons* are end-stopped and can, therefore, more easily fit the patterns developed by the couplet. In *Autumn*, for example, Thomson wrote,

> Presents the dow*n*y peach; the shi*n*ing plumb,   (664)
>
> The tankards f*o*am; and the strong table gr*o*ans.   (499)

In one line the parallel adjectives consonate while their nouns alliterate; in the other, the parallel subjects alliterate and their verbs assonate. Also in *Autumn* the parallel verbs alone can alliterate:

> Sudden, the ditches swell; the meadows swim,   (333)
>
> To swim along, and swell the mazy dance;   (586)

or they can assonate:

> To j*o*y at anguish, and del*i*ght in blood,   (396)
>
> To r*ai*se the Virtues, anim*a*te the Bliss.   (596)

Perhaps Thomson's best balanced consonance is in a zeugma found in *The Castle of Indolence*,

> Sere*ne* yet war*m*, huma*ne* yet fir*m* his mind,   (1.65)

where the primary adjectives end in [n] and the secondary adjectives in [m].[13]

The caesural sound balance favored so much by writers of the heroic couplet is found surprisingly often in Thomson's blank verse. Here two lines in a row in *Winter* emphasize the medial caesura, one with assonance, the other with assonance and alliteration:

> Frosty, succ*ee*d; and thr*o*' the bl*ue* Ser*e*ne,
> For S*i*ght too f*i*ne, th'etherial N*i*ter fl*i*es.   (693–94)

Close by, the first of two lines has a caesural consonance of [l] while the second has a double assonance in a chiasmus that Pope or Dryden might have written:

Where sits the Sou*l*, int*e*nse, coll*e*cted, coo*l*,[14]
Br*i*ght as the Sk*i*es, and as the S*ea*son K*ee*n.   (702–3)

Although anaphora was even more a favorite rhetorical weapon with eighteenth-century poets than with their successors—except perhaps Walt Whitman—many of them[15] were aware that the device could be made more subtle by reducing the number of repeated words and combining them with consonant or vowel echoes. Here Thomson contrived a kind of anaphoric alliteration:

How **d**ead the Vegetable Kingdom lies!
How **d**umb the tuneful!   (*Winter* 1027–28)

And in *Winter* he can be discovered creating an assonance that has something of the effect of anaphora. In 1726 he wrote,

To lay their Passions in a gentle Calm,
And **w**oo lone **Q**uiet, in her s*i*lent **W**alks,   (38–39)

which in 1730 was transferred to *Autumn* thus:

To s*oo*th the throbbing **P**assions into **P**eace
And **w**oo lone Qu*i*et in her s*i*lent **W**alks.   (908–9)

His final version had retained the sounding second line entire, but the first line added not only the [p] alliteration but the word *soothe* so that the two initial stressed syllables would have the same vowel.

Since there are a number of run-on lines in *The Seasons*, Thomson did not in that poem so often as Pope or Dryden emphasize line endings with a vowel or consonant repetition in the final stressed syllables, even though his blank verse will be found to have more such terminal echoes than any blank verse written outside the eighteenth century. Three times in *Winter*, for example, there are successive terminal alliterations, among them "**b**itter **B**read," "**w**intry **W**inds" (335–36); and three times there are successive ter-

minal assonances, among them "double Sons," "brightest
Skies" (591–92). The end rhymes of *The Castle of Indolence* attract far more phonic repetitions at the ends of lines,
perhaps as many as are to be found in the heroic couplet.
There are seven of them, in fact, in two stanzas of that
poem (1.72, 77).

Blank verse may not be so suitable for sound parallelism
as the heroic couplet, but Thomson's blank verse was
eminently suited for other kinds of emphasis and for the
fitting of sound to sense. Just as much as any poet from
Chaucer to Pope, for example, he tied adjective to noun
with a vowel or consonant echo. Often one can catch him in
the act of altering a word in order to achieve this kind of
binding. In 1728 he wrote "homely Fowls"; in 1744 he
wrote "household fowls." In the same way "hilly Wave"
became "inflated Wave," and "employless Greyhound"
was changed to "vacant Greyhound." "Mighty Pride"
already had the assonance, but Thomson improved the
image by exchanging *Mighty* for *Tyrant* even though he
carefully kept the vowel echo.[16]

Because of the nature of its content Thomson's blank
verse may have more attempts at extended onomatopoeia
than Pope's heroic couplets, as many perhaps as Dryden's
Georgics. In an early Lucretian attack on luxury, he wrote,

> A Season's Glitter! In soft-circling Robes.
>
> (*Summer* 1727.300)

Then seeing an opportunity not only to add a more scathing
image but to tie sound to sense by means of phonic echoes,
in particular a consonance, he revised the line to read,

> A Season's Glitter! Thus they flutter on.   (1744.348)

In "shiver every feather" he repeated the final [v] of the
onomatopoeic *shiver*. With a nearby word *restless* he
echoed in Popeian fashion the initial [r], the final [s] phonestheme, even the initial weak [l], of the even more

onomatopoeic *rustling*, and he extended the sound of the same word by placing it close to *incessant*.[17]

One of Thomson's great teachers in the poetry of nature and reflection was Lucretius. But the author of *De Rerum Natura* was also a master of the sense-echoing phrase,[18] attempting to convey with language the crackling of fire, the running of water, the movements of humans and animals. And he tried musical instruments in such lines as "tympana tenta tonant palmis et cymbala circum" (2.618). Although Thomson had no occasion to give us the instruments of an orchestra, he often hoped to suggest the sounds of nature. With the phonesthemes [s] and [l] and the diphthong [aʊ], he believed he was capturing the owl's sad sound:

> Assiduous, in his Bower, the wai*l*ing Owl
> Plies his sad Song.   (*Winter* 142–43)

With the same [l] and [s] to go with other appropriate sounds—some of them phonesthemes—final [d], [n], and [nd], initial [w] and [st], he tried the equally sad wail of the nightingale, at the same time making the passage more acoustically attractive with at least five assonances in five lines:

> she sings
> Her Sorrows thro' the Nigh*t*; and, on the Bough
> Sad-si*tt*ing, s*t*i*ll* at every dying Fa*ll*
> T*a*kes up ag*ain* her her lament*a*ble St*r*ain
> Of w*ind*ing Woe, till w*i*de ar*ound* the Wood[s]
> S*i*gh at her Song, and with her Wail res*ound*.
>   (*Spring* 720–25)

The consonants [l] and [n], as well as [s], are favorites for imitating in language the softer sights and sounds of nature. In *Spring* when

> the L*i*ly dr*inks*
> The latent R*ill*, scar*ce* *oo*zing thro' the Gra*ss*,
> Of Growth luxuriant,   (495–97)

Thomson not only repeated the vowel of the sound-sense *ooze*; he alliterated and consonated the [l]'s of *Lily*, echoed the [s] of *grass*, and provided three [ɪ]'s, one of the front vowels Dryden also liked for such scenes. And as with Dryden, another front vowel, [i], was a favorite with Thomson if his nature scene was more or less calm. In *Spring*, for example, he made a plea for walking

> Where the Breeze blows from yon extended Field
> Of blossom'd Beans,*   (502–3)

and in an *Autumn* paean to his friend Dodington's country seat, the poet ran nine stressed front vowels—all close to [i]—through four lines, beginning the passage thus,

> In this glad season, while his last, best beams
> The sun sheds equal o'er the meeken'd day,   (641 ff.)

and in 1744 adding another such vowel to the first line in this fashion,

> In this glad Season, while his sweetest beams, . . . (654)

The same vowel, combined with a medley of other phonic recurrences, was—again with Thomson as well as with other poets—apparently best for sleepy scenes, as in this primitivistic account of a happy, carefree, but lazy, awakening in an early spring:

> The first fresh Dawn then wak'd the gladden'd Race
> Of uncorrupted Men, nor blush'd to see
> The Sluggard sleep beneath her sacred Beam.
> (*Spring* 242–44)

Although Thomson was less idealistic about the backward Eskimos described by travelers, he was even more onomatopoeic with their cold, lifeless sleeping, his seven-

---

*Although one cannot be sure, the modern [i] of *Beans*—and in the next quotation—*season* and *beams*, all *e²* words in Wyld's categories, probably were standard for Thomson's and Pope's day. See note, p. 120.

word image, with five heavy syllables, thick and slow with
[s] and [z] consonance and two assonances:

> Immers'd in Furs,
> Doze the gross Race.   (*Winter* 943–44)

Just as yellow was perhaps Thomson's favorite color,
light was one of his favorite images, and following a well-
established tradition he was liable to let the sound of [ɔɪ, aɪ]
control such images. In *Summer* the sun suffuses the
"lively Diamond" with "Collected Light" (142–43), and
unheeding men "pass / An idle Summer-Life in Fortune's
Shine" till time comes "Behind, and strikes them from the
Book of Life" (346–47, 351). Thomson's other works make
constant use of this phonestheme, for example, "A Poem
Sacred to the Memory of Sir Isaac Newton, " which re-
counts the great scientist's many interests in the physical
world, including his experiments with light and the refract-
ing of light. Here, in three passages of six, seven, and eight
lines that tell of those experiments, Thomson subdued his
other sound echoes in order to let the diphthong [aɪ,ɔɪ]
dominate.[20] And his last important poem, *Liberty*, because
of the nature of its subject, echoes the phonestheme in
dozens of passages, whether Thomson was speaking of
physical brightness or of the light of virtue or knowledge.[21]

As with all his auditory effects, one can often discover
Thomson working for improvement in his fitting of sound to
sense. In attempting to imitate the sound of winter winds,
he wrote in 1730,

> Muttering, the winds at eve, with hoarser voice
> Blow blustering from the south.   (*Winter* 701–2)

This version he altered slightly in 1744 to read thus:

> Muttering, the Winds at Eve, with Blunted Point,
> Blow hollow-blustering from the South.   (988–89)

The first pair of lines is rich in echoes, but the final pair has more and may be even better as a representation of the winds Thomson had in mind. While he gave up the [s] consonance of the onomatopoeic "hoarser voice," its replacement, "blunted point," produced all sorts of effects. First, it kept the vowel that was needed to assonate with *Winds*. Second, it repeated the final, stressed [t] of *Muttering* not once but twice. Third, since the words *Muttering* and *Blustering* were a bit far apart for the assonance to be heard best, *blunted*, inserted half way between, caused the three-syllable vowel echo to be most effective. And fourth, *blunted* added a third [bl] to the initial echoes in the very onomatopoeic *Blow* and *blustering*. Throughout his career Thomson worked in this fashion at such sound-sense patterns.

There is no doubt, then, that the popular modern defense of Thomson's so-called neoclassical diction and luxuriant language needs to note how much the consonant and vowel echoes affect the quality of that language. Bernard Fehr,[22] for example, talks of sentence syntax, versification, and descriptive epithets when he analyzes "a lavish display of rococo" in seven lines of *Autumn*, but he does not notice that in the seven lines there are five assonances—one of three syllables—and three alliterations—also one of three syllables. Geoffrey Tillotson defends the image in *Winter* (261–62) of "The **bl**e*a*ting K*i*nd" that "*Eye* the **bl**e*a*k heaven" without regard for the two assonances and the alliteration that must have helped determine Thomson's choice of words. The Thomson line that has perhaps evoked the most divergent opinions is one in *Spring* (361),

A sh*o*reless *o*cean tumbled round the gl*o*be,"

from an eighteenth-century comment that the image is inappropriate to Bonamy Dobrée's belief that the line is "miraculous." It may be that the words were selected here for sound as much as for sense. At least, the image strikes the eye no more than the three [o]'s resound in the ear. It may be too that Thomson's poems do not "fill the ear more than the mind" but that, at their best, the oral appeal is related to the intellectual and emotional involvement. But whether any reader condemns or admires those poems, their "luxuriant language" depends very much on the phonic echoes that were as important to the eighteenth century's blank verse as to its heroic couplet.

5

Graces of Harmony
in Varied Verse

"There is sound and sense, and truth and nature in the trifling compass of ten little syllables"—Goldsmith.[1]

For Thomson was by no means the only eighteenth-century writer whose medium was blank verse. There were, for example, Edward Young (1683–1765) and Robert Blair (1699–1746), who had published their best work before Pope and Thomson were dead. Young's *Night Thoughts* and Blair's *The Grave*, almost as widely read and internationally influential as *The Seasons*, are not only in blank verse but in the tradition that demands a strong emphasis on the repetition of vowels and consonants for sound and for sense.

Young, in spite of excesses often pointed out, is both historically and intrinsically worth considering in any study of poetry. His *Night Thoughts* owes much to *Job*, of which he wrote a paraphrase in 1719, to Shakespeare,[2] to Milton, to the Christian manuals of devotion, and especially to Pope, for whose *Essay on Man* he was writing a sequel: "Man too he sung: immortal man I sing" (451). And, like Pope, he is quotable.[3] Frequently his famous lines are made more quotable with phonic echoes, as when he put an assonance and two alliterations in the first of these lines:

> How sad a sight is human happiness,
> To those whose thought can pierce beyond an hour!
>
> (306–7)

Often, in fact, Young was heavy handed with his alliteration. Here, although five lines have four assonances, half of the stressed syllables are involved in consonant repetitions:

> The cobweb'd cottage, with its ragged wall
> Of mold'ring Mud, is royalty to me!
> The spider's most attenuated thread
> Is cord, is cable, to man's tender tie
> On earthy bliss; it breaks at every breeze.[4]   (175–79)

But Young employed just as many vowel repetitions, although they are seldom so thick in a given passage. In one group of eight lines (72–79) he contrived five adjective-noun assonances and no other noticeable echoes, and in this five-line passage, heavy with alliterations and consonances, there is still one assonance for every line:

> War, Famine, Pest, Volcano, Storm, and Fire,
> Intestine broils, Oppression with her heart
> Wrapt up in triple brass, besiege mankind.
> God's image disinherited of day,
> Here, plunged in mines, forgets a sun was made.
>   (241–45)

There is no doubt that Blair's *The Grave* depends even more on acoustic ornament than does *The Night Thoughts*. In fact, his blank verse, while often paraphrasing Shakespeare,[5] is much like that of Thomson, especially in the thick onomatopoeic recurrence of phones, as in this passage, so reminiscent of lines in *Winter*:

> The wind is up:—hark! how it howls!—Methinks,
> 'Till now, I never heard a sound so dreary:
> Doors creak, and windows clap, and night's foul bird,
> Rook'd in the spire, screams loud; the gloomy aisles
> Black-plaster'd, and hung round with shreds of
>   'scutcheons
> And tatter'd coats of arms, send back the sound,
> Laden with heavier airs, from the low vaults,
> The mansions of the dead.—Rous'd from their slumbers,

In gr*im* array the gr*is*ly spectres r*ise*,
Gr*i*n horrible, and obstinately s*u*llen,
Pass and repass, h*u*sh'*d* as the f*oo*t of Nigh*t*.
Again the scr*ee*ch-*ow*l shr*ie*ks—ungr*a*cious s*ou*nd!
I'll hear n*o* **m**ore—it **m**akes *o*ne's bl*oo*d r*u*n chill.

(33–45)

Here the eerie images are emphasized not only by the slow tempo, as in the last lines, but also by the repetition of *gr* and [I] in *grim, grisly, grin,* by the initial [d]'s, by words like *creak* and *clap, screech* and *shrieks, no* and *more,* by the echo in two nearby words of phones in the sound-sense *hush'd,* by the two polysyllabic assonances of [U,ʌ], and perhaps most of all by the [aU] that runs persistently through the passage to remind us of the howling wind outside. Blair did not, of course, know the word *phonestheme,* but this passage is evidence enough that he, like his great contemporaries, was aware that the sounds of words, lexically prepared for, are an important element in setting a scene or evoking an emotion.

As with Thomson, since two-thirds of Blair's blank verse lines are end stopped, they often make use of terminal echoes but only rarely of balanced sounds, and like Thomson's they tend to concentrate their echoes in important or purple passages, as when they describe the "ungracious sound" of the shrieking screech-owl, list among the "sullen dumb" of the "Dull Grave" such citizens as

The Roman C*ae*sars and the Gr*e*cian ch*ie*fs,
The b*o*ast of st*o*ry, (124–25)

or conclude with five lines like these,

We **m**ake the gr*a*ve our bed, and the*n* are g*one.*
Th*u*s at the sh*u*t of *e*ven, the weary bir*d*
L*ea*ves the wi*de* air, and in some l*o*n*e*ly br*a*ke
C*o*wers d*own* and d*o*zes till the d*aw*n of d*a*y;
Then claps his w*e*ll-fl*e*dged w*i*ngs and bears aw*a*y.

(763–67)

The sound effects are so thick in Blair's blank verse that of the first two hundred lines of *The Grave* almost half have assonances, more than one of four have alliteration, and one of eight has a polysyllabic echo. In this respect he and Young are less in the tradition of Milton than they are in that of Shakespeare, Dryden, Pope, and Thomson.

And it can be demonstrated that the blank verse of Restoration and eighteenth-century tragedy is also in that tradition. Like Dryden's the decasyllabics of Thomas Otway (1652–85), Joseph Addison (1672–1719), and Nicholas Rowe (1674–1718) are imitative of Shakespeare's; and like Dryden's tragedies, theirs repeat sounds even more than do the plays of Shakespeare. Sudden short bursts of echoes, like this one of Jaffeir's, occur regularly in *Venice Preserved*:

> but if you think it worthy
> To cut the thr*oa*ts of *r*everend rogue*s* in *r*obe*s*,[6]
> S*e*nd me into the curst, ass*e*mbled S*e*nate. (2.3.128–30)

Nor is it unusual to find Syphax in Addison's *Cato* putting initial [f] in four stressed syllables of one line,

> Fly from the fate that follows Caesar's foes, (1.4.126)

or Sempronius using a four-syllable alliteration and a three-syllable assonance in a line and a half of the same play,

> Through winds and w*a*ves and storms he works his w*ay*,
> Imp*a*tient for the battle, (1.3.15–16)

or a three-syllable consonance and an assonance in another line,

> St*uck* on a for*k*, and bla*ck*'ning in the s*u*n. (3.5.56)

Of the three dramatists Rowe, the editor of Shakespeare, is most like Shakespeare in metaphor and subject, and he has even more recurrences of small units of sound than Otway

or Addison, as when Hastings announces his loss of love to
Alicia in six lines over twenty important syllables of which
are stressed even more, and at the same time made more
ear appealing, by their repetition of vowels or consonants
(*Jane Shore* 2.1.103–8):

> Patient I bore the painful bondage long:
> At length my genrous love disdains your tyranny;
> The bitterness and stings of taunting jealousy,
> Vexatious days, and jarring joyless nights,
> Have driv'n him forth to seek some safer shelter,
> Where he may rest his weary wings in peace;

or when, in a speech describing Jane's sorrow, he ends with
a line in which every stressed syllable is involved in an
assonance:

> She never sees the sun but through her tears,
> And wakes to sigh the livelong night away.   (1.1.72–73)

Such lines, typical of dramatists from Dryden to Rowe, and
including Young and Thomson, are some evidence that
eighteenth-century tragedy was as dependent on phonic
echoes for its ear appeal as are twentieth-century plays as
highly ornamented as *J.B.* or *Murder in the Cathedral.*

Along with the heroic couplet and blank verse, one of the
most important of eighteenth-century poetic forms was the
octosyllabic line employed in satirical or light poems and
called the Hudibrastic. In this form Samuel Butler's
Hudibras was the popular model for over one hundred
years, both in England and in the American colonies. Butler was a master not only of debasing imagery and jarring,
polysyllabic, demeaning rhymes but of internal phonic
echoes. He could echo a sound for onomatopoeia,

> As if Divinity had catch'd
> The Itch, of purpose to be scratch'd,[7]   (1.1.163–64)

frequently run a stressed vowel through two lines,

Or, like a Mountebank, did wound
And stab her self with doubts profound,[8]   (1.1.165–66)

occasionally emphasize three of the four accented syllables
in a line with an assonance,

Or Knight with Squire jump more right,   (1.1.620)

And some for Brooms, old Boots and Shoes,   (1.2.549)

find three proper names with the same stressed vowel,

Didst inspire Withers, Prin, and Vickars,   (1.1.640)

or provide a neat caesural sound balance in the fourth and
eighth syllables,

With Mouth of Meal and Eyes of Wall,   (1.1.418)

Quoth Hudibras, I smell a Rat.   (1.1.815)

He could even select his Latin quotation for the sounds:

That Cane et angue Pejus hate us.   (1.1.742)

Nevertheless, Butler's octosyllabic couplets, like those of
his imitators such as Swift and Prior, have far fewer repetitions of single phones than do the decasyllabics of Dryden
and Pope, no doubt the chief reason being that in the
Hudibrastic the rhyme words are so close to each other that
it is not only harder but less necessary to employ echoes
internally.[9]

Such a conclusion holds for those eighteenth-century
poets who employed other kinds of short lines. Ambrose
Philips's (1675?–1749) "namby-pamby" trochaic style, for
example, devised for children, unfairly traduced by Pope
and Gay, and parodied as often as the trochaics of
Hiawatha, does not at all depend for its effects on phonic
repetitions: "To Miss Charlotte Pulteney" has at most five
alliterations in its thirty lines, three of them being found in
the repeated phrase "Like the linnet." And the light ballad

quatrains in the vers de société of Prior and Parnell have just as few internal echoes.

Perhaps the better known of the short-line poems that are most clearly exceptions are the serious octosyllabics such as Parnell's "A Night-piece on Death" (1722) and Dyer's "Grongar Hill" (1726), both of which are meditative nature poems, one an early example of the Graveyard tradition, the other a late topographical work in the tradition of *Cooper's Hill* and *Windsor Forest*. Parnell's poem has even more vowel than consonant echoes and ends with a generous display of acoustical decoration,

> S*ee* the gl*ad* Sc*e*ne and unfold wi*de*,
> Cl*a*p the gl*ad* W*i*ng and tow'r away,
> And m*i*ngle w*i*th the bl*a*ze of d*a*y.

Dyer apparently published three versions of *Grongar Hill* in 1726, two of which are rhythmically rough odes many of whose lines are pentameter, the third—and probably the final version—having 158 four-beat lines, about half of which are trochaic catalectic, that is, seven syllables each. While the last poem, now the only one read, has less assonance than Parnell's "Night Piece," it has much more alliteration and considerably more consonance than are found in other short-line poems of the period. Sometimes its alliteration is garish. Three times Dyer ran initial *l* along a number of successive stressed syllables—once through three (42),[10]

> What a landskip lies below,

once through four (66-67),

> Gaudy as the op'ning dawn,
> Lies a long and level lawn,

and once through five (84-85),

> Yet time has seen that lifts the low,
> And level lays the lofty brow.

Of these consonant repetitions only the four-*l* line is hinted at in the original poem (66–67):

> Light as the Lustre of the rising Dawn,
> Spreads the gay Carpet of yon level Lawn.

But most of the time Dyer's phonic echoes are more subdued and more functional. He was able to balance vowels in the manner of Dryden and Pope (92):

> Between the cradle and the grave,

a line not suggested by the earlier version; or line 110,

> The naked rock, the shady bower,

which was reworked from line 73,

> The naked Rock, the rosy Bower.

He balanced consonants (29, 38):

> And groves and grottoes where I lay,
>
> Adds a thousand words and meads.

And he could balance both vowels and consonants, as in this neat chiasmus (59):

> The gloomy pine, the poplar blue.

Dyer also liked to bind noun to epithet with a sound repetition—"lonely van," "modest Muses," "mountains round"; and more than any other short-line poet of his day he repeated sounds at the end of the line—"riding high," "sides I wind," "waving wood." There are, in fact, twenty-six of these terminal echoes in *Grongar Hill*, all helping to make it one of the most pleasing of serious, octosyllabic poems of the eighteenth century.

Besides its blank verse poems and plays and the many varieties of iambic and trochaic octosyllabics, the period from 1660 to 1780 liked the lilting anapaest. Here Dryden, one of the most varied of poets,[11] was again an important model, employing anapaestic rhythm in songs like those of Comus in *King Arthur* (1691) and Mercury in *Amphitryon* (1690). Such a rhythm provides much less opportunity for all the kinds of sound balance and emphasis that go with the heroic couplet, the chief and almost only function of phonic echoes in anapaests being to emphasize the few stresses, as in this line from Mercury's song (4.1),

> The Legend of Love no Couple can find,

or in Swift's "Clever Tom Clinch Going to Be Hanged," where six of the last seven lines have such emphasized stresses, for example,

> Take Courage, dear Comrades, and be not afraid,
> Nor slip this Occasion to follow your Trade
> My Conscience is clear, and my spirits are Calm.

The most ear pleasing of eighteenth-century anapaestic poems may be William Shenstone's "A Pastoral Ballad," which has as many phonic repetitions as most poems written in the heroic couplet. More than once Shenstone used the same vowel in every accented syllable in a line; twice it was the vowel of "die":[12]

> Repine at her triumphs, and die,   (144)

> Then the violets die with despight.   (155)

And in two successive lines (148–49) he has four initial [f]'s and an assonance in key syllables:

> He throws it at Phyllis's feet.
> "Oh Phyllis, he whispers, more fair . . . "

In the hands of poets from Dryden to Shenstone such emphasis abetting echoes helped to keep the anapaest alive and vibrant, ready to be willed to nineteenth-century poets like Byron, Keats, and Browning.

There is perhaps no theme in Restoration and eighteenth-century literature more persistent than that of the limitation of man's reason and the superiority of faith. The theme is reflected in Dryden's sun-faith, moon-reason image that opens *Religio Laici* and is found again in Prior's "Exodus" and Gay's "Contemplation on Night"; it is in the attack on pride in Rochester's "Satyr Against Mankind," Pope's *Essay on Man*, and Swift's Third Voyage; it is in the Graveyard poets and in Dr. Johnson's concern with the vanity of human wishes. The eighteenth century, then, though often called an Age of Reason, was certainly an Age of Fideism. The extreme manifestation of its placing faith first is the rise of Methodism. And so it is no longer surprising to note that the great period of the heroic couplet and the "prose poem" was also a great period of religious verse, from Bishop Ken (d. 1711) and his "Evening Hymn" which introduced the Doxology, to Augustus Toplady (1740–78) and "The Rock of Ages." It includes hymn writers such as Dryden, Nahum Tate, and Joseph Addison; it includes Edward Perronet, author of the Coronation song, "All Hail the Power of Jesus' Name," and the sailor-turned-minister, John Newton, who wrote "Amazing Grace" and as many popular hymns as his friend William Cowper; it includes Isaac Watts and Charles Wesley, who still dominate almost every Protestant hymnal. And except for Toplady, whose "Rock of Ages" is the plainest of popular religious songs, all these hymn writers, like their fellows in other genres, helped establish the strong eighteenth-century tradition that demanded ear-pleasing ornaments for its poems.

As one would expect, Dryden's religious songs have all the devices of sound. His best known hymn, beginning "Creator Spirit" (1693), has an assonance in each of the first four of its octosyllabic lines and a three-syllable alliteration in the fifth; it has balanced sound, both in nouns and in verbs,

> Thrice Holy Fount, thrice Holy Fire,
> But, oh, inflame and fire our Hearts!

and a terminal echo for every five lines.

Although Isaac Watts (1674–1748), honored and prolific, was the most varied in form of the British hymnists, he perhaps employed internal echoes less than any of his great colleagues. His most famous song, "O God, our help in ages past," one of the least decorative of religious poems, has hardly a single assonance in its thirty-six lines. On the other hand, "The Day of Judgment," with very irregular but strong and attractive rhythm, repeats phones deliberately, although with restraint, as in the first stanza:

> When the fierce Northwind with his airy Forces
> Rears up the Baltick to a foaming Fury;
> And the red Lightning with a Storm of Hail comes
>   Rushing amain down;[13]

and one of his many children's songs, "A Cradle Hymn," begins with eight lines each of which has an internal echo and in another line makes use of a double sound balance,

> See his Face, and sing his Praise!

Charles Wesley (1708–88), even more popular as a hymnist, master of rhetoric and, especially, of all the devices of repetition, echoed small units of sound far more than did Watts. In "Hymn For Christmas-Day" he has an obviously intended internal assonance in each line of this stanza:

> Joyful all ye Nations rise
> Join the Triumph of the Skies;
> Universal Nature say,
> "Christ the Lord is born to Day!"

"Morning Hymn," about "Christ, the true the only Light," stresses the vowel of *light* nine times in the first five lines; "Wrestling Jacob," sometimes called Wesley's greatest poem, has the refrain

> Till I Thy Name, Thy Nature know

and a double sound balance in

> Faint to revive, and fall to rise;

"Jesu, Lover of my Soul" has two such balances in two successive lines,

> Raise the Fallen, cheer the Faint,
> Heal the Sick, and lead the Blind.*

Among Wesley's *Hymns for Children*, one—very Blakean—in quatrains of trochaic tetrameter acatalectic lines opens with one of the most echo-laden short-line stanzas possible:

> Gentle Jesus, meek and mild,
> Look upon a Little Child,
> Pity my Simplicity†
> Suffer me to come to Thee;

and includes one dominated by the very appropriate phonestheme [I]:

> I shall live the Simple Life
> Free from Sin's uneasy Strife,
> Sweetly ignorant of Ill,
> Innocent, and happy still.

Finally, "For Easter-Day," sung by millions once a year, has stanzas like this, where there are two very effective consonances and two assonances,

> Vain the Stone, the Watch, the Seal;
> Christ has burst the Gates of Hell!
> Death in vain forbids His Rise
> Christ has open'd Paradise.

---

* By Wesley's time the *ea* words here and in the quotations below were surely pronounced with [i]. For Thomson and *-easy*, for example, see chapter 4, p. 120, and, especially, chapter 1, n. 36.

† Singers always stress the final vowel of *Simplicity*.

The high standards in hymnology set before 1760 were kept by later religious poets of the century such as Perronet (1725–92), Newton (1725–1807), and William Cowper (1731–1800). In the Olney Hymns of Cowper, for example, although the phonic echoes are quieter than those of Charles Wesley, they are abundant and effective. One of his opening short-line stanzas,

> *Oh*! for a clo*s*er w*a*lk with G*o*d*
>   a Cal*m* of heavenly fra*me*
> A *l*ight to sh*i*ne upon the road
>   That leads me to the La*mb*,

employs a consonance in place of end rhyme and in addition has an alliteration and three assonances. Cowper's most popular hymn, beginning "There is a fountain filled with blood," has at least fifteen such internal sounds in its twenty-eight lines.

One of these hymnists, Dryden, was ultimately a Roman Catholic, others like Addison were Anglicans, Watts and Toplady were obviously Calvinists, and Wesley was Arminian. Addison wrote only a few hymns, Watts wrote hundreds, Wesley wrote over 6,000. Some of the best hymns of the period were translations from Latin, Dryden's "Creator Spirit," for example; others, like John Wesley's "Give to the Winds thy Fears," were from Dryden's great German contemporary, Paul Gerhardt; still others—by Watts, for example—were reworkings of the Psalms. Some of the hymns were set to music out of Palestrina and the Reformation; others took music from the Scotch Psalter; the setting of Addison's "Creation" was adapted from a

---

* *God* [gɔd] is a common rhyme with *road* in the eighteenth century (see *Ess. on Man* 2.115–16; 4.331–32, e.g.). Even more often it rhymed with *abode*, as in Dryden, Pope, Prior. See Wyld, *Colloquial English*, pp. 253, 257, on this rhyme. At any rate, *God* and *walk* provide a perfect assonance, while *frame* and *Lamb* consonate but do not rhyme.

chorus in Haydn's oratorio; and many gave birth to rousing new tunes during the Methodist revival. But whatever their theology, their origin, their tune, or their literary quality, the hymns of this great period of hymnology passed on a tradition not only of reverence and biblical quality but of echoing language that made the songs appeal even more to the ear.

The eighteenth century was a hymn writing period and it was also the age of the ode—the Pindaric, the Horatian, the Miltonic—and from Cowley, Dryden, and Prior to Gray and Collins the ode was employed for every serious subject and for some light ones.[14] It assumed many forms—Cowley's rough, long "Pindarics," the changing rhythms of Dryden's and Pope's St. Cecilia poems, Prior's short stanzaic patterns, and Collins's finished products of all kinds.

After Dryden and Pope, William Collins (1721–59) and Thomas Gray (1716–71) may have been the practitioners of the ode most conscious of the acoustic effects of language, and like the writers of heroic couplets, blank verse, and hymns they knew the value of internal echoes for making language pleasing. The second and third lines of Collins's "Ode to Fear," for example, have a three-syllable alliteration and a three-syllable assonance:

> With all its shadowy Shapes is shown;
> Who see'st appall'd the unreal Scene;[15]

the seventh line alliterates parallel adjectives:

> I know thy hurried Step, thy haggard Eye;

and the first stanza of the same poem's Epode has four assonances in its four lines,

> In earliest Greece to Thee with partial Choice,
>   The Grief-full Muse addrest her infant Tongue;
> The Maids and Matrons, on her awful Voice,
>   Silent and pale in wild Amazement hung.

Collins, furthermore, had all the techniques that made repetitions onomatopoeic and functional, and he knew how to employ consonance, as when he ended the "Ode to Evening" with two short lines that have five final nasals:

> Thy gentlest influence own,
> And hymn thy fav'rite name!

In the middle and late eighteenth century only Thomas Gray's Pindarics have the aural appeal of the odes of Collins. Gray's "The Bard," for example, has as many internal echoes as it has lines, one of the highest proportions in any long poem in English, especially when we note that almost half of the 144 lines are short. Dr. Johnson, of course, condemned the odes of Gray for this very reason, insisting that their sound effects are "glittering accumulations of ungraceful ornaments."[16] It is true, no doubt, that to some readers the alliteration and assonance in "**R**uin seize thee, **r**uthless King" may provide "ungraceful ornaments" for the very first line of "The Bard"—or is it the imagery?—but surely Gray's repetitions are often graceful, not only in other lines from the same ode,

> Modred, whose magic song
> Made huge Plinlimmon bow his cloud-top'd head,[17]
>
> (33–34)

but in lines from, say, "The Progress of Poesy":

> Woods that wave o'er Delphi's steep,
> Isles, that crown th'Egaean deep,
> Fields, that cool Illisus laves,
> Or where Maeander's amber waves
> In lingering Lab'rinths creep.   (66–70)

While Dr. Johnson's charges were no doubt directed at Gray's alliterations—and these five lines have four—perhaps the most "glittering" ornaments here are the assonance and -er repetition in "Maeander's amber," the balancing of *Isles–Fields* and *crown–cool*, the terminal echoes, and the adjective-noun linkings; perhaps the eight stressed *l* syllables are designed for coolness; and surely the total effect of the phonic echoes is not, as Johnson thought, ungraceful.

There are, of course, other kinds of poems in the eighteenth century. Of the countless ballad stanzas and fables, for example, those of John Gay are only the best. There is also the six-line octosyllabic stanza of John Byrom's strange "Careless Content," which revived the alliterative tradition of *Beowulf* and the Pearl Poet. And there is Gray's four-line, decasyllabic stanza of the "Elegy," the first stanza of which has seven internal phonic repetitions in stressed syllables and the whole of which has many sounding lines, among them these two,

> Now drooping, woeful wa*n*, like [w]o*ne* forlor*n*,
> Or craz'd with care, or cross'd in hopeless love.

(107–8)

Nevertheless, it is the heroic couplet that for most readers still rules the period, if not in quantity at least in quality, for after Dryden and Pope it was the chief form of Swift, Gay, Charles Churchill, Dr. Johnson, Crabbe, and Goldsmith. Of the many, Gay and Dr. Johnson, although quite unlike each other, can be taken as representative of a group no two of whom are really alike yet all of whom helped to make the couplet one of the most ear appealing of poetic media.

Intimate with those important Tory writers who thrived under Queen Anne and the first George—Swift, Pope, Parnell, and Prior—John Gay (1685–1732) may be one of the most underrated poets in the English language, for he is typically presented as "a docile friend of the great wits" who "got help from them in developing a vein of realistic humor in his verse."[18] Gay was, in fact, their friend because he also was a brilliant wit to whom they suggested work that they must have known he could do better than they—*The Beggar's Opera*, best of its kind in English; *The*

Shepherd's Week, surely the best of burlesque pastorals; and *Trivia*, a city eclogue that even rivals Swift's "Description of a City Shower." One of the wittiest and most observant of poets, he was also one perfectly aware of the sound of words.

That would be true even if we did not have *The Beggar's Opera*. More than those of any other contemporary of Pope, his heroic couplets abound in ear pleasing echoes of all kinds. "Friday," one of the seven pastorals in *The Shepherd's Week*, tells how "**Bl**ouzel*i*nda, **bl***i*thesome mai*d*, is dea*d*" and loses no opportunity to alliterate or assonate the heroine's name, the penultimate syllable of which Gay pronounced as Spenser and Shakespeare pronounced it in *Rosalind*.[19] As Grubbinol and Bumkinet sing the "**d**oleful **d**irge" to "bew*a*il her f*a*te," Blouzel*i*nda "**l**yes," she is "**l**ost," she "exp*i*red," she "**d**ied." The name occurs 11 times in "Friday": 5 times it alliterates and 5 times it assonates. "Saturday," the story of the drunken Bowsybee who charms everyone at the autumn fair with his songs, has a consonant or, more often, a vowel echo in almost every one of its 128 lines. And *Trivia; or, the Art of Walking the Streets of London*, as important to the social as to the literary historian and critic, has just as high a proportion of sound effects, a fact that may be unexpected when one considers the realistic rather than poetic nature of this, perhaps Gay's best, verse.

Some of his couplets resound with vowel echoes, as when in *Trivia* he paused at the beginning of Book 2 to review his poem,

> Thus far the M*use* has trac'd in *u*seful l*ays*,
> The proper *i*mplements for w*i*ntry w*ays*;[20]

or again when he condemned the rich young fool,

> There fl*a*mes a fool, begirt with tinsell'd sl*a*ves,
> Who w*a*stes the wealth of a whole r*a*ce of kn*a*ves;
>
> (2.581–82)

or in one line only, when he selected echoing as well as concrete words to list the contents of the "fishy stalls,"

Red-speckled trouts, the salmon's silver joul;   (2.415)

or in a four-line appeal to Fortescue when he alliterated four stressed syllables but assonated fourteen,

Come, F——, sincere, experienc'd friend,
Thy briefs, thy deeds, and ev'n thy fees suspend;
Come let us leave the Temple's silent walls,
Me bus'ness to my distant lodging calls.   (2.475–78)

Prior, in "To a Lady," compared the coy damsel's killing eyes to the darts of the Parthian, who slew as he fled; Gay made a similar—but much more sound effective—comparison of the lethal Parthian darts with the London mud flung back by speeding carriage wheels,

The Parthian thus his jav'lin backward throws,
And as he flies, infests pursuing foes.   (2.295–96)

Here the caesural consonance of *flies* and *foes* is not unique, since Gay, in the tradition of Dryden and Pope, employed much consonance effectively. In a sad "Ballad" his heroine "cast a wistful look" before "She bow'd her head and dy'd." In "Thursday" Hobnelia introduces one of her folk charms thus,

And while I knit the knot repeat this strain,   (114)

while in "Friday" Bumkinet sadly announces, making use of both the [d] and [l] phonesthemes,

So shall my doleful dirge bewail her fate.   (30)

And *Trivia* (2) closes with a couplet that carries five final *t*'s:

O rather give me sweet content on foot,
Wrapped in my virtue and a good surtout!

Gay liked to employ these echoes functionally, in all the ways popular with Dryden and Pope. In one perfectly balanced line of "Rural Sports" he has a polysyllabic alliteration, but at the same time he assonated the parallel verbs as well as the parallel objects,

Climb round the poles, and rise in graceful row.   (76)

And in the same poem he effected a similar double sound balance in a chiasmus,

Is moved by flatt'ry, or with scandal hung.   (16)

But Gay was also original with his sound effects, as in this couplet from one of his best poems, "The Epistle to Paul Methuen," where with Gay's—and Swift's—pronunciation of "yet" as [yɪt] we have two successive caesural echoes as well as echoing consonants in each opening trochee.

Be Bolder y*et*, you must go farther st*i*ll,
Di*p* dee*p* in ga*ll* thy mercenary qu*ill*.   (25–26)

Far more characteristic of him than of Chaucer or any other early British poet are the assonances that bind the lines of a couplet together. At least half a dozen couplets in "Saturday" are tied together with four stressed vowels alike. Sometimes, in fact, the same stressed vowel occurs five times in two successive lines, as in *Trivia* (2.13–14),

Before proud g*a*tes attending asses br*ay*,
Or arrog*a*te with solemn p*a*ce the w*ay*;

or (2.319–20),

Winter my theme conf*i*nes; whose n*i*try w*i*nd
Shall crust the slabby m*i*re, and Kennels b*i*nd.

And once in *Trivia* he even has three couplets in a row each of which has a stressed vowel occurring four times (2.143–48).

Perhaps Gay was most adept at letting his echoes help with the image he hoped to fix for his reader. Three final

[l]'s went with falling water even more than two [ɔ]'s, the sound in British *water*:

> Lu*ll*ing as fa*ll*ing w*a*ter's ho*ll*ow noise. (*Trivia* 2.379)

And throughout *Trivia*, which depends for its success chiefly on the hundreds of carefully pictured sights and sounds and smells of London street scenes, Gay has such sound reinforcements. Not only does [l] go with falling water; it goes, whether initial or final, with easy laziness, helped out here by the consonance of the [z] in *lazy*:

> In gi*l*ded chariots whi*le* they lo*ll* at ease,
> And la*z*ily insure a life's disea*s*e.[21] (1.69–70)

The final [z] and medial [i] of *wheezing* are echoed in a most onomatopoeic line:

> Nor wh*ee*zing a*s*thma h*eaves* in vain for breath. (2.508)

Breaking ice on the Thames becomes "**cr**acking **cr**ystal" (2.389), and the *yolk* of broken eggs is emphasized by the double repetition not only of its [o] but its final [k] when, "*h*alf-*h*atched," the thrown eggs

> Among the *r*a*bb*le rai*n*: some *r*a*n*dom throw
> May with the tri*ck*ling y*o*l*k* thy chee*k* o'erfl*ow*.
> (2.224–25)

Gay's other poems are as onomatopoeic, *The Shepherd's Week*, for example. Like Pope and Dryden, he liked monosyllabic lines for slowness, and like them he echoed sounds in such lines to emphasize slowness or related images and emotions. Here, in "Thursday; or The Spell," the slow line shows in the ashes the snail that spells the *L* that starts the name of Lubberkin,

> Slow craw*l*'[d] the snai*l*, and if I right can spe*ll*. (55)

One of Gay's most attractive sound-sense passages is in "Friday; or, The Dirge" where Grubbinol bemoans the fate of Blouzelinda:

When Blouzelind expir'd, the weather's bell
Before the drooping flock toll'[d] forth her knell;
The solemn death-watch click'd the hour she dy'd,
And shrilling crickets in the chimney cry'd;
The boding raven on her cottage sate,
And with hoarse croaking warn'd us of her fate.

(99–104)

Here, where the ear filling echoes may be intended to
contribute to the elevated style of the burlesque, are the
phonesthemes [o] and [d] for sadness and death, the [l]'s for
tolling, the initial [k] beginning with the onomatopoeic
click'd and carried through five other words to stop in the
onomatopoeic *croaking*, slow, successive stresses—as in
"death-watch click'd" and "hoarse croaking"—and altogether three consonances, three alliterations involving
eleven syllables, and seven assonances involving twenty
syllables, all in addition to the three end rhymes. John Gay,
as W. C. Brown has been one of the few to emphasize,[22]
was not only a burlesque and descriptive poet fully quali-
fied to be placed in the company of the best Tory writers of
the Queen Anne period but he was one of the most artful
manipulators of phone echoing words.

Having been trained on the language not only of Dryden
and Pope but of their native and foreign models, Dr.
Johnson's ear was, like theirs, well educated. One by-
product of editing Johnson's poems, the editors of the Yale
edition say, was the "realization that he had a keen ear for
the musical qualities of verse."[23] Moreover, his criticism
includes many theories about the sound of poetry. In the
Rambler, in certain articles in the *Dictionary*, and especially in his "Lives" of Cowley and Pope, he left a large and
consistent system of prosody, which has been analyzed by
Jean Hagstrum, Joseph E. Brown, and, even more, by Paul
Fussell.[24] Johnson was relatively a conservative in the use
of the medial caesura, in his reluctance to recognize how
much sound supports sense, and in matters of rhythm,

believing, for example, that the standard iambic meter should admit few trochaic substitutions, no more than one to a line, and that an important element in verse is "to relieve the ear without disappointing it." [25] Following this rule he found fault with the "dissonances" of Cowley and the frequent trochaic substitutions in Milton's basically iambic decasyllabics, although he did insist that verse by being too regular could become "tiresome and disgusting." In spite of his conservative prosody, however, Johnson was fully aware of the importance of style and language to a poet, who, Imlac concluded his lecture, "must by incessant practice familiarize to himself every delicacy of speech and *grace of harmony.*" [26] But to Imlac's creator the "graces" had to be unobtrusive in serious poetry.

Johnson's conservative prosody is perhaps best demonstrated in his attitude to and use of alliteration. In the *Dictionary* he defined *alliteration* as the "beginning of several words in the same verse with the same *letter,*" [27] a definition that, while acceptable to Charles Churchill[28] and other poets of the time, does not lay emphasis on the repetition of consonants primarily for sound: To Johnson *alliteration* had to do with the beginnings of words only and included initial vowel repetition as well as the weak echo of *d* in "despised, distressed" ("Vanity," 341), a conclusion verified by his dictionary illustration selected from Milton, "Behemoth biggest born," where one of the three initial *b*'s comes in an unstressed syllable. Furthermore, although his definition claims that for alliteration to exist "several" words in the "same verse" must begin with the "same letter," he condemned the two-syllable alliterations of Gray as excessive and therefore "below the grandeur of a poem that endeavours at sublimity." [29] Johnson's own poetry reflects this conservatism about initial echoes. "The Vanity of Human Wishes," perhaps his best poem, has no more than 80 alliterations in its 360 lines, a low ratio in comparison with, say, *The Rape of the Lock* or *Mac*

Flecknoe; and it has even fewer if we allow him his own definition and restrict the count to echoes that occur at the beginnings of words. Furthermore, only four times in "Vanity" did he break his own rule about not having three or more words begin with the same letter.

One of the most noticeable facts about Johnson's few alliterations is that they so often reinforce balance and emphasis. Every variety of sound parallelism inherited, developed, or invented by Dryden and then imitated by Pope can be found in "Vanity." There are two syntactically balanced nouns that alliterate in line 16,

> Each gift of nature, and each grace of art;

two possessives that alliterate in line 92,

> Sign her foes' doom, or guard her fav'rites' zeal;

and a perfectly balanced alliteration in the nouns of this chiasmus (262),

> The fruit autumnal and the vernal flow'r.[30]

So while Dr. Johnson's campaign against alliteration extended to his own poetry, his few alliterations are made to serve his cognitive ends, his rhetoric, even more than they do his ear. About one-half, in fact, of those in "Vanity" emphasize some kind of balance.

Although Johnson, both in theory and in practice, had a bias against initial phonic echoes, he apparently had no quarrel with medial vowel repetitions. Walter Jackson Bate has said of the late eighteenth-century prosodists that "most of these writers gave careful attention to the particular auditory effects . . . of stress, pause, balance, assonance, and the like,"[31] but Johnson and his contemporaries did not use *assonance* for vowel echoes and his *Dictionary* defines the word simply as "resemblance of sound."[32] Nevertheless, his poetry has one of the highest ratios of stressed vowel echoes in British literature,

the reason undoubtedly being that since assonance is much
less obtrusive than alliteration it can be used much more by
poets trying to conceal their art. There are over 130 assonances in "The Vanity of Human Wishes,"[33] nearly twice
as many as there are of consonant echoes at the beginnings
of words. And as a sharp contrast to the paucity of three-
syllable alliterations in that poem, 10 of the assonances are
polysyllabic, as in

> Where w*a*sted *n*ations r*ai*se a single *na*me,   (186)
>
> Fresh praise is try'*d* till m*ad*ness f*i*res his m*i*n*d*.   (231)

Another important contrast is in the fact that while
"Vanity" has so many stressed vowel repetitions few of
them are employed for balance. One of the best of the few is
in a pair of adjectives that also consonate and go with
alliterating nouns,

> And pour on m*i*sty **D**oubt res*i*stless **d**ay.   (146)

Another that is effective is in the participles of a chiasmus,

> And sm*oa*k'd in kitchens, or in auctions s*o*ld.   (85)

One of the most interesting of the vowel echoes was not in
the first draft of "Vanity." According to Boswell, the word
garret in the following line was replaced by *patron* after the
famous experience with Chesterfield,

> Toil, envy, want, the p*a*tron, and the j*ai*l;   (160)

but when one knows how much Johnson employed assonance, one wonders if the new word was not chosen at least
in part because it permitted the last two nouns in a series to
echo the vowel, as the three nouns of this line in "London"
were selected for their assonance,

> Here m*a*lice, r*a*pine, *a*ccident, conspire.   (13)

Dr. Johnson also has caesural and terminal balance of
sounds, and less often than Gay he bound together the lines

of a couplet with four or five stressed vowels alike; but a unique feature of his poetry is its astonishingly frequent use of what has been called vertical sound repetition. Like Thomson he sometimes began successive lines with similar sounds, if not similar words—a kind of anaphoric phonic echo. In "London," for example,

> And here the fe*ll* attorney pr*ow*ls for **prey**;
> Here **fa***ll*ing **h***ou*ses thunder on your head,
> And here a **f**emale atheist talks you dead,   (16–18),

the first important word of each of three successive lines is an adjective that begins with *f*, the *f* word in each line going with "here" to increase the effect of the anaphora.[34] In the same poem, there is an even better example in only two lines:

> Some **pl***ea*sing bank where verdant osiers **pl***a*y,*
> Some **p***ea*ceful **v***a*le with n*a*ture's **p***a*intings g*a*y. (45–46)

Here the couplet has five [e]'s and four initial [p]'s, but, more important, the second word in each line is an adjective, the two adjectives beginning with the same consonant and the same vowel sound, all of which continues the anaphoric effect of repeating *Some*. "London" and "Vanity" together have at least seven couplets with vertical sound repetitions,[35] the best of them, no doubt, being in this one from "Vanity":

> With fatal h*eat* imp*e*tuous **c**ourage glows,
> With fatal sw*eet*ness *e*locution flows.   (17–18)

Here there is the traditional anaphora in the repetition of the two initial words, and there is the vertical rhyme in the final words. But between the second word and the last of the first line there are three stressed sounds that are to be

---

*By Johnson's time the modern [i] for *ea* words such as *pleasing*, *peaceful*, and, in the next quotation, *heat* must have been standard for London speech (see chap. 1, n. 36).

found just below, and in the same order—the [i] of *heat* and *sweetness*, the [ɛ] of *impetuous* and *elo-*, and the [k] of *courage* and *-cution*. So many vertical echoes perhaps should not be called accidental, especially when one notes that Johnson's friend Goldsmith also liked them.[36]

Dr. Johnson, then, may have complained about alliteration and about attempts to find onomatopoeia in Milton and other poets, but his own poems show a calculated use of consonant echoes, especially for parallelism in structure, and a far greater use of assonance, about which he offered no theories. The last four lines of *The Deserted Village*, according to Boswell, were added by Johnson: they have only one alliteration, but they have five assonances, one of them polysyllabic. In "The Vanity of Human Wishes,"

> And sloth's bland opiates shed their fumes

was altered by Johnson to

> And sloth eff*use* her opiate f*u*me*s* in vain,[37]

thus giving an alliteration and a consonance but also an effective vowel repetition. Johnson's favorite couplet in "Vanity," according to Mrs. Thrale,[38] was

> Th'incumber'd *o*ar scarce leaves the dreaded c*o*ast
> Through purple billows and a fl*o*ating h*o*st,   (239–40)

lines with no unusual sound effects except the four [o]'s that bind them together and provide a terminal echo.

Of the famous portrait of "Swedish Charles" in the same poem, T. S. Eliot, defending eighteenth-century poetry against such charges as one made by Joseph Wood Krutch, says that if these lines "are not great poetry, I do not know what is."[39] Eliot was no doubt considering the passage from many points of view—the perfect structure, the images, the sentiment, the generalized vocabulary that states much, the classical balance, and what W. C. Brown calls "Johnson's own special kind of organ music."[40] But it is a

telling fact that of all Johnson's poetry the passage is one of
the most heavily ornamented with phonic echoes. In the
thirty lines (190ff.) there are five alliterations only, but one
is polysyllabic:

He comes, nor want nor cold his course delay.

There are five sound balances—in this zeugma, for example:

No dangers fright him and no labors tire.

There is a couplet bound with four stressed [e]'s that go
with another assonance and an alliteration:

The march begins in military state,
And nations on his eye suspended wait.

There are adjective-noun echoes and terminal echoes, as in
this couplet, which has an alliteration and a five-syllable
consonance and in which every stressed syllable echoes a
vowel:

The vanquish'd hero leaves his broken bands
And shows his miseries in distant lands.

And altogether the thirty lines have more than twenty
internal vowel echoes. It is, in fact, these many assonances, more than the balanced alliterations, that supply
for Johnson the graces of harmony he found to be necessary to the lyric poet.

Such graces are obviously a marked characteristic of the
best poems of a period of poetry obviously aware of the
sounds of words. Furthermore the blank verse, the ode, the
hymn, the many stanza patterns, the three-syllable foot,
the frequent trochaic substitutions—all make those poems
as varied in their rhythms and line lengths as are the poems
of any period before 1900. But just as dramatic blank verse
dominated the late Elizabethan age and the short lyric rules
today, the heroic couplet was supreme in the Restoration

and eighteenth century. And the heroic couplet was itself varied, as varied as any poetic form, at least in the hands of the great poets who worked with it. Dryden and Pope were only the best of those poets. After them, Cowper and then most writers of the nineteenth and twentieth centuries may have avoided the challenge of writing couplets,[41] but Pope's contemporaries Swift and Gay, as well as his successors Johnson, Goldsmith, and Crabbe, not only accepted the challenge but learned from it and thrived on it. Among the lessons they learned and passed on was how to employ phonic echoes to help make any restricting poetic medium acoustically appealing.

6

The Continuing Echo

"When sound, and colour, and form are in a musical relation, a beautiful relation to one another, they become as it
were one sound, one colour, one form, and evoke an emotion that is made of their distinct evocations and yet is one
emotion"—Yeats.[1]

Because certain young nineteenth-century writers rebelled
against what they considered to be the binding couplet and
the trite diction of the eighteenth century and because
Blake found that period to be unspiritual while Arnold
found its best poets to be prose writers, the nineteenth
century created one of the most persistent myths in the
history of literature: that *lyrical* means *subjective* or *per-
sonal* or *exact* and that eighteenth-century poetry is not
lyrical because it is *prosaic* or *objective* or *universal*. After
Matthew Arnold the myth can be found perhaps in its most
dogmatic form in one of Lytton Strachey's statements that
"music and imagination seem to us the most essential
qualities of poetry. . . . But the eighteenth century knew
none of these things."[2] It is now being assumed that the
myth has been laid to rest by critics and scholars like Eliot,
Wimsatt, Winters, and Empson, who are aware that writers from Dryden to Johnson did not almost dry up the
springs of poetry but rather made them flow faster and
sweeter for poets like Keats, who, in spite of his com-
plaints, studied Dryden for *Lamia*, or Byron, who found
Pope superior even to the best of the Renaissance poets.
Arnold and Strachey have not been completely stilled,
however, for their voices continue to be heard, sometimes
in important places, as when the already influential *Encyclopedia of Poetry and Poetics* (1965) insists that "during

the seventeenth and eighteenth centuries, alliteration lost its importance somewhat. While it was used as an occasional ornament by some poets, . . . it was largely ignored by others. . . . With the Romantic poets a new vogue set in" (p. 16). That such an opinion is contrary to the fact is now obvious.

Just as obvious is the fact that the Restoration and eighteenth-century poets employed all the ornaments of sound as much and as distinctively as the poets of any period. Furthermore, since some nineteenth-century writers were more prone to license in their verse forms, since they sometimes argued for an aesthetic that insisted on poets employing the language of common men, and since at other times they believed in the sacred nature of the prophet's first words, they would tend to produce less sophisticated language, to avoid a display of the cognitive and acoustic devices that went with the correctness of an Alexander Pope or the polish demanded by a Dr. Johnson. As a result, certain well-known British and American poets after Johnson belong to a relatively spare verse tradition, the most important of them perhaps being Wordsworth and Whitman, each of whom—no matter how appealing in other ways—has, for example, fewer uses of phonic echoes than any of a number of eighteenth-century poets.[3]

On the other hand, there is a large group of writers after 1780—both British and American—whose poems are relatively heavy with vowel and consonant repetitions. Blake, for example, has a remarkable array of internal echoes, as many perhaps as Housman, who, a hundred years later, was another poet with a good ear and a preference for rhymes and short lines. A typical four-line stanza from Blake's "The Will and the Way" has two sounding vowel echoes, one polysyllabic, and a three-syllable alliteration:[4]

I asked a thief to steal me a peach:
He turned up his eyes.

> I asked a l*i*the lady to l*ie* her down:
> Holy and meek, she cries.

But he also knew the value of consonance and often let it substitute for end rhyme, as in "Spring" or "Night":

> Come and li*ck*
> My white ne*ck*;
> . . . .
> Let me ki*ss*
> Your soft fa*ce*.

> But, if they rush drea*d*ful,
> The Angels, most hee*d*ful,
> . . . .
> Saying: "Wrath by his mee*k*ness,
> And, by his health, si*ck*ness."

Moreover, he fitted sound to sense with his echoes, for example, running twelve [o]'s through the ten lines of his "Dedication to the Designs of Blair's 'Grave,'" which opens not only with an [o] assonance but with the phonestheme [d] alliterating and consonating:

> The **d**o*o*r of **D**eath is ma**d**e of g*o*l**d**.

"A Cradle Song," reminiscent of the many children's hymns by Watts and Charles Wesley, is possibly Blake's most acoustically appealing and onomatopoeic poem. It does not, however, depend on initial consonants for its effect, since it has no really noticeable alliteration. Instead, to go with the end rhymes and three internal rhymes, its thirty-two lines assonate at least eight different vowels and diphthongs, some being extended polysyllabic echoes and one being the phonestheme [i], which comes in thirty-four stressed syllables of this softest and sweetest of sleepy songs, the first and third stanzas being representative:

> Sw*ee*t dr*ea*ms, form a sha*d*e
> O'er my lovely infant's h*ead*
> Sw*ee*t dr*ea*ms of pl*ea*sant str*ea*ms

By happy, silent moony beams.
....
Sweet sm*i*les, in the n*i*ght
Hover over m*y* del*i*ght;
Sweet sm*i*les, mother's sm*i*les,
All the l*i*velong n*i*ght begu*i*le.

Housman's echoes of single phones, though obvious and plentiful, are not so varied as those of Blake and some other poets, partly perhaps because he depended so much on refrain and incremental word repetition, partly because of his more limited subject matter, and partly because his vocabulary has so many expressions that are favorites, among them common names such as *Teme, Ludlow, Severn, Bredon* and ordinary words—usually short—such as *lads, man, love, lovely, steeples, sleep, bells, forlorn, grave, hill, holt,* and *hollo.* Although

The r*ai*n, it streams on sto*ne* and h*i*llock
The boot cl*i*ngs to the cl*ay*   (p. 119)[5]

shows Housman's most nearly typical use of alliteration, assonance, and consonance, decorative but at the same time onomatopoeic for the rain and the clinging clay, he could sometimes provide balanced sounds with balanced rhetoric:

O wide's the world, to rest or roam,
With change abroad and cheer at home,
Fights and furloughs, talk and tale,
Company and beef and ale.   (p. 97)

Because of his pessimism and concern with death, one would expect Housman to make even more use than he did of such phonesthemes as [o], [ʌ,ʊ], and [d]. All three are, however, found echoed in "The Immortal Part," [ʌ,ʊ], for example, coming six times in this stanza, which has no other internal vowel echo:

> 'This tongue that talks, these l*u*ngs that shout,
> These thews that h*u*stle *u*s about,
> This brain that fills the sk*u*ll with schemes,
> And its h*u*mming hive of dreams,—'　　　　　(p. 64)

It may be that Housman has as many final nasals—one of the most popular of phonesthemes—as any poet,[6] but what may be a more nearly unique fact is that one of his favorite small sound-sense units is the initial cluster [st]. In poem after poem he has "starting still," "steadfast station," "straight . . . striking," "The stars of heaven are steady" (p. 180), or, in three lines, *Stand, still, strip, stain* (p. 148). "Eight Oclock" begins "He stood, and heard the steeple" and ends "And then the clock collected in the tower / Its strength, and struck" (p. 115). But the most extended use of [st] comes in that unnamed poem (p. 76) where in "the Grecian Gallery" the poet says,

> I met a statue standing still.
> Still in marble stone stood he,
> And stedfastly he looked at me.

When the statue urges the weak man to "stand and bear it still," to "Stand, quit you like stone, be strong," the listener gains courage and "stept out in flesh and bone / Manful like the man of stone." So while he was a poet of pessimism, Housman's [st]'s may be one small evidence that he urged courage and resolution, as in his many poems about soldiers, including those mercenaries who defended what "God abandoned" because "They stood, and earth's foundations stay" (144).[7]

Among the highly ornamental poets of the nineteenth century, Byron most clearly shows the influence of the ear-conscious eighteenth century, not only in the Popeian balance, antithesis, and zeugma in "English Bards and Scotch Reviewers" but in its terminal and balanced assonance as well as the twenty-one phonic echoes in the first twenty-six lines. *Don Juan* is heavy with vowel repetitions; and the song in *Childe Harold* beginning "The castled crag of Drachenfels" has a proportion of echoes rivaling that of the most attractive passages in Dryden, Pope, and Thomson. But *Childe Harold* looks back in many ways. For example, Byron's storm descriptions at Lake Leman employ the language of Dryden's *Aeneis* (4.232–33, 5.911–12), especially in the "fork'd lightning" of one storm (*CH* 3.95) and the "rattling crags" of another (*CH* 3.92):[8]

> From peak to peak, the rattling crags among
> Leaps the live thunder! Not from one lone cloud,
> But every mountain now hath found a tongue.

One of Byron's most consistently ear-appealing shorter poems is "Stanzas for Music," written in twenty couplets of fourteen or fifteen syllables to a line and unlike anything by Dryden or Pope. Here the long lines lend themselves well to internal echoes, as in this typical stanza:

> Though wit may flash from fluent lips, and mirth distract
>   the breast,
> Through midnight hours that yield no more their former
>   hope of rest;
> 'Tis but as ivy-leaves around the ruined turret wreath,
> All green and wildly fresh without, but worn and grey
>   beneath.

The experiments of Tennyson and Hopkins with the sounds of words are, no doubt, even better known than those of Blake, Byron, or Housman, while Poe's alliteration is so heavy that it has sometimes been condemned as facile or cheap.[9] But Poe employed as much assonance and almost as much consonance, and his revisions demonstrate that like Pope before him he labored to add phonal repetitions.[10] For one of many possible examples, there are the rough and unsatisfactory lines,

> Whose entablatures intertwine
> The mask—the viol—and the vine,

which became the famous couplet,

> Whose wreathed friezes intertwine
> The viol, the violet, and the vine.

Between the relatively unornamental poets of the nineteenth and early twentieth centuries and those who continued the tradition of a consciously abundant use of phonal repetitions, there are the many who employed such repetitions less often, perhaps irregularly, but still deliberately, artistically, sometimes heavily. In this group belong poets from Keats[11] and Coleridge to Hardy and Yeats. And among these belong Shelley, Browning, and Emily Dickinson. Shelley and Browning provide good examples of the irregular use of sound effects. "The Cloud," besides its end and internal rhymes, has much more alliteration and assonance than "To a Skylark," while "Adonais," in Spenserian stanzas, has proportionately much less than Shelley's sonnet, "England in 1819," which is in his richest style:

> An old, mad, blind, despised, and dying king—
> Princes, the dregs of their dull race, who flow
> Through public scorn,—mud from a muddy spring,—
> Rulers who neither see, nor feel, nor know,
> But leech-like to their fainting country cling,
> Till they drop, blind in blood, without a blow,—
> A people starved and stabbed in the untilled field,—
> An army, which liberticide and prey
> Makes as a two-edged sword to all who wield;—
> Golden and sanguine laws which tempt and slay;
> Religion Christless, Godless—a book sealed;
> A Senate,—Time's worst statute unrepealed,—
> Are graves, from which a glorious Phantom may
> Burst, to illumine our tempestuous day.

In these fourteen lines there are more than thirty stressed syllables and over fifty phones involved in internal echoes. What is most important about the repetitions here, however, is that they go with slow, predominantly monosyllabic lines, that [ʌ,ʊ] is a prominent vowel, that there is so much consonance, especially of the phonestheme [d], that there are two three-syllable alliterations (*dying–dregs–dull*; *blind–blood–blow*) and three three-syllable assonances (*blind–despised–dying*; *dull–public–mud*; *see–feel–leech*), and that everywhere Shelley was attempting to make his sounds—especially his echoes—reflect the ugly, blind, starved death-in-life he saw around him, as Pope had made his sounds help with the picture of a sterile land of dunces.[12]

Although Browning's sound echoes come more irregularly than those of Shelley, he has far more of them than one might expect if the dramatic nature of much of his work is considered. Often one of his traditional poems—"Evelyn Hope," "Any Wife to Any Husband"—is almost without ornament except for the end rhymes, but on the other hand he has rhyming poems whose abundant internal sound effects indicate how conscious he was of all the possible phonic echoes, the most obvious example being "Love Among the Ruins." The irregular use of these echoes is seen best in the famous dramatic monologues, where Browning could go for lines without apparently feeling the need to appeal in any way to the ear. And then, as in "Andrea Del Sarto," would come a burst of echoes, especially of alliteration:[13]

> Love, we are in God's hand.
> How strange now, looks the life he makes us lead;
> So free we seem, so fettered fast we are!
> I feel he laid the fetters: let it lie!   (49–52)

or of alliteration and assonance:

Such frank French *eyes*, and such a fire of souls
Profuse, my hand kept plying by those hearts.

(160–61)

Perhaps the most artistic as well as the most regular use of initial, medial, and final phonic echoes in any of the great monologues—a surprising fact, no doubt, to some readers—is found in "The Bishop Orders His Tomb at Saint Praxed's Church." Even here, however, certain groups of lines stand out, as with these two which fit sound to sense so well:

Clammy squares which sweat
As if the corpse they keep were *oozing* through—

(116–17)

or this much longer passage, every line of which has at least one internal echo and which features not only [d], [ʌ,ʊ], and [o] but [st]:

No gaudy ware like Gandolf's second line—
Tully, my masters? Ulpian serves his need!
And then how I shall lie through centuries,
And hear the blessed mutter of the mass,
And see God made and eaten all day long,
And feel the steady candle-flame, and taste
Good strong thick stupefying incense-smoke!
For as I lie here, hours of the dead night,
Dying in state and by such slow degrees,
I fold my arms as if they clasped a crook,
And stretch my feet forth straight as stone can point,
And let the bedclothes, for a mortcloth, drop.   (78–89)

Across the ocean and later in the century, Emily Dickinson is not only unique with her invigorating images and quick twists of wit; she is intriguing in her use of phonic recurrences, of which she has an amazing number if we consider her preference for short lines and short poems. Among the short-line poets of stature, perhaps only Blake

and Housman have so many. But far more than Blake or
any poet before her, she replaced end rhyme with consonance, something that long-line poets have never done
except unwillingly. The Locomotive poem is just the best
known of many for such effects: in its four short unrhymed
stanzas, each *B* line consonates with its *D* line, eighteen
syllables altogether consonate, and in addition there are six
alliterations (three of them polysyllabic) and six assonances. Almost as famous, "A Bird Came Down the Walk"
has end rhymes in two of its five stanzas, but it has end
consonance in three to go with many other sound effects, as
in the last lines:

> c*au*tious
> I *o*ffered hi*m* a cru*m*[b],
> And he unr*o*lled his feathers
> And **r**ow*ed* him softer h*ome*
>
> Than *o*ars divide the *o*cean,
> Too **s**ilver for a sea*m*,
> Or **b**utterflies, off **b**anks of noon,
> Leap, pl*a*shless, as they swi*m*.

Surely Emily Dickinson's good ear is almost as important
to her success as her clear eyes and her delightful mind.

One of the many ways in which the twentieth-century
poets feel themselves to be different, "freer," is this use of
end consonance to replace rhyme. Auden has done it;
Richard Wilbur has done it. And so has Ransom, for example in "Bells for John Whiteside's Daughter," which has
five rhymes in five stanzas but which has end consonance
for the other lines ("li*tt*le"–"scu*tt*le," "rea*d*y"–"stu*d*y,"
etc.).

Another, more important, characteristic of the twentieth
century is its rougher rhythms, in the Donne rather than
the Pope tradition. Because there are more spondees and
as many trochaic substitutions, sound echoes are today
often found in consecutive syllables: Dylan Thomas's in

"house-high hay," Spender's "like lank black fingers,"
Robert Graves's "wax-manniquin" and "Claims kin,"
Robinson Jeffers's "the northwest wind wakening / Their
wings to the wild spirals of the wind-dance," or—all in one
poem—Marianne Moore's "frock-coat skirt," "tucked
under," "stick; / stagger." A fine example of phonic echoes
in consecutive stressed syllables of rough rhythms occurs
in these predominantly monosyllabic lines from W. S.
Merwin's "Blue Cockerel":

> the spread red hand
> Of his comb thrown back, beak wide, and the one *eye*
> Glaring like the sun's self, . . . *seen* rimmed in red secret.

Nevertheless, regular rhythms are still preferred and, as
with all other periods of English poetry, the writers of our
day are unanimous in employing their phonic echoes to
emphasize the stresses, as in this line from Dylan Thomas's
"If I were Tickled by the Rub of Love":

> Broke through her straws, breaking my bandaged string;

or these lines from Robert Lowell's "Man and Wife":

> once hand on glass
> and heart in mouth
> outdrank the Rahvs in the heat
> of Greenwich Village, fainting at your feet—
> too boiled and shy
> and poker-face[d] to make a pass,

where fourteen stressed syllables of perhaps eighteen are
made more emphatic by a consonant or vowel repetition.
  Today critics would hardly attack Thomas or Lowell for
such heavy ornamentation, not only because their echoes
are no doubt usually subdued, even if they are thick, but
because of the almost universal admiration for Hopkins,
Verlaine, and other poets even more obviously concerned
with the possibilities of letting the sound of language embel-
lish, suggest, or reinforce the literal meaning. One of the

chief facts about the literary history of the twentieth century is that, just as the generation immediately before us was so busy tracing and interpreting patterns of imagery, our generation is rather feverishly finding and analyzing patterns of sound, not only in poems but in prose. And the busiest of the searchers are getting more and more attention,[14] from the ingenious followers of Noam Chomsky and transformational grammar to brilliant analysts like Roman Jakobson and Manfred Bierwisch who seem able to please both houses—the linguists and the aestheticians. It may be that the Russians have been more busy at it than the Western world. Among them Brik and Bryusov[15] have been pioneers in the study of the vowel and consonant echoes that, since the very recent popularity of poets like Yevtushenko, are now commonly known to be so important to Russian poetry. Pasternak, most popular of the Russians, has told us in the fourteenth chapter of *Dr. Zhivago* how, for him, at the moment of inspiration the language is the "dominant thing . . . and turns wholly into music." And his "music," one reader tells us, depends most on "an interplay of vowels and of serried consonants,"[16] while another reader finds Pasternak's poems constantly producing "sound metaphors,"[17] what Pope and his age called representative meter.

The question of sound metaphors, or whatever we call them, is only one of the many problems that students of language are attacking. Certain nonlinguists, however, including William Wimsatt,[18] still agree with Dr. Johnson that language is "iconic" and has only some auditory possibilities, that while one art may have parallels with another the dependence of one art on the techniques of another— poetry on painting or music—can probably not be demonstrated. But even such an authoritative warning is hardly going to keep poets like Pope, Pasternak, or Poe from trying to make words do the work of music, nor is it liable to curtail attempts of other critics, as well as of grammarians, to study the many ways of using language as sound.

Just as there is a conservative opinion and a liberal opinion about the relationship between sound and sense, there are still two positions with regard to the possibilities of echoing small units of sound in poetry. One, rather old fashioned now, argues that "excessive alliteration, assonance, and rhyme suggest calculation, contrivance, effort," that these effects are "comparatively easy to produce" and "suggest an unwarranted sacrifice of sense to the mere jingling of sounds, and, therefore, a cheap form of ornamentation."[19] The other position, which avoids the word *excessive*, contends that a

> preoccupation with what Hopkins calls 'graces' may be artificial and mechanical—like the preciosity of Euphues . . . and much of the alliteration in Middle English verse and even in Swinburne. On the other hand, it may manifest itself in a genuine sensibility which, released from the burden of creative thinking, and challenged by the perfection of an earlier 'Augustan' form, spontaneously chooses a newer mode, a more brilliant *décor*, which will recapture the reader's or hearer's attention.[20]

Each of these traditions has its adherents among poets of the twentieth century.

Three modern poets who are to be classed as relatively unornamental are Frost, Pound, and William Carlos Williams, although Frost by no means eschewed alliteration and assonance so much as did Wordsworth.[21] Pound's famous "Portrait d'une Femme" or a poem like "The River Merchant's Wife: A Letter" has perhaps no significant assonance and almost no alliteration; and "Apparuit," one of his most ear appealing compositions, has few echoes after the first stanza. Williams's poems have even fewer. It is true that three of the eleven stanzas of "The Yachts" have quite noticeable internal echoes, in these lines especially, where three of the pairs of like sounds are in adjacent stressed syllables:

> the be*st* man knows
> to p*i*t again*st* its bea*t*ings, and s*i*nks them p*it*ilessly.
> Mothlike in m*i*sts, sc*i*ntillant in the minute
>
> **br***ill***iance** of clou*d*less d*a*ys, with **broad be***ll***ying** s*ai*ls
> they **gli***de* to the **wind** tossing **green water**
> from their sharp prow*s* while over them the **crew crawl***s*.

But these lines are highly unusual for Williams, "Gulls," for example, with two assonances and three alliterations in its twenty-seven lines, being typical of his usual spare style.

More dependent on phonal repetitions, but in that respect still not in the tradition of Dryden and Hopkins, are Americans like MacLeish, Stevens, and Eliot. MacLeish will employ echoes of all kinds in a poetic drama like *J.B.* or in an onomatopoeic poem such as "'Dover Beach'—A Note to That Poem," where there are assonating phrases like "fine and wild smother" but where alliteration dominates the welter of watery sounds. Although "You, Andrew Marvell" depends less heavily on sounds for its success, it has many [i]'s and [l]'s for sleep and softness and lines like these:

> To f*ee*l **cr***ee***p** **u***p* the **c**urving *ea*st
> . . . .
> And d*ee***p**en on Palmyra's **str***ee***t**
> The **wh***ee***l** **ru***t* in the **r**uined **st**one.

Some of Steven's favorite short lyrics have surprisingly few repetitions of any kind, "Peter Quince at the Clavier," for example. But here and there "Sunday Morning," a longer poem with longer lines, is thick indeed with attention-getting phonic echoes.[22] And although the very short lines of "Cortège for Rosenbloom" should not be expected to have many internal echoes, in it Stevens was able in a stanza with only one rhyme to involve in repetition fifteen phones and all ten stressed syllables, even to effect three striking parallel sounds to go with structurally parallel words:

To a jangle of d*oo*m
And a ju*m*ble of word*s*
Of the *i*ntense p*o*em
Of the str*i*ctest pro*se*
Of R*o*senbl*oo*m.

Eliot's least ornamented important poem is perhaps *Four Quartets*, which, in spite of his admonition not to work "too close to musical analogies," is an example of his own attempt—at least in its symphonic structure—to employ a musical analogy. The opening fourteen lines of the first movement, however, have only two assonances that seem intentional. But later on Eliot stressed the same vowel at least four times in one line,

> The problem once solved, the brown god is almost forgotten,

and he began "Little Gidding" with very obvious assonance and alliteration to go with some nine final nasal sounds:

> M*i*dw*i*nter Spr*i*ng *is* *i*ts own season
> Sempiternal though sodden towards sundown.

Perhaps the most pleasing of the echoes in the *Quartets* accompany these images:

> the tor*n* sei*ne*,
> The sha*t*tered l*o*bsterp*o*t, the br*o*ken *o*ar.

"Prufrock" repeats phones more consistently; but of all Eliot's best known poems, "Sweeney Among the Nightingales" may repeat most. There are more than twenty assonances and ten alliterations in its forty short lines. And in these two stanzas every line has at least one such echo:

> Apeneck Sw*ee*ney spr*ea*ds his kn*ee*s
> *L*etting his arms hang down to *l*augh,
> The z*e*bra stripes al*o*ng his *j*aw
> Sw*e*lling to m*a*culate gir*a*ffe.
>
> And s*a*ng within the bl*oo*dy woo*d*

When *A*gamemnon crie*d* alou*d*,
And let their l*i*quid s*if*tings fall
To s*tain* the s*tiff* disho*n*ored shroud.

Among the echoes are two terminal consonances, two
adjective-noun couplings, and a pair of parallel participles
that assonate, all in the eighteenth-century tradition that
Eliot defended. But in spite of their sometimes lavish display of ornament, these three poets—like Yeats and
Spender in Britain—cannot be placed in the group that,
following Poe, Swinburne, and Hopkins, has experimented
so much with word and phone repetitions.

In this very large group belong such minor poets as
James Wright and Peggy Schumacher, such widely read
ones as Theodore Roethke, Marianne Moore, Dylan
Thomas, and e. e. cummings, and the controversial but
popular anomaly Vladimir Nabokov, the Russian who also
writes in English. One of Wright's distinctive experiments
is found in "The Avenger," which—thick with echoes,
including a number of end consonances—has ten short-line
stanzas with almost as many pairs of lines tied together by
letting the first syllable, always stressed, of one line alliterate or assonate with the last syllable, always stressed, of
the preceding line, as here:

St*ri*kes the **b**ee and rabbit **bl***i*nd,
Blow*s* the sparrow out of *eyes*,
. . . .
Had I caught her in the d*ar*k
Sn*ar*led in an alien lover's hair.

And any of Wright's poems will be as decorative, perhaps
as experimental. "Lament for My Brother on a Hayrake,"
for example, with only one end rhyme has more than
one internal phonic echo for each of its seventeen lines
and in addition, twelve echoes of single phones at the
ends of lines—*eyes–sacrifice, face–pass, shroud–down–
cloud*, etc.

The alliteration of Roethke, Thomas, and Moore is too

well known to be discussed here, but their heavy assonance
and almost excessive emphasis on consonance are not
well known. Roethke's "The Gibber," for example,
has a short-line stanza every final syllable of which has a
stressed [aɪ]:

> The weeds wh*i*ned,
> The snakes cr*i*ed,
> The cows and br*i*ars
> Said to Me: d*i*e;

and Thomas's "Twenty-Four Years" has a vowel repetition in nearly every line, while this passage from "Fern
Hill" will show that his vowels were even more important
to him than were his consonants:

> Nothing *I* cared, in the la*m*[b] wh*i*te d*a*ys, that t*ime* would
>   t*a*ke me
> Up to the sw*a*llow-thr*o*nged l*o*ft by the sh*a*dows of my
>   h*a*nd,
>   In the moon that is always r*i*sing,
>   Nor that r*i*ding to sl*ee*p
>   I should h*ear* him f*ly* with the h*i*gh f*ie*lds
> And wake to the farm for*e*ver fl*e*d from the childless land.
> Oh as I was young and *ea*sy in the m*e*rcy of his m*ea*ns,
>   T*i*me held me gr*ee*n and d*y*ing
>   Though I sang in my chains l*i*ke the s*ea*.

In these nine lines there are five alliterations but there are
at least ten internal assonances. Moreover, the echoing
initial consonants involve only twelve syllables while the
vowels are found in twenty-four. A unique fact about
Thomas's assonance, only recently studied,[23] is that he
constantly used it, as he did alliteration and consonance,
as a substitute for end rhyme. The stanza from "Fern Hill"
has two different rhymes but only three different vowels in
the stressed syllables at the ends of the lines, which rhyme
or assonate as follows: *a b c a' a' b a' c' a*. Three lines
from Marianne Moore's "Combat Cultural," widely an-

thologized and typical, show an equal concern for assonance:

> I recall a documentary
> of Cossacks: a visual figure, a mist
> of swords that seemed to sever.

Robert Graves, like Edmund Wilson, believes that
Nabokov is "tone-deaf." But then to Graves, John Keats
was tone-deaf too.[24] Nevertheless, while there are poets
who no doubt employ phonic echoes as a cheap and easy
way to attract attention, Nabokov, perhaps because of a
Russian heritage that depends so strongly on such devices,
is one who both loads his English poems with vowel and
consonant repetitions and continually experiments with
them. The thirty-four-page poem near the beginning of
Pale Fire ranges from riotous word plays such as

> The brain is drained
> And a brown ament, and the noun I meant
> To use but did not, dry on the cement,[25]

to less playful passages of Eliot-like philosophy that have
far more than Eliot's sound effects,

> For we die every day; oblivion thrives
> Not on dry thighbones but on blood-ripe lives,
> And our best yesterdays are now foul piles
> Of crumpled names, phone numbers and foxed files.[26]

But the "heroic couplets of *Pale Fire* burn dimly beside the
extravagances of something like Nabokov's "Ode to a
Model," which is one of the closest of twentieth-century
approximations to Hopkin's Welsh *Cynghanedd* style, al-
beit the subject is hardly Hopkinsian and vowels, rather
than consonants, dominate. The first two stanzas may be
enough:

> I have followed your model,
> in magazine ads through all seasons,

from d*ead* l*ea*f on the *s*od
to r*ed* l*ea*f on the br*eeze*,

from your l*i*ly-whi*te* *arm*p*it*
to the t*i*p of your bu*tt*erfly *eye*lash,
ch*arm*ing and p*iti*ful,
s*i*lly and st*y*lish.

In this tour de force of sound exceeding even Auden's
experiments in "rider to reader" and "The Age of Anxi-
ety," every end word repeats at least the important vowel
of some other end word and even four final unstressed
syllables are made to engage in echoes: "mode*l*"–
"pitifu*l*," "eyela*sh*"–"styli*sh*."

Nabokov may not be an important poet, but his effects do
show to what extremes the ornamental school can go and is
going. No great twentieth-century poet—Eliot, Pound,
Yeats, Frost, Stevens—belongs to this extreme school, all
of them normally preferring more subtle or more widely
separated ornamentation. Nor does any important
twentieth-century writer—unless we include Dylan
Thomas—make such varied uses of alliteration or depend
so much on assonance and consonance as the best of the
eighteenth-century poets did.

They have, however, been as willing to retouch their
lines. Early versions, for example, of poems by Spender,
Alastair Reed, Richard Wilbur, Conrad Aiken, and Robert
Graves, all prove how hard each artist struggled to perfect
his work.[27] And among the reasons for moving or replacing
words was the hope to improve not just the image or the
rhythm or the structure but the sound. Spender, in "The
Landscape Near an Aerodrome," replaced *rich* with *furred*
to get "With burring furred antennae," one of his best
internal phonic echoes. Even a better example is found in
Aiken's "The Fountain," one short passage of which first
read,

while the goldfinch (?) under the eaves
for the last time, and the Hill

draws closely about it its Joseph's Coat of colors,
and geese honk by the tide-line.

The final, and much more acoustically effective, draft reads,

The goldfinch caught in a ring of light
taps at the eaves and Sheepfold Hill
once more wears its Joseph's coat colors
while wil[d] geese honk at the tideline.

Seven syllables involved in echoes were increased to at least sixteen, a three-syllable assonance of [o] was kept even though one of the [o] words was exchanged for another, and three [aɪ]'s—one a bit weak—became four in the last line. What seems true from a study of these and other moderns, as well as of their immediate predecessors such as Poe, is that, like the craftsmen of the eighteenth century, they strove for perfection not just of form and of image but of sound.

What can now be concluded will sometimes be hesitant when the conclusions involve a comparison of eighteenth-century sound effects with those of other periods, for the best comparison may need a longer review of poetry before 1660 and after 1780. But for poets from Dryden to Johnson what is offered here may suggest points of departure for students of older British poetry, of modern poetry, and even of poetries in other languages. Among the facts and suggestions advanced are these.

First, in England and at least since Shakespeare's day, what the twentieth century calls "assonance" is now known to have been as important to poets as alliteration has always been; and with dozens of great poets who have hoped to be less conspicuous with their art, vowel echoes—internal, muted, unnoticed by the eye—have been even more important than eye-catching echoes of initial consonants.

Second, the repetition in stressed syllables of a final

consonant or consonant cluster without a vowel was not a device widely employed by poets during the centuries when English words were changing so fast, especially in their final syllables; but by the end of the seventeenth century, consonance, even though without a name, was known to be another subtle sound effect. And while most nineteenth-century writers used it less consciously than, say, Dryden, the twentieth century—since Hopkins and Dickinson—has made much use of it internally and far more use of it as a substitute for end rhyme, as with Edna St. Vincent Millay, e. e. cummings, and Marianne Moore.

Third, contrary to a widely held notion, the eighteenth century was one of the prinicipal users not only of alliteration but, more particularly, of the subtler echoes involving medial vowels and final consonants. But the fact that poets from Dryden to Johnson are sometimes wrongly reputed to have avoided alliteration and the fact that no one has before demonstrated their great reliance on assonance and consonance are strong indications that their phones echo so artistically that the art has been unnoticed by those readers who read with the eyes only.

Fourth, eighteenth-century poets, as much as those of any period, corrected and polished their lines not just to make their images sharper, their transitions smoother, their rhythms and rhymes better, or their rhetoric more effective but to provide more internal phonic recurrences that would increase their poetry's acoustic appeal.

Fifth, the chief reason these poets had for altering language to add echoes was simply to provide more ornament, more pleasurable sounds. And this is still the chief reason. Today, however, as in the nineteenth century, a somewhat greater number of short-line poems has tended to make internal phonic echoes less necessary in rhyming lines, where the rhyme occurs so often. On the other hand, as with blank verse in other periods, the preference today for unrhymed poetry or the attempt to avoid blatantly full rhymes, has been a powerful force in increasing internal echoes as well as in the substitution—say with Roethke, Owen, and Thomas—of much end consonance, end assonance, and even end alliteration for rhyme. Just as Dryden and Pope strained so successfully to make their limited media more varied, poets today seek ways to overcome their self-imposed limitations.

Sixth, another very important reason for the eighteenth-century writers to polish their echoes was to strive for the fitting of sound to sense, for representative meter. Their varied subject matter, the wide range of their moods, the exactness of many of their images—such variety gave opportunities for the countless sound metaphors that run through the best of their many kinds of poems. And this is an aim, a characteristic, of much of the best poetry of all times. It is found today, for example, in Robert Lowell's "go*bb*ets of blu*bb*er," in e. e. cummings's "m*u*d-l*u*scious," in Eliot's "To spi*t* ou*t* all the bu*tt*-ends of my days and ways," of Peggy Schumacher's "*fr*a*c*tured ice *fr*agments" and "bri*tt*le pe*t*als," or in Pasternak's hearing a horse gallop through one of his entire poems. Furthermore, Dryden, Pope, Thomson, and their contemporaries—like Spenser, Shakespeare, and Milton; like Homer, Lucretius, and Virgil—not only knew, or intuited, that certain sound units go best with certain emotions or ideas but were aware of the necessity of providing the lexical support that would prepare the reader, consciously or unconsciously, to associate the sounds with the sense and thereby feel the effect more completely and more forcefully. In short, their continued experiments with the language of poetry led these poets to discover many of the sounds that today our phoneticians and literary critics are calling phonesthemes. Before the name was, the fact existed. And so poets after 1660, with models like Shakespeare, made frequent and artistic use of sound-sense echoes, initial or final, of single consonants such as [n] and [m], [d], [l], or [s] and [z]; they alliterated consonant clusters that are suggestive—[st], [gl], [tw]; and they assonated front vowels for peaceful nature, [i] for sleep, [ɪ] for little, dainty images or satiric diminution, [ʊ,ʌ] for death, dullness, drabness, [o] for sadness, and [aɪ]—or [əɪ]—for brightness. It may be that poets of our day, studying the experiments and theories of psychologists and linguists, will realize even more than their great predecessors how to employ these phones-themes creatively, but even without such scientific help Pope employed [d] more than Wilbur Owen did later, or [o] more than Poe. In fact, it is apparent that no important eighteenth-century poets, and few moderns, have felt that language is merely discursive. They have worked instead at trying not only to select a dominant sound or sounds for a particular passage, or to find words that will suggest or echo a nearby key word, but in every way to force the sound of language to reinforce the cognitive and affective content of the poem.

Seventh, the most distinctive use of vowel and conso-nant echoes in the age of Dryden and Pope was to aid the structure, the rhetoric, the idea. Such a reinforcing of the cognitive message is, of course, ornamental and emotional as well as cerebral. It is found at its most effective best in the heroic couplet with its end rhyme, its caesura, and its dependence on classical rhetoric, but it is a device that rubbed off on other poetic forms of the period. The rebel-lious nineteenth-century writers, with their de-emphasis on intellectual poetry, and the moderns, with their free verse, have—like their predecessors—let echoes emphasize the stresses both in regular lines or in irregular, rough rhythms. And, also like earlier poets, they have very often coupled adjectives with nouns, not only by means of alliteration but even more often with assonance, for example, in Spen-der's short "The Express"—"jazzy madness," "streamline brightness," and "honey buds"—and, sometimes, with

consonance, as in John Ciardi's "A P*i*nstripe u*n*icor*n*." On
the other hand, few poets now make a conscious effort to
place echoes in balancing words. It takes a rather studied
search to find a Stevens with three parallel sound units in
the short "Rosenbloom" or three alliterating nouns in a
series,

> Among the choirs of w*i*nd and wet and w*i*ng;

or an Elinor Wylie with two terminal assonances in successive unrhymed lines,

> Avoid the l*a*thered p*a*ck
> Turn from the st*ea*ming sh*ee*p;

or a cummings with balancing nouns that assonate,

> b*i*rd by snow and st*i*r by st*i*ll;

or a Moore effecting a double balance—adjective with
adjective and noun with noun—in "unc*o*nquerable c*ou*n-
try of / unp*o*mpous g*u*sto." It takes somewhat less effort, however, to find parallel echoes in certain other
twentieth-century poets—Pound and Eliot, for example,
who are known admirers of Dryden and Pope and Johnson.
Eliot neatly balances his verbs in

> She y*aw*ns and dr*aw*s a stocking up,

and again at the beginnings of successive lines,

> L*i*cked its tongue into the corners of the evening,
> L*i*ngered upon the pools that stand in drains,

where the initial consonant-vowel repetitions make the
parallelism almost as emphatic as the anaphoric assonance
in Pound's

> I have pl*a*yed with God for a woman
> I have st*a*ked with my God for truth.

Balance like that takes us back to Dr. Johnson, to

Goldsmith, or to Pope, who opened his Prologue to Addison's *Cato* with three such lines:

> To wake the soul by tender strokes of art,
> To raise the genius and to mend the heart,
> To make mankind in conscious virtue bold.

Although such balance is indeed a distinctive feature of poets from 1660 to 1780, it is only one of the many ways they had of embellishing and varying verse. Their acoustic devices could, in fact, be studied even more by an experimental twentieth century that is so concerned with the language of literature. A great many modern poets have, of course, engaged in that study. Besides Mark Van Doren, who trained himself on Dryden's "music," Auden has called "modest" Dryden "The master of the middle style."[28] The middle style must be concerned with the graces of harmony, however, for Auden—by common consent a master of sound effects himself—believes that "the unsaid inner meaning is revealed in the music and the tonality of the poem,"[29] a creed that surely controls a line like "Dark and deeper than any sea-dingle." An Auden then, or an Eliot, would agree with Dryden that the idea, the emotion, must be clothed in language that is ornamental; and they would agree with Pope that language can itself suggest, emphasize, prolong, even combine a thought and a feeling. For while the eighteenth century wrote great prose, it was also an age that continued, deepened, perfected the traditions of English poetry. And nowhere did it perfect poetry more than in the ear-appealing use of small units of language. Its poets knew, as well as Blake did, that after the arrival of inspiration, "Every word and every letter [must be] studied and put into its fit place."[30] And they knew, as well as any poets have known, that the sounds of individual vowels and consonants can be artistically managed to help evoke the "one emotion" that Yeats insisted would result if "sound, and colour, and form are in a musical relation, a beautiful relation to one another."

Notes

Chapter 1

1. For the quotations in this paragraph see John Dryden, "Dedication of the *Aeneis*," in *Of Dramatic Poesy and Other Critical Essays*, ed. George Watson (New York: Dutton, 1962), 2:234–46, hereinafter called *Essays*, ed. Watson; Empson, *Seven Types of Ambiguity* (1947; rpt. New York: Meridian Books, 1963), p. 13; Pound (see Scher in n. 2 below); Eliot, "The Music of Poetry," in *Modern Writing*, ed. Willard Thorp and Margaret F. Thorp (New York: American Book, 1944), p. 404 (also *On Poetry and Poets*, New York: Farrar, Straus and Cudahy, 1957, p. 32); Aiken (see n. 2 below: Brown, *Music and Literature*, p. 195); Spender, "The Making of a Poem," in *The Making of a Poem and Other Essays* (New York: Norton, 1962), p. 60 (on this page will be found also the quotation heading this chapter); and for Verlaine and others like Valéry and Hopkins on "music," see W. H. Gardner, *Gerard Manley Hopkins* (New Haven: Yale Univ. Press, 1949), 2:101, and the *Encyclopedia of Poetry and Poetics*, ed. Alex Preminger, Frank J. Warnke, and O. B. Hardison, Jr. (Princeton: Princeton Univ. Press, 1965), p. 682, hereinafter cited as *Princeton Encycl*.

2. Although René Wellek (with Austin Warren) in *The Theory of Literature* (New York: Harcourt, Brace, 1942) was an early important voice to protest against the "romantic" or "sentimental" use of music terms in literary criticism, Calvin Brown (in *Music and Literature: A Comparison of the Arts*, Athens: Univ. of Georgia Press, 1948; in *Tones into Words: Musical Compositions as Subjects of Poetry*, Athens: Univ. of Georgia Press, 1953; and in several articles, e.g., "The Musical Analogies in Mallarmé's *Un Coup de dés*," *Comparative Literature Studies*, 4, 1967, 67–79, and "Musico-Literary Research in the Last Two Decades," *Yearbook of Comparative and General Literature*,

no. 19, 1970, pp. 5–28) has been one of the best and most persistent advocates of a clear separation of terms when one treats the similarities between music and poetry. Another important spokesman is John Hollander in *The Untuning of the Sky: Ideas of Music in English Poetry, 1500–1700* (Princeton: Princeton Univ. Press, 1961; rpt. Norton, 1970) and in numerous articles, for example, "The Music of Poetry," *Journal of Aesthetics and Art Criticism*, 15 (December 1956), 232–45, and "The Poem in the Ear," *Yale Review*, 62 no. 4 (Summer 1973), 486–506. See also S. P. Scher, "How Meaningful is 'Musical' in Literary Criticism," *Yearbook of Comparative and General Literature*, no. 21 (1972), 52–56, who reviews the use and misuse of the term *music* in literary criticism but neglects Calvin Brown while pointing to a number of German music critics and historians who have confused music with poetry. In spite of Wellek, Brown, Hollander, and others who know their music as well as their literature, many critics have been and are still using "musical" in talking of poetry, for example R. P. Blackmur, John Crowe Ransom, Jacques Barzun, and David I. Masson, while Robert P. Newton, "The First Voice: Vowel Configuration in the German Lyric," *JEGP*, 68, (1969), 580–81, is one scholar who believes that the arguments of the Wellek-Brown school "either do not hold, or are not compelling."

3. Brown, *Music and Literature*, pp. 23ff. For the last quotation in this paragraph, see ibid., p. 39, and to go with the discussion of repetition in verse given here in the next paragraph, note Brown's statement, p. 47, "Music demands far more repetition than literature can tolerate."

4. For the quotation from Hollander, see "The Poem in the Ear," p. 489; for his own splendid analyses of the odes and other poems to music, see especially his *The Untuning of the Sky* (n. 2 above). For the "discursive" versus the "musical" meaning as insisted on by "romantics," see E. J. Kearns, "'Discursive Meaning' and 'Musical Meaning' in the Romantic Theory of Art," *Durham University Journal*, 65 (December 1972), 65–78.

5. For one among many short histories of rhyme, see George L. Raymond, *Rhythm and Harmony in Poetry and Music*, 2nd ed. (New York: Putnam, 1909), pp. 133–35; but for extended treatments see Lanz and others listed in n. 50 below. For a

popular and useful recent discussion in one of the many hand-books, see John Frederick Nims, *Western Wind; An Introduction to Poetry* (New York: Random House, 1974), pp. 204–20.

6. See, for example, Laurence Perrine, *Sound and Sense*, 2nd ed. (New York: Harcourt, Brace, 1963), p. 149. Perrine does not here insist that alliteration be restricted to accented syllables, but he adds that restriction on p. 152. See also Edgar V. Roberts, *Writing Themes about Literature* (Englewood Cliffs, N.J.: Prentice Hall, 1964), p. 112. Lawrence J. Zillman, *The Art and Craft of Poetry* (New York: Macmillan, 1966), p. 58, prefers this definition but, without *consonance*, is more liberal and illustrates *alliteration* with "Lost Lenore" when the *l* of Lenore is not stressed.

7. That is, Ulrich K. Goldsmith, chairman of Germanic Languages and Literature at the University of Colorado.

8. For the first of these two quotations see *NED*, s.v. "Alliteration"; for Churchill, see his *The Prophecy of Famine*, l. 86.

9. For brief, though sometimes uncertain, sometimes conflicting, histories of alliteration see *Princeton Encycl.*, pp. 16ff.; Raymond, p. 122; and many special studies, such as Gardner, *Hopkins*, pp. 137–38. For Aeschylus's alliteration see W. B. Stanford, *Aeschylus in His Style* (Dublin: Univ. Press, 1942), p. 83, who agrees with the conclusions of a long essay on alliteration in W. Porzig, *Aischylos* (Leipzig: E. Wiegandt, 1926), pp. 73–94. For the argument about Latin folk poetry see *Princeton Encycl.*, p. 15, which says yes, and William Beare, *Latin Verse and European Song* (London: Methuen, 1957), which says it has little. For Ennius's "curious exaggeration" of alliteration see Rosamund E. Deutsch, "The Pattern of Sound in Lucretius" (Diss. Bryn Mawr, 1939), p. 5; and for Lucretius see ibid., pp. 9ff., and E. E. Sikes, *Lucretius* (Cambridge: Cambridge Univ. Press, 1936), pp. 44–48, as well as Sikes, *Roman Poetry* (London: Methuen, 1923), pp. 260–61.

10. The *Princeton Encycl.*, p. 16, says that the Germans have used it "only as an occasional ornament." My scansion of the lines of dozens of poets after the period of Germanic alliterative poetry bears out this conclusion: Walther von der Vogelweide almost never echoed an initial consonant in stressed syllables, nor did Luther, whose famous "Ein Feste Burg" has only four

alliterations in its thirty-six lines. German poets during the "baroque" period and the *Aufklärung* had little more, as with Paul Fleming, Gunther, Hagedorn. Of the greatest Germans, Goethe employed it often, although the *Princeton Encycl.*, p. 16, says, "In Goethe it is less numerous than in Schiller and the romantic poets."

11. *Princeton Encycl.*, p. 15.

12. Hugh Paul Thieme, *Essai sur l'histoire du vers français* (Paris: É. Champion, 1916), quotes this opinion from older studies, that of Kohler (1890) especially, but does not necessarily agree with it.

13. See Philip A. Wadsworth, *Young La Fontaine* (Evanston, Ill.: Northwestern Univ. Press, 1952), pp. 51–56; and for the quotation, La Fontaine (2.4).

14. Peter France, *Racine's Rhetoric* (Oxford: Clarendon Press, 1965), pp. 28–39.

15. Gardner, *Hopkins*, 2:148. For another description of *Cynghanedd*, see the translation, with introductory essays, by H. Idris and David Bell of *Dafydd ap Gwilym: Fifty Poems* (London: Honourable Society of Cymmrodorion, 1942). Idris and Bell distinguish four types of *Cynghanedd*.

16. For the opinions given in this paragraph, see, for the first—but with different phrasing—J. P. Dabney, *The Musical Basis of Verse* (London: Longmans, Green, 1901), pp. 116–17; see also David Masson (n. 39 below) and his "kinaesthetic associations" as well as Kenneth Burke's chapter (n. 38 below) on the repetition of related consonant sounds. For the second opinion, see *Princeton Encycl.*, p. 785, as well as C. F. Main and Peter J. Seng, *Poems: Wadsworth Handbook and Anthology* (San Francisco: Wadsworth, 1961), p. 179, who believe that since the fourteenth century most poets have used alliteration sparingly and only for special effects. And for the third, see Coventry Patmore, *English Metric Critics* (1857), as quoted in Gardner, *Hopkins*, 2:159.

17. Among the many are these three: August Brink, *Stab und Wort im Gawain* (Halls: M. Niemeyer, 1920); J. P. Oakden, *Alliterative Poetry in Middle English*, 2 vols. (Manchester: Manchester Univ. Press, 1930; rpt. 1968); and Virginia E. Spencer, *Alliteration in Spenser's Poetry* (Diss. Zurich, 1898). The treat-

ment of assonance that follows is indebted to my article, longer
and fuller, "The Historical Importance of Assonance to Poets,"
PMLA, 88 (1973), 8–19, and to a response to that article made by
Nathaniel B. Smith in *PMLA*, 88 (1973), 1182–83, who has helped
especially with early French poetry. For the opinion, repeated in
this paragraph, that vowels are more "sonorous," more "musical," than consonants—except perhaps for the liquids and
nasals—see Wilbur L. Schramm, *Approaches to a Science of
English Verse*, Univ. of Iowa Studies, Series on Aims and Progress of Research, no. 46 (1935), p. 42; Woldemar Masing,
Sprachliche Musik in Goethes Lyrik (Strassburg, 1910), p. 9; and
Nims, pp. 179–87, who believes vowels "in a way [are] like
musical notes" and divides them into "low," "middle," and
"high" frequency vowel sounds.

18. See *NED*, s.v. "Assonance," and handbooks such as Perrine; Nims, especially pp. 183–87; Chad Walsh, *Doors into
Poetry* (Englewood Cliffs, N.J.: Prentice Hall, 1962); Roberts;
Main and Seng; and Lewis Turco, *Poetry: An Introduction
through Writing* (Reston, Va.: Reston [Prentice Hall], 1973).

19. *A Note on Consonants, Vowels, Phones:* There is not total
agreement about which sounds are consonants and which are
vowels. The analysis of Henry Cecil Wyld, *A Short History of
English* (London: J. Murray, 1914), whose book has gone through
many editions, is still usable (3rd ed., rev. and enl., 1927). In
chapter 3 he describes the processes by which consonants and
vowels are articulated, classifies them as to types, and concludes
with a statement about the more "sonorous" quality of vowels.
Each consonant or vowel sound, even though affected by
neighboring sounds in speech, is normally considered a single
sound, a phone. For other studies of the differences between
consonants, vowels, and semivowels, as well as between phones
and phonemes, see Daniel Jones, *Outline of English Phonetics*,
9th ed. (Cambridge: W. Heffer and Sons, 1960), and *The
Phoneme: Its Nature and Use* (Cambridge: W. Heffer, 1950). See
also chapter 3 of J. Vendryes, *Language: A Linguistic Introduction to History*, trans. from the French by Paul Radin (London:
Routledge and Kegan Paul, 1925, 1949), and—for a popular but
respected analysis—Roger Brown, *Words and Things* (Glencoe,
Ill.: Free Press, 1925), who explains (pp. 22ff.) that "what we

think of as vowels and consonants are not single invariant sounds but rather categories of varied individual sounds (phones)" while "the phoneme is often called the smallest unit of speech that 'makes a difference' to a listener or speaker." Brown distinguishes *phonetic* description from *phonemic* description of speech sounds thus: "Phonetic transcription is a culture-free system for recording any speech. It does not take account of all the physical differences in speech—that would be impossible. It does take account of all the differences that are significant in any language. Phonemic transcription of a language represents as different sounds only those that are thought of as different by native speakers. It reproduces the local feeling about the language. A phonetic transcription, a culture-free description, must precede the discovery of any local phonemic system." Phonetic symbols are placed in square brackets normally—e.g., [b]—and phonemic symbols between slashes—e.g., /b/. The much respected Trager-Smith system lists nine vowels in English, three semivowels (y, h, w), and twenty-one consonants. See Harold Whitehall, "From Linguistics to Criticism," *Kenyon Review*, 18 (Summer 1956), 411–21. Throughout the present study, the repetition of initial semivowels (y, h, w) will be referred to as alliteration rather than as assonance, a practice that seems to be universal.

Because a reader of poems need concern himself only with a phonetic, not a phonemic, transcription of small sound units in language, I shall employ phonetic symbols for vowel and consonant sounds; and where they are used they will, with few exceptions, be those of the IPA. In general, the symbols for the consonants are letters of the alphabet; [š] will, however, be employed for the sound of *sh* in *shut* or *sash*, while [č] represents the first and last sounds in *church*. For the vowels and diphthongs the following phonetic symbols will in general be the only ones needed since fine distinctions in sound will not here be necessary and since only stressed syllables are being considered: [i]: *we*, [ɪ]: *sit*, [ɛ]: *set*, [e]: *fate*, [æ]: *bat*, [a]: *ah* or British *bath*, [ɔ]: *law* or British *plot* or *bottom* (these two words would today have IPA symbol [ɒ] in American English, at least, but the British sound is so close to [ɔ] that I am avoiding the attempt to separate [ɒ] from [ɔ] in the seventeenth- and eighteenth-century poets), [o]: *go*, [u]:

fool, [ʊ]: *full*, [ʌ]: *cut* or *custom*, [aɪ]: *while*, [ɔɪ]: *boy* in modern American English, or—for the seventeenth century—perhaps [əɪ]: or [ʌɪ]: (spelled *oi* or *oy*, as in *enjoy*; close to [aɪ] in modern American *die*), [aʊ]: *how*, [ju]: *fuse*. It is important to note that I am also avoiding the phonetic symbols for vowel length, for example, the colon, as in [i:], the reason being that an English vowel, at least since early Modern English, will have much the same quality of sound whether it is long or short. For a phoneticist's discussion of that fact, see, for example, Thomas Pyles, *The Origins and Development of the English Language*, 2nd ed. (New York: Harcourt, Brace, Jovanovich, 1971), pp. 40–43. For consonant clusters IPA symbols will normally be combined, e.g., *cl* in *clap* is [kl].

20. Quoted from the *Encyclopaedia Britannica* (1964), s.v. "Assonance." The *Americana* (1963) uses almost the same words. A similar approach is taken by certain books on prosody, for example, Paull F. Baum, *The Principles of English Versification* (Cambridge, Mass.: Harvard Univ. Press, 1922), p. 167; and Max Kaluza, *A Short History of English Versification* (New York: Macmillan, 1911), pp. 174–75.

21. Coventry Patmore, *English Metric Critics* (1857), quoted in Gardner, *Hopkins*, 2:101.

22. Russell Astley, "Stations of the Breath: End Rhyme in the Verse of Dylan Thomas," *PMLA*, 84 (1969), 1595–1606. An interesting, distantly related, moot opinion is that offered by Coleridge in *Table Talk*: "Brute animals have the vowel sounds; Man only can utter consonants." But Coleridge was not denying the importance of vowels; he was leading to a conclusion, also moot, that "it is natural, therefore, that the consonants should be marked first, as being the framework of the word."

23. For J. R. Lowell, see *My Study Windows* (Boston: J. R. Osgood, 1871), p. 327; for Hopkins, see Gardner's study of Greek vowel repetitions, 2:125–31; for Dryden's quoting of Virgil, see "Preface to *Fables Ancient and Modern*," in *Essays*, ed. Watson, 2:276.

24. For the Digby Ms. in the Bodleian, see the edition, ed. Rosalyn Gardner, H. H. Hilton, Jr., and W. S. Woods (Columbus, Ohio: H. L. Hedrick, 1950). Nathaniel B. Smith, whose work on "Figures of Repetition in the Old Provençal Lyric" is to

appear shortly, has more examples of assonance, often a kind of subassonance, in Arnaut Daniel and other poets. See n. 17.

25. Maurice Grammont, *Le Vers français* (Paris: Delagrave, 1947), p. 349. See, however, for a different opinion, W. Theodor Elwert, *Französiche Metrik* (Munich: M. Hueber, 1961), pp. 88–89, who argues that in French poetry such final vowel echoes are so common that they have been accepted as genuine rhymes ("als ein echter Reim gegolten"); he suggests that they be called "rimes faibles."

26. For these lines and many others like them, see Robert P. Newton, p. 577.

27. Main and Seng, p. 180.

28. In nine of the most famous—Sonnets 15, 18, 30, 55, 60, 64, 73, 97, 116—there are, without counting rhymes, at least forty-two vowel echoes in stressed syllables, or about one to every three lines, and only thirty-one alliterations.

29. *East* was pronounced something like [ɛst] by Shakespeare, Spenser, and their contemporaries. Kökeritz (see n. 36), showing that with these writers *east* and *feast* rhymed with such words as *rest*, *west*, *best*, *jest*, used the symbol [ę], which is, he tells us, the sound in *get* while, for him, [ɛ] is the short form of the vowel in French *même*. The distinction is a fine one now often made by phoneticists but not noted by the IPA.

30. Norman Nathan, *Judging Poetry* (New York: Putnam, 1961), p. 347. For examples of various definitions, see *NED*, s.v. "Consonance."

31. Roberts, p. 112. The *Princeton Encycl.*, p. 152, has only this definition in a very brief article, as does Sylvan Barnet, Morton Berman, and William Burto, *The Study of Literature: A Handbook of Critical Essays and Terms* (Boston: Little, Brown, 1960), p. 351.

32. Gardner, *Hopkins*, 1:140, calls such exercises "novelties."

33. In his sound "game," in addition to the alliteration and consonance, Auden also assonated the alternate end words— *began* and *flash*, *flush* and *gun*, etc.

34. Although *consonance*, even with this definition, will continue to be ambiguous to many readers, the alternate expression *slant rhyme*—see Walsh, p. 95, or X. J. Kennedy, *An Introduc-*

tion to Poetry (Boston: Little, Brown, 1966), p. 132, for example—is even less satisfactory.

35. As, for example, in R. F. Brewer, *Orthometry: The Art of Versification and the Technicalities of Poetry* (London: Deacon, 1893; new and rev. ed., Edinburgh: Grant, 1918, 1923).

36. *A Note on Eye Rhymes, Rhymes, and Vowel Sounds.* The question of when a rhyme, originally good, may have become an eye rhyme or some other inexact rhyme is impossible to determine for any given group of English poets before, say, 1800. For Helge Kökeritz on eye rhymes, especially for Shakespeare and Shakespeare's day, but also for the seventeenth and eighteenth centuries, see his *Shakespeare's Pronunciation* (New Haven: Yale Univ. Press, 1953), pp. 31–35; for certain of his special examples and theories, see pp. 242–44. While often following H. C. Wyld, Kökeritz disagrees with Wyld on several important points. For example, Kökeritz believes that "as a criterion of early NE pronunciation Shakespeare's rhymes and, for that matter, the rhymes of any sixteenth- or seventeenth-century English poet are not so dependable as the reliable phonetic spelling or the homonymic pun" (p. 31). Kökeritz's explanation is that by Shakespeare's time a rhyming tradition was already strong.

For Wyld's theories, see his *Studies in English Rhymes from Surrey to Pope* (London: J. Murray, 1923) as well as his other books on the history of the English language. In *Rhymes*, pp. 10–12, he says, "It is scarcely possible to conceive a conspiracy among poets to spoil their verse by adopting bad rhymes, and the same bad rhymes. It seems reasonable then to argue . . . that these rhymes were 'good' and satisfactory to the ears of poets and readers in that age [1500–1800]." On the other hand, he goes on, one must consider the tradition a poet works in: "A poet may continue to rhyme words together, after they have ceased to be true rhymes, because such rhymes are traditional, and occur again and again in the verse of his predecessors. . . . This adherence to outworn traditional rhymes is greatly encouraged when the words to be coupled in rhyme agree in their spelling, when they constitute what are called *rhymes to the eye*." Wyld believes that "on the whole it is safe to say that most poets are conservative and prefer to adhere" to an immediate past tradition. Because, then, of the tension that perhaps existed over real versus eye rhymes, Wyld tests the rhymes of poets from Surrey to Pope by reference to private letters, rhyme manuals, and the works of grammarians such as Hodges (1643), Wallis (1654), and Cooper (1685), pointing out that the grammarians had little or no influence on the great mass of speakers (p. 16). As a result he is able to conclude, for example, that Dryden's *fate–height* and Swift's *meat–say't* were good rhymes for them. See also his statement that Puttenham (1589) urged poets to make rhymes spell alike as well as sound alike, a request not followed by poets after him (see below).

Wyld's most important conclusion, however, in his preface to *Rhymes*, is one to which I can subscribe after my thirty years of studying rhymes from 1600 to 1800: "The most interesting result which this inquiry has led to is the conviction that the language of the great poets—and others—of the sixteenth and seventeenth centuries is a true mirror, often even in minute details, of the living spoken English of their age . . . , [and] it seems more probable that the poet intended a real rhyme, as certainly many of his readers would believe. . . . At the same time it would be very unwise to assume that Spenser, Shakespeare, Milton, Dryden, and Pope never made bad rhymes. They certainly did so now and then, but, I believe, not very often considering the thousands of lines they composed." And, one might add, no more often than poets of the nineteenth and twentieth centuries. See also Dean Tolle Mace, "Sound and Sense in Augustan Poetic Theory," *RES*, n.s. 2:138, who speaks confidently of "the inevitable phonetic accuracy" of Pope's rhymes.

In all the discussion of eye rhymes no one seems to have pointed out that it is far easier to make a case for good rhymes not spelled alike than for rhymes which are spelled but not pronounced alike. For example, one must contend not only with *Rome–room* but with *jail–scale, Queen–scene, praise–days, care–Bear, exprest–breast, Dunce–once, there–despair, beget–wit, roll–stole, great–complete, size–pies,* a list which constitutes about one-fifth of the non-eye rhymes in the first *Dunciad* and all of which were good rhymes in Pope's day. The same kind of statement can be made, however, for Dryden, or Waller, or Prior, or Swift.

For the sounds of vowels in the seventeenth and eighteenth centuries, see Wyld, *Rhymes;* Wyld, *A History of Modern Colloquial English* (London: T. Fisher Unwin, 1920); Wyld, *The Historical Study of the Mother Tongue* (New York: Dutton, 1906); William Edward Mead, *The Versification of Pope* (Diss. Leipzig, 1889); E. J. Dobson, *English Pronunciation: 1500–1700*, 2 vols. (Oxford: Clarendon Press, 1957); K. Luick, *Historische Grammatik der englischen Sprache* (Leipzig: Tauchnitz, 1921); Thomas Pyles, *The Origins and Development of the English Language* (New York: Harcourt, Brace, and World, 1964); R. E. Zachrisson, *Pronunciation of English Vowels, 1400–1700* (Göteborg: W. Zachrissons Boktryckeri, 1913); and Constance Davies, *English Pronunciation from the Fifteenth to the Eighteenth Century* (London: J. M. Dent, 1934). For Shakespeare's day see Wyld, Luick, Zachrisson, Dobson, and Kökeritz. Although these historians of sound changes do not always agree on the question of how a vowel was pronounced at a given time and place, there is such substantial agreement that a study of assonance rests upon firm ground. Here are a few of the problems a modern, especially a modern American, speaker must face when he reads poets from Shakespeare to Pope.

First, for the diphthong *oi*, note that while Swift ridiculed Dr. Gibbs for three times rhyming *oi* with *i* or *y* (as *destroy* with *defy*), Swift's close friend Pope continually rhymed those sounds, as did his other friends Gay and Prior, no one of whom Swift—in print, at least—accused of having false rhymes. Swift never used the rhyme himself and thought it reflected the pronunciation of a Scotsman or "my lady's maid." See *The Prose Works of Jonathan Swift*, ed. Temple Scott, 12 vols. (London: Bell, 1897–1908), 4:231ff. Dryden and his contemporaries surely pronounced the *oi* of *join* and the *i* of *fine* in much the same way, something like [əɪ], or [ʌɪ], the same sound occurring in the final syllable of "Rosalind," as Kökeritz, p. 218, is not the only one to show. See Wyld, *Colloquial English*, pp. 223–26, who describes two accepted standard pronunciations for several centuries, both leading eventually to "Received Standard" [aɪ]. Wyld is apparently followed by Pyles (see pp. 171, 173, 187), although Kökeritz (p. 216) disagrees about the exact sequence of changes ME *i* underwent to arrive at modern [aɪ]. The most extended treatment of the development of ME *oi* and ME *ui* is in Dobson, 2:810–26, to which should be added his section on the dipthongization of ME *i* to PresE [aɪ]. Note Dobson's statement (2:661, again 667) that "the difference between [əi] and [ʌi] is so slight it is not of great importance which sound was actually used" in the sixteenth and seventeenth centuries.

Second, Dryden, Swift, Gay, and Pope, to mention only four, pronounced *yes* to rhyme with *miss* and *yet* and *get* to rhyme with *sit*, just as Spenser and Shakespeare rhymed *yet* (*yit*, *yitt*) with *sit*, *unfit*, *wit*, etc., and just as *Devil* was spelled and pronounced *Divel* or *Divil* by many poets besides Dryden and Pope. In fact, while Wyld gives evidence to show that [ɛ] for [ɪ] was common "among the upper classes and others during the whole of the sixteenth, seventeenth, and the first third of the eighteenth centuries" (*Rhymes*, p. 82; see also his *Colloquial English*, pp. 226–29), Kökeritz (pp. 186–90) with even more evidence shows that [ɪ] was common for [ɛ], not only in *get*, *yet*, etc., but in *sense*, *engine*, *hence*, etc. Dobson, 2:570–71, treats this raising of ME *ĕ* to *ĭ* and the lowering of ME *i* to *e* only briefly (see also 2:503–4, for shortening of ME *ę̄* to [ɪ]), agreeing with Wyld that "in London English the *e*-forms belong to a lower-class dialect" and that the raising and lowering were both dialectal. In other words, for some poets from Spenser to Pope, at least, *him* and *them* had the same vowel and *since* and *sense* had the same sound. For the same phenomenon in the Southern U. S. today, at least for [ɛ] becoming [ɪ] before nasals, see John S. Kenyon and Thomas A. Knott, *A Pronouncing Dictionary of American English* (Springfield, Mass.: Marriam, 1944), p. xliii.

Third, from Shakespeare through the eighteenth century, evidence is strong that, as in our day, [r] often had strange effects on preceding vowels in stressed syllables. There is the well-known development of modern *ar* from ME *er*, as in *star* and *far*. This development leads to some variation even in Modern English, however ("p*e*rson," "p*a*rson"; British and American "cl*e*rk" and "d*e*rby"). Because of the variability in this sound, Dryden, Pope and their contemporaries could rhyme *air*, *appear*, *care*, *hear*, *car*, and *far*, or *heard* with *reward* and *hard* with *dared* (see Kökeritz, pp. 178–79; Dobson, 2:517–19: "such rhymes are to be accepted as accurate"; and Wyld, *Rhymes*, pp. 63–67,

83–84, for three of many treatments, not only of *e* and *a* but of *ea* before *r*). For assimilation of *r* after vowels and development of the vocalic *r* [ər]—for example *bust*, *word* rhyming with *ford*, *herd*, *bird*, *curd*—see, for only one treatment, Kökeritz, pp. 249–54.

Fourth, one of the most difficult of phonetic problems for vowels of the sixteenth, seventeenth, and eighteenth centuries is that concerning the pronunciation of the sound often expressed by *ea*, as in *sea* and *beast*. Wyld (*Rhymes*, pp. 48–62; *Colloquial English*, pp. 205–12), followed in general by Zachrisson and Kökeritz (pp. 194–204; see also Pyles, pp. 172, 174, and Dobson, 2:818–25), gives the now accepted discussion of the early (fifteenth-century?) development of two vowel sounds often related. First, there is ME [e:], usually spelled *e* or *ee* as in Chaucer's *be* and *queene* but pronounced as in modern *bay* (Wyld's *e*[1]), and its development to modern [i], as in *be* and *queen*. Then there is ME [ɛ:] (Wyld's *e*[2]), usually spelled *e* or *ea*—as in the Latin word *beste* and Anglo-Saxon *great*—a sound which, apparently by Shakespeare's death, became, Wyld argues, [e], so that the vowel in Dryden's and Swift's rhyme *sea–obey* or in Pope's famous *obey–tea* and his less famous *shade–mead* had the sound of *a* in *ale*. But, as Wyld, Kökeritz, Dobson, and others agree, this [e] was in competition with a less popular colloquial pronunciation that early adopted the [i], and it was this pronunciation that in the eighteenth century won out; that is, the [e] slowly disappeared from Standard English (not from Dublin Irish or some Appalachian American dialects) and [i] took over—*sea* [se] was supplanted by *sea* [si]. So the sound of ME *e*[1] and that of ME *e*[2] became the same sound and would remain the same, except in a very few words, such as *break* and *steak*. Hence this sound was evidently in flux in the sixteenth, seventeenth, and eighteenth centuries; and writers of Shakespeare's day, and of the seventeenth century especially, were aware of more than one pronunciation for *sea*, Dryden rhyming it usually with words like "*day*" but, often also, with words like "*me*" and "*decree*" (Dobson, 2:642–43, believes the raised [i] in the seventeenth century "was not accepted in any but careless speech"); other writers, as Kökeritz says, may have been following a rhyming tradition in coupling *ea* words with *e* or *ee* words; and still others may have been pronouncing this sound according to the part of England from which they came. In sum, as Dobson, 2:629, says, it is often difficult to determine exactly how a poet of this period pronounced the *ea*: he may have said [e] in what most phoneticists believe to have been the standard way, or [i] in the tradition of Wyld's e^1, or even [ɛ:] in the ME way, which obviously lingered on in certain words, as when Shakespeare, and many poets after him, rhymed *east* with *detest, rest, west* (see n. 29 above), three words that, whether Latin or AS, had [ɛ], or [ɛ:], in ME. Note Wyld's warning (*Rhymes*, pp. 58–59, 86–93) "to be careful in attributing the new type of pronunciation of the genuine B (e^2) words to poets of the sixteenth and seventeenth centuries," and Kökeritz's long explanation (pp. 194–204) to go with his conclusion, "The unstable quantity of ME $\bar{e}$ is a notable feature of sixteenth- and seventeenth-century pronunciation." (See also Dobson, 2:606–43, for another long discussion of these complicated developments and variations within dialects.)

One interesting disagreement between Kökeritz and Wyld—to some perhaps a quibble, but not to students of assonance— comes in the explanation of how ME [ɛ:] (Wyld's e^2) became [e:] in the eighteenth century (after 1650, Dobson, 2:623, thinks) and then obsolete. Wyld describes the change as one movement: Kökeritz posits an intermediate stage for "about 1600," a sound which he calls [ę:], that is, a mid-front vowel "between [e:] in G *sehen* and [ɛ:] in Fr *même*" (p. 199) and found in modern *tell*. And, as a matter of fact, Dryden—late in the seventeenth century—rhymes *stream* five times in the *Georgics* (1:290–91; 591–92; 3.395–96; 4.45–46, 397–98), once with *beam(s)*, (another [ɛ:] word in ME), and once even with *name*, but three times he rhymed it with *stem, contemn*, and *stem*, two words of ON and OF origin that are thought to have had [ɛ] before as well as after Dryden's time (see Dobson, 2:631–634, for this variant even earlier and for an attempt to explain the [ɛ] pronunciation sometimes found in *steam* and *stream*). If we accept Kökeritz's [e:], that is, [ɛ], the rhymes are all good, with the possible exception of *name*, and even there the vowels could have been the same or very close, if we remember that the ME [a:] in *name* went through [ɛ:] before reaching modern [e:] (see Pyles, p. 174, e.g., who thinks the [e] in such words became standard "probably in the early years of the eighteenth century"). The point is that we cannot be sure exactly how Dryden, even Pope, pronounced the *ea* words from ME [ɛː], but we can see how often such poets rhymed Wyld's *e*¹ and *e*² words (Wyld, p. 60, 91–92), how often the [ɛː] sound seems to have lingered in many words where Wyld and others—but not Kökeritz—find [eː], and how close the sounds in *name* and *beam* could have been. With Kökeritz's explanation, in fact, Pope's *obey–tea* rhyme would perhaps have a diphthong, close to but not exactly the same as the vowel, or vowel glide, in Pope's *name*, which for him may have still been near [ɛː], as Pyles, for example, explains. Wyld, *Historical Study*, p. 314, suggests that the word was apparently pronounced [nɛəm] by some speakers at the end of the seventeenth century, while Dobson, 2:618, explains how *tea* "vacillates between the forms *tay* . . . and *tee*" until the middle of the eighteenth century. By that time the rhymes of Thomson and other poets show clearly that [i] was becoming accepted in *ea* words such as *ease* and *sea*. For example, in *The Castle of Indolence* (1748) Thomson has the following *e*² words rhyming [i]: *ease–trees–degrees–fees*: *meads–exceeds–breeds*; *sea–me–free–lea*; *speaks–cheeks*; *stream–teem*; *beads–reeds–weeds*; *please–trees–fees*. *Ease* and *sea*, in fact, never certainly rhyme [ɛ] or [e] in that poem. Dobson, 2:642–43, shows that he believes one cannot be sure until after 1700 how a poet pronounced ME *ē* and ME *ā*. "It is clear," he says, "that the raised pronunciation (i.e. [i]) was not accepted in any but careless speech in the seventeenth century."

Fifth, an even more difficult problem for readers of sixteenth, seventeenth, and eighteenth century poetry, especially for students of rhymes and assonances, in the relationship among, the separation of, the possible identity of, the vowel sounds in the following groups of rhymes found by the hundreds in poems from Spenser and Shakespeare to Pope: *strove–grove–move–love–above*; *song–throng–strong–tongue–sung*; *mood–stood–blood*; *doom–home–come*; *cuts–puts*; *bush–blush*; *fool–dull–pull*; *sun–alone*. What is confusing to twentieth-century readers is that among these words are several vowel sounds which today are different from the others. Historians of the English language have great difficulty deciding what sounds the vowels had at a given time, but they do show conclusively (1) that the existence of numerous dialects helps account for some of the variation, (2) that certain of the vowels involved changed faster with some regions or social groups than with others, and (3) that differences between British and American English today continue to confuse the picture. A reading of Wyld (*Rhymes*, pp. 75–82; *Colloquial English*, pp. 232–39, 254–56); Pyles, pp. 171–74; Kökeritz, pp. 229–44; and Dobson, 2:583–94, 674–87, will help to show what the problems are but will also go far toward solving some of them satisfactorily.

The two chief ME vowel sounds which are reflected here are the short *u* in words like *run* (Wyld has three related vowels that move along with *u*, these being OE *y*, as in *thrush*; ME *u* of French origin as in *judge*; and a new *ū* out of earlier *ō*, as in *blood, flood, done*) and *ō*. By common consent the *u* was often, though perhaps not in every dialect, unrounded and lowered sometime around the fourteenth and fifteenth centuries, giving us the two modern sounds in *pull* [ʊ] and *butter* [ʌ], while the *ō* sound—at uncertain times, varying with the regions, and with no phonological reasons to account for the changes—first went to [u] (as in modern *fool*) before ending up today as any one of three sounds, [u] in *fool*, [ʊ] in *good*, and [ʌ] in *blood*. In one set of *ō* words— *rood, spoon*—the [u] remained; in another large group it was shortened earlier to [ʊ] and then, in many words, underwent unrounding and further shortening to give us modern *blood, done, brother* (see *u* above). For the period including Shakespeare and Pope these vowels now give so much trouble partly because some analysts (Kökeritz, Pyles) believe in a strong influence of tradition and of eye rhymes (that is, that all these poets rhymed words that did not in their day sound alike); partly because of disagreement over when the later shortening, that of [ʊ] to [ʌ], took place; partly because the seventeenth and eighteenth century grammarians could not themselves agree on what the vowels in *food, wood,* and *bud* sounded like; and—for Americans—partly because the British [ʌ] is central-back, therefore very close to [ʊ], and not low mid-center, as for most Americans (see Wyld, *Colloquial English*, p. 225: the vowel in *cut* is mid-back-[tense]; and, for another Britisher's distinction between the two [ʌ]'s, see David I. Masson, "Wilfred Owen's

Free Phonetic Patterns," *Journal of Art and Art Criticism*, 13[1954–55], 363n.).

To illustrate the problems concerning these vowel sounds and to suggest how poets from 1600 to 1750 may have pronounced them, one can start with Kökeritz (pp. 229–44), who over and over confesses about Shakespeare's [u], [ʊ], [ʌ] vowel sounds that certain questions "must remain . . . open," that certain of the vowels may have had certain sounds, that certain spellings or rhymes or contemporaneous statements seem to indicate a certain sound, etc. But Kökeritz does have some strong convictions, for example, those regarding Shakespeare's rhyming of *strove–love–move*. "If exact," he says, "*strove:Love* would indicate the use of a pronunciation [strʌv] which had developed like *struck*; such a form is still current in several dialects, as in [drʌv] for *drove*. Yet other rhymes like *Jove:love:grove:love* and *over: lover* rather point to its being an eye rhyme, originally based on [u:] for ME ō in *strove* (as in *Jove*, *grove*, *over*), which was linked with [ʊ] or [u:] in *love*" (p. 233). (See Dobson, 2:676, n. 2, for another explanation.) Then, after finding unacceptable Ben Jonson's statement that for his time "prove" and "love" had the same vowel, Kökeritz concludes that by Shakespeare's day such rhymes were inexact even though they had once been good (pp. 243–44). In fact, Kökeritz is able to place almost no confidence in the rhymes of Shakespeare or Spenser or other poets (see especially pp. 236, 237, 243). Pyles (p. 173) quotes Kökeritz on the distribution of [u], [ʊ], [ʌ] in the sixteenth and seventeenth centuries but obviously is not in total agreement with him, just as Dobson, 2:674ff., sometimes disagrees with Wyld and Luick about the development of "ME ǭ" (see pp. 674–76, 679–80 especially).

An answer to some of the problems involved in the question of the sixteenth and seventeenth century distribution of [u], [ʊ], and [ʌ] hinges on when, in many words, the later shortening of ME ō, that of [ʊ] to [ʌ] took place. While Kökeritz has Shakespeare and Spenser often using [ʌ], in *blood*, for example, Wyld puts "the late or second shortening . . . as late as the end of the seventeenth or the beginning of the eighteenth century" (*Colloquial English*, p. 239), that is, not until Pope's day, while Luick (secs. 529–32) concludes that the transition to [ʌ] was still going

on as late as 1800. Furthermore Luick (sec. 525) believes that
most of the problems Kökeritz has trouble with can be solved by
positing the middle sound [ʊ] for most of the words in the sixteenth and seventeenth centuries which today have [u], [ʊ], [ʌ].
For the ME *u* Wyld believes that "the sound had attained . . . its
present stage by the third quarter of the seventeenth century"
although there were two distinct developments, one in which
"the unrounding does not always take place, or rather, perhaps, a
new rounding has sometimes taken place, as in *bull, pull, put,
push* . . . ," and the other found in words with the unrounded
vowel of *pulse, bud, butter, mug, mud,* etc. "It is therefore
probable," he says, "that we have here a duality due to difference
of dialect, perhaps of Social rather than Regional character"
(*Colloquial English*, pp. 323–32). For the ME *ō* Wyld argues that
contemporaneous evidence is no help to us in deciding whether
the words that did not remain [u] were pronounced with [ʊ] or
[ʌ], even though he believes that they "correspond very largely"
with our [ʌ] type. But so long as we are not sure of the existence
of [ʌ] in the seventeenth century, he concludes,

> we cannot say with certainty whether the forms with 'short
> *u*' are the descendants of those which had [u] in the fifteenth
> century, and are the ancestors of our [ʌ] type, or whether
> they are the beginnings of our second or later shortening
> which has produced our [ʊ] in *cook*, etc. *It does not follow
> even when once the* [ʌ] *forms had come into existence in
> some dialects, that they were used in the best type of Lon-
> don or Court speech.* (*Colloquial English*, p. 238—with [ʊ]
> and [ʌ] substituted for Wyld's symbols for the sounds in
> modern *cook* and *cut*; italics mine).

But for our treatment of rhymes and assonances involving [u],
[ʊ], and [ʌ] in poems from Shakespeare to Pope, Wyld's conclusions in his study (*Rhymes*, pp. 75–82) are most important. First,
he is sure that "it is impossible to explain the distribution of the
three types. We cannot even say why the vowel in some words
should have undergone the early shortening, while that in others
did not . . . the two shortening processes occurred only in the
speech of some sections of the community, while among other
groups of speakers one or other of these tendencies did not

obtain; in yet other groups perhaps neither shortening took place." Second, he points to a number of fluctuations in the use of the three sounds today and shows that the same fluctuations existed in Dryden's day. *Soot*, for example, not only rhymes with *cut* for some twentieth-century speakers but "there is evidence that this word was habitually so pronounced in the seventeenth century," while *groom*, *broom*, and *soon* sometimes had a long vowel, [u], and sometimes a shorter one, [ʊ] or [ʌ]. *Blood, flood, good, foot, cut, soot, hood, but, took* are only a few other words, Wyld shows, that in Dryden's day vacillated between [u] and [ʊ] or perhaps between [ʊ] and [ʌ]. Not only, then, were *good* and *stood* perfect rhymes with *mud* and *bud* for some seventeenth-century writers, but "the rhymes of *love* and *above* with *move* and *prove* . . . were perfectly good. There is evidence on the one hand that *prove* could be pronounced with the same vowel which we now have in *love*, and on the other that this word and *above* could be pronounced with the sound which we now have in *prove* and *move*." Finally, Wyld says, "All things considered, it seems more probable that the poets who, in the sixteenth and seventeenth centuries, appear to us to confuse the various types in their rhymes are in reality, basing them upon a pronunciation according to which the agreement in sound was perfect."

Some rhymes, Wyld does believe, were imperfect, however, for example Swift's *over–lover*. But for Spenser these words and *hover* rhymed; so Swift perhaps had [ʊ], a sound close to the one many British and American speakers today have for *hover*, the other popular pronunciation being with [ɒ], as in American *plot*. Again Wyld (*Colloquial English*, p. 236) is puzzled as to "why the vowel in *done* was shortened but not that in *moon* and *spoon*." Actually, for some speakers of the seventeenth century even the vowel in *moon* was apparently shortened. For example, in the *Georgics* Dryden rhymes *moon* four times, and every time the rhyme word has a shortened vowel—*sun–run–shun–sun* (1.571–72, 583–84, 371–72; 2.679–80)—while *sun* rhymes not only with *done*, *begun*, *run*, *shun*, etc., but with *alone* and *zone* (*Georgics* 1.632–33, 322–23). Dryden, like Shakespeare before him and Pope after him, rhymed *long* and *song* with *wrong* and similar words but just as often with *tongue*, *young*, *hung*, *strung*. Furthermore, while he rhymed *come* with *some*, *drum, bum, plum,* he rhymed it far more often with *home* and even with *groom* and *bloom.* We know also that a favorite pronunciation of the name *Bolingbroke,* from Shakespeare's character to Pope's friend, was with the [ʊ], possibly [ʌ], for the first *o* and [ʊ] for the second (Kökeritz, pp. 241–42, e.g.), just as *Cromwell* was pronounced with [ʊ] in the stressed syllable (Wyld, *Colloquial English,* p. 103) and words like *bomb* had the same [ʊ] as they do today for many people. Wyld (*Rhymes,* p. 128) points out that Dryden rhymed *Rome* with *home* in the "new-fangled" way and that Pope rhymed it with *doom,* but Dryden rhymed it far more often with *come* as well as with *doom* and Pope also rhymed it with *dome.* (See Dobson, 2:680–81, however, who believes with Kökeritz that *Rome* in the sixteenth and seventeenth centuries had [u:] and should have rhymed only with words like *doom.*) With Pope and his predecessors *dull* rhymed with *fool* on the one hand but also with *full* on the other. Today in standard English *fool* has [u], *full* has [ʊ], and *dull* has [ʌ], all of which perhaps indicates that Wyld is right in believing that [ʌ] had not been reached in the seventeenth century, at least in court circles, and that [u] and [ʊ] were close together for many speakers.

If we disagree with Wyld, then, and argue that the seventeenth- and eighteenth-century poets were conspiring to displease their readers by using rhymes that were not "real rhymes based on pronunciations current in their day" (Wyld, *Rhymes,* p. 98), we must go on to argue that Dryden, Pope, and their contemporaries had not dozens but hundreds of imperfect rhymes, not merely eye rhymes. But if we accept Wyld's and Luick's arguments about [u], [ʊ], [ʌ] and those of Kökeritz regarding [ɛ:], [e], [i], as well as the conclusions of Wyld (*Rhymes,* pp. 86–93) and other historians for other vowels and diphthongs, then the following groups of words contained vowels in stressed syllables that were either identical or so close that the poets' ears could detect little difference: *love–move–strove; come–home–groom–doom–Rome–womb; tongue–long–throng–sung–*(even)*song* (Dryden rhymes *song* with *young, tongue, hung, strung* as often as with *long* and similar words); *sun–alone–none–one* (for *one* and *alone* see Wyld, *Rhymes,* p. 126)–*throne–son; cull–dull–full–wool–fool–pull; bush–blush; cuts–puts; pair–Star–appear–where–be-*

ware–care–prepare; *devil–civil*; *obey–tea–away*; *break–neck*; *streams–Thames*; *beast–feast–guest–rest–dress'd*; *join–line–toil–pile*; *sea–way–be*.

When employing IPA symbols for these sounds, I shall let [ɛ] stand for the *ea* words that derive from Wyld's *e*² or that for any reason seem to have retained the ME long *e* of *bell*—for example, *feast* and *beast*; [əɪ] for the sound in *join* and *line* (but remember Dobson's statement, quoted earlier, that the difference between [əɪ] and [ʌɪ] is "so slight" as to be of no real importance); [ɔ] for the sound in *God*, which in the eighteenth century rhymed often with *abode*, *road*, *unawed* as well as with words having modern [ɒ], the sound in *pod*, *rod*, *nod* (see Wyld, *Rhymes*, p. 101); [ɪ] for the vowel in *yet* and *devil* as well as for that in *civil*; and [ʊ,ʌ] for the vowel sound—or sounds, if they were not really identical—in all the words listed above from *love* through *puts*. The [ʊ,ʌ] device, both cumbersome and arbitrary, is simply an attempt to remind readers that to Dryden and Pope *fool*, *full*, *dull* had vowels that sounded alike. My own opinion is that the sound was not [ʌ] for educated Londoners until after Pope's day, certainly not the American [ʌ]; but perhaps those readers who disagree on this point will remember that the three words rhymed with Dryden and Pope and that with them and their contemporaries *one*, *lone*, *love*, *Rome*, *strung*, *come*, *home*, *full*, *blush*, *puts* were therefore apparently assonating words.

37. There is, for example, the suggestion of Dell H. Hymes concerning one problem of dividing words into syllables according to sound ("Phonological Aspects of Style: Some English Sonnets," in *Essays on the Language of Literature*, ed. Seymour Chatman and Samuel R. Levin, Boston: Houghton Mifflin, 1967, p. 40, hereinafter called *Essays*, ed. Chatman and Levin). Hymes suggests that "syllable boundaries are not always clear-cut. Of consonants occurring between nuclei, a single consonant [may be] counted in the preceding syllable if its nucleus is a simple vowel, not if its nucleus is a diphthong. Of two or more consonants between nuclei, the last [may be] counted in the following syllable but not in the first." Such a theory does not, however, consider whether the first syllable is stressed, nor does it consider whether the preceding single vowel is long, say [u:] in "moody,"

or short, say [ɛ] in "messy." For more hesitation over, and explanation of, syllable boundaries, see John Thompson, *The Founding of English Metre* (New York: Columbia Univ. Press, 1961), p. 12n., and Vendreyes, pp. 54ff. Webster's various editions, as well as other dictionaries, have long attempted to indicate syllable boundaries even as they admit that tradition forces them to do so and that one often needs to have a word in context before deciding where the syllables end and begin. Throughout the present study I hope to avoid dogmatism about whether a consonant, for example, is final in a stressed syllable or initial in the following weaker one, although I do believe that most readers will agree on most of the traditional syllabic divisions. For example, there is probably no argument about the [l] consonance in "va*ll*-ey li*ll*-ies" and "l'a*l*-tre ste*ll*-e" or that [k] is final in *slacker*—all in chapter 1; but there may be some professional hesitation over "moody madness" in chapter 1 or over "vocal oak," "oraculously spoke," and "sleepy poppies"—all in chapter 2—since the [k] of *vocal*, at least, is initial with most orthoepists and the [d] of *moody* is initial with some although final with others. It is obvious to me, however, that, in context, the repetition of [d] in "moody madness" and of [k] in "vocal oak" clearly affects the ear. While trying to avoid controversial examples of consonance wherever possible, I cannot always avoid them in long passages, nor do I want to avoid affective repetitions, as in "moody madness." For a short, but professional, treatment of syllabication see *Webster's Third New International Dictionary*; and for shorter and more popular ones, see *Webster's Seventh New Collegiate Dictionary* (1965), p. xlv. In the case of *moody*, for example, this and all editions of Webster's break the word after *d* while the *American Heritage Dictionary* breaks it before the *d*. More than once in this book I point out such specific, really minor, problems in marking consonance.

38. See Burke's "On Musicality in Verse," *The Philosophy of Literary Form* (1941; rpt. New York: Vintage Books, 1957), pp. 296–304. *Consonantal acrostic* is found, Burke says, in "tyrannous and strong" because the combination "*t–r–n–s* is reordered to *s–t–r–n–g*." *Tonal chiasmus* occurs in "the ship drove fast" in that the "structural frame of 'drove' (*d–v*) is reversed in 'fast' (*f–t*), with the variation of a shift from the voiced *d* and *v* to the

corresponding unvoiced *t* and *f*." In the phrase describing *diminution* the initial *b*'s in "But" and "by," even though unstressed, provide an example of alliteration for Burke, while the *s*'s give an example of his *colliteration*.

39. See, for example, his articles in the *Princeton Encycl.* as well as his "Vowel and Consonant Patterns in Poetry" (1953) and "Thematic Analysis of Sounds in Poetry" (1960), both reprinted in *Essays*, ed. Chatman and Levin, and, for two more only, the essay on Owen quoted in n. 36 above and "Word and Sound in Yeats' 'Byzantium,'" *ELH*, 20 (1953), 136–60.

40. *A Note on Metrics:* For metrics in general and for the metrics of the seventeenth and eighteenth centuries in particular, there are several assumptions on which the present study is based. First, the meter of that period, as with the period of Ralegh and Shakespeare, is basically accentual rather than temporal, although timing was as important to Dryden, Pope, and their contemporaries as to other great poets. Second, although the relative stress theorists have argued well for four categories of accent in poetry, for a study of phonic echoes two grades will suffice—one that includes syllables with some obvious stress, one composed of all other syllables. John Crowe Ransom, for one, in "The Strange Music of English Verse," first printed in the *Kenyon Review*, 18 (Summer 1956), and often reprinted, believes two grades of stress sufficient for the normal reader. Third, in spite of Otto Jespersen's famous attempt of 1900 to effect a universal discarding of traditional terms for the several kinds of metrical feet, and in spite of Robert Frost's even more famous assertion that all rhythm is basically iambic, for English poetry after Shakespeare the old terms—at least *iamb*, *trochee*, *anapest*, *dactyl*, *spondee*, and *pyrrhic*—can be conveniently employed. Fourth, although most of the poetry of the period from Dryden to Johnson, as with other periods since 1500, is basically iambic, it contains many deviations from the norm, the favorite substitutions being trochees, spondees—as with the first two words of Ralegh's "Nymph's Reply"—and pyrrhics. Fifth and last, in spite of the fact that Dryden, Pope, and Thomson—like Milton, Shakespeare, and Byron—counted syllables, they probably all read their poems naturally enough for a student of sound effects to place the stresses with considerable confidence, with

perhaps as much confidence as for the poetry of any period, that is, where a good dramatic or poetic reading would place them. The following studies can be recommended as a beginning: Paul Fussell, *Theory of Prosody in Eighteenth-Century England* (New London: Connecticut College, 1954); John Thompson, *The Founding of English Metre* (New York: Columbia Univ. Press, 1961); Seymour Chatman, *A Theory of Meter* (The Hague: Mouton, 1964); Karl Shapiro, *A Bibliography of Modern Prosody* (Baltimore: Johns Hopkins Press, 1948): Shapiro and Robert Beum, *A Prosody Handbook* (New York: Harper and Row, 1965); Jakob Schipper, *A History of English Versification* (Oxford: Clarendon Press, 1910); Otto Jespersen, "Notes on Metre," *Essays*, ed. Chatman and Levin, originally read in Danish in 1900 and reprinted here from his book *Linguistica* (Copenhagen: Levin and Munksgaard, 1933); W. K. Wimsatt, Jr., and Monroe C. Beardsley, "The Concept of Meter: An Exercise in Abstraction," *PMLA*, 74 (1959), 585–98, reprinted in *Essays*, ed. Chatman and Levin; various articles by John Hollander, Harold Whitehall, and Seymour Chatman; Graham Hough, *Style and Stylistics* (London: Routledge and Kegan Paul, 1971); *Style in Language*, ed. Thomas A. Sebeok (Cambridge, Mass.: M.I.T. Press, 1960); Roman Jakobson, "Linguistics and Poetics," reprinted in Sebeok as well as in Chatman and Levin; and Harvey Gross, *Sound and Form in Modern Poetry* (Ann Arbor: Univ. of Michigan Press, 1964; 1965). Calvin Brown, "Can Musical Notation Help English Scansion," *Journal of Aesthetics and Art Criticism*, 23 (Spring 1965), 329–35, like Wellek agrees with Wimsatt in rejecting all "musical theories of metre (as argued in America, for example, by Northrop Frye and D. W. Prall)." Besides Roman Jakobson's linguistic system of prosody, attacked, for example, by Jonathan Culler in *Style*, 5, no. 1 (Winter 1971), 53–67, see Morris Halle and Samuel Jay Keyser, "Chaucer and the Study of Prosody," *College English*, 28 (1966), 187–219, and the heated exchange their article drew in *CE* and elsewhere, Wimsatt's, for example, in "The Rule and the Norm: Halle and Keyser on Chaucer's Meter," *Literary Style: A Symposium*, ed. Seymour Chatman (London and New York: Oxford Univ. Press, 1971), pp. 197–215. See also Charles L. Stevenson, "The Rhythm of English Verse," *The Journal of Aesthetics and*

Art Criticism, 28 (Spring 1970), 327–45, who argues for a prosody that discards old terms such as *foot* while talking much of metrical and non-metrical stress, and Roger Mitchell, "Towards a System of Grammatical Scansion," *Language and Style*, 3 (Winter 1970), 3–29, who defends his system as best for scanning writers of "non-metrical" verse. One can see that today, more than ever, John Hollander's 1956 caution is necessary: "Prosody is a particularly treacherous study right now" ("The Music of Poetry," pp. 232–33).

41. See, for example, the *Princeton Encycl.*, pp. 590–91.

42. Yeats's words, in "The Symbolism of Poetry," *Essays* (London: Macmillan, 1924), pp. 192–93. Quoted also by Masson, "Vowel and Consonant Patterns in Poetry," *Essays*, ed. Chatman and Levin, p. 4.

43. "Sound in Poetry," *Princeton Encycl.*, pp. 785–86, and also in *Essays*, ed. Chatman and Levin, pp. 11ff.

44. See J. J. Lynch, "The Tonality of Lyric Poetry: An Experiment in Method," *Word*, 9 (1953), 211–24. Hymes believes, for example, not only that the [aɪ] of *silent* is the most conspicuous and important sound in Keats's sonnet on Chapman's Homer (p. 39) but that "if the dominant sounds of a poem must always include some or all of a small set of consonants, the poet may choose a word summative in theme which contains them and place it strategically so as to exploit the cumulative effect which his language unavoidably offers" (p. 51). And while he concludes that "in some sense, then, there must be appropriateness to the nexus of sound and meaning if the poem is to be regarded as good," he adds this caution, "I would say that a sonnet which showed no unity of sound and meaning was not a good one, but there are many ways in which unity can occur. So the absence of a summative word is not critical, and its presence does not guarantee the unity of the other dimensions in the use of sound" (p. 53).

45. See his *Traité de phonétique*. This volume went through many editions after 1908, the year of the first edition. See also his *Le Vers français*, later and fuller. Grammont sums up his conclusions (p. 246) about the power of vowels thus: "Nous avons vu les voyelles claires exprimer un léger bruit, un doux murmure et au contraire les voyelles graves peindre un bruit éclatant; nous

avons vu d'autre part les voyelles claire peindre des objets petits, mignons, délicats ou des scènes gracieuses; il est tout naturel que les voyelles graves et particulièrement les éclatantes s'appliquent aux idées contraires, qu'elles conviennent à la description d'un personnage ou d'une scène grande, majestueuse, suscitant l'admiration" (p. 269). For Masson's equally extreme conclusions, see *Princeton Encycl.*, p. 786.

46. Paul Delbouille, *Poésie et sonorités*, Bibliothèque de la Faculté de philosophie et lettres de l'Université de Liège, fasc. 163 (Paris: Société d'édition "Les Belles lettres," 1961), pp. 44–45, cites a long list of French and other scholars and critics who have been influenced by Grammont. To his list one can add, especially, M. M. Macdermott, *Vowel Sounds in Poetry* (London: Kegan Paul, 1940). Masson is only one disciple of Grammont and Macdermott.

47. See Walsh, for example, p. 85, who is very skeptical about sound-sense relationships.

48. *Lives of the English Poets*, The World's Classics (London: Oxford Univ. Press, 1906, 1912), 2:329–30.

49. Raymond (pp. 314ff.) cites the great composers to show how they can, in music, represent the barking of a dog, the braying of an ass, the sobbing of a child, etc., and then concludes that the associative and imitative effects in music "correspond exactly to poetic" effects, not only in the use of representative words but of phrases and sentences as well. Elsewhere (p. 143), Raymond (in 1909) anticipates the "dominant" sound theory of Hymes and Lynch by talking of the recurrence of certain important sounds in a poem just as a piece of music emphasizes a key note. For a good discussion of the expression of ideas and emotions in music, see Calvin Brown, *Music and Literature*, pp. 64–68.

50. René Wellek and Austin Warren, "Euphony, Rhythm, and Meter," *Theory of Literature* (New York: Harcourt Brace [Harvest Books], 1956), rpt. in *Discussions of Poetry: Rhythm and Sound*, ed. George Hemphill (Boston: Heath, 1966), pp. 64–65. For Wimsatt see "One Relation of Rhyme to Reason," *MLQ*, 5 (1944), 323–38; and for Henry Lanz, *The Physical Basis of Rhyme* (Palo Alto, Calif.: Stanford Univ. Press, 1931). Wellek

and Warren in *Discussions* (p. 65) say that "there is nothing in English to compare with Viktor Zhirmunsky's book on rhyme, which classifies the effect of rhyme . . . and gives its history in Russia and in the main European countries" (*Rifma, ee istoria i teoriya* [*Rhyme: Its History and Theory*], Petrograd, 1923).

51. Jakobson, "Linguistics and Poetics," *Style in Language*, ed. Sebeok, pp. 350–78 (see esp. p. 368); and Levin, "The Conventions of Poetry," in *Literary Style: A Symposium*, ed. Seymour Chatman (London and New York: Oxford Univ. Press, 1971), pp. 177–93 (see esp. p. 186).

52. See Jakobson, p. 367. Hopkins, one of the few poets to discuss the power and effect of rhyme, notes particularly that "there are two elements in the beauty rhyme has to the mind, the likeness or sameness of sound and the unlikeness or difference of meaning" (quoted in ibid., p. 368).

53. See, for example, Dabney, p. 21, and n. 21 above.

54. See Levin (n. 49) for one strong support of the thesis of this paragraph. See also my article (n. 17 above).

55. Dwight L. Bolinger, "Rime, Assonance, and Morpheme Analysis," *Word*, 6 (1950), 136. Firth's definition is in his book *Speech* (London: Ernest Benn, 1930), pp. 45–54. But see students of language before Firth who treat the same phenomenon at great length but without the term, for example, Otto Jespersen, "Sound Symbolism," in *Language: Its Nature, Development and Origin* (London: George Allen and Unwin, 1922), pp. 396–411. For Masson's longer definition of *phonestheme* see his "Vowel and Consonant Patterns in Poetry," p. 11. Nims, pp. 179–94 in his handbook, without using the terms *phonestheme* or *phone*, provides many attractive analyses of the relationship between sound and sense in poetry.

56. For example, Jespersen, p. 396; Bolinger, p. 133; or Masson, "Vowel and Consonant Patterns in Poetry," p. 11: acoustic patterns "are often dormant unless activated by the proximity, or lexical existence, of similar patterns."

57. For these statistics, see Bolinger, p. 133. For the information about specific phonesthemes that have been argued for, see also Jespersen, who has six classes of "sound universals"; Levin; Jakobson; Christine Tanz, "Sound Symbolism in Words,"

Language and Speech, 14, pt. 3 (July–September 1971), 266–73, who emphasizes the controversial nature of such a study but still supports it with evidence; Valter Tauli, *Introduction to a Theory of Language Planning*, Studia philologia scandinavicae upsaliensia, 6 (Uppsala: Universitetet, 1968), who has a chapter on "Phonemic Shape"; U. Weinreich, "On the Semantic Structure of Language," in *Universals of Language*, ed. Joseph H. Greenberg (Cambridge, Mass.: M.I.T. Press, 1963), p. 117 especially; Grammont; Lanz; M. Chastaing, "Le Symbolisme des voyelles," *Journal de psychologie*, 55 (1958), 402–23, 461–81; Chastaing, "La Brilliance des voyelles," *Archivum Linguisticum, 14* (1962), 1–13; Stephen Ullmann, "Semantic Universals," in *Language and Style* (New York: Barnes and Noble, 1964), pp. 63–97; Robert P. Newton (see n. 2 above); and, for a corrective to the extremists, Paul Delbouille and, say, Gordon M. Messing.

Messing, in "Sound Symbolism in Greek and Some Modern Reverberations," *Arethusa*, 4, no. 1 (Spring 1971), 5–25, after arguing that many linguists of the twentieth century, including Jespersen and Ullmann, have supported sound symbolism, at great length quotes and paraphrases Dionysius of Halicarnassus (*De Compositione Verborum*, chapter 14) on the emotional and intellectual effects of the sounds of words, even phones. To Dionysius *l* is sweet and pleasing to the ear; *r* is harsh but noble; *m* and *n* imitate such sounds as those made by a horn; *s* is "graceless" and "unpleasant," and its hissing sound is "akin to that of a brute beast"; *z*, on the other hand, is pleasant; and long vowels are also "pleasant" while short ones "castrate the sound." Messing, believing that Dionysius represents the theory of sound symbolism in its most extreme form, nevertheless permits the great modern Greek scholar W. B. Stanford to defend such theories as those of Dionysius: the Greeks, Stanford believes, carried onomatopoeia far beyond simple sound-sense words such as *croak*, although Dionysius "may have exaggerated" (p. 11). Messing, who places Wellek somewhere between the extremes of Stanford and Dionysius, Hymes and Lynch, on the one hand and Ransom and Richards on the other, concludes very negatively, almost in the words of Dr. Johnson, "On the whole I rather doubt that sounds in themselves have any significance in Greek or any other language, aside from the limited category of onomatopoeic words" (pp. 21–22), and he thinks that Pope did not intend the subtle harmonies attributed to him. One can, of course, list ad infinitum the names of supporters and condemners of sound-sense relations. Gilbert Highet, for example, in *Juvenal the Satirist* (Oxford: Clarendon, 1954), pp. 175–76, provides examples of alliteration, rhythm, and what he calls assonance that help Juvenal imitate "tittering Greeks," "the belching" of a courtier, or "the wailing of a defeated army." See also Highet's "Sound Effects in Juvenal's Poetry," *Studies in Philology*, 48 (1951), 697–706.

58. X. J. Kennedy, p. 123.

59. Ullmann, p. 70. Ullmann gives a number of other examples of this effect of [l], in five languages.

60. Masson, "Wilfred Owen's Free Phonetic Patterns," pp. 362–63.

61. Jespersen, p. 401.

62. Ullmann, "Semantics and Etymology," in *Language and Style*, ed. Sebeok, p. 41. See also Jakobson, p. 317. Ullmann's statement here quoted leads, of course, to the question of synesthesia, and on pp. 85–88 he has a fine essay on this popular subject which takes us to "synaesthetic metaphors" that have always been used by poets and that we find in Baudelaire's *Correspondences*, Proust's rainbow colored music and white, black, or blue silence, or Sartre's green and yellow smells. As an example, however, of what many readers of poems may find to be an extreme approach to sound-sense literary criticism, see this excerpt from Masson, "Owen," p. 367: "In the following lines [Owen's *Insensibility* (4.6–9)] he evokes much of the more cosmic horror and mystery of war; and music fuses with statement:

> He sings along the march
> Which we march taciturn, because of dusk,
> The long, forlorn, relentless trend
> From larger day to huger night.

How is this evocation achieved? At the semantic and affective levels, by adjectives which release great reservoirs of emotion, and by the abstractness and vagueness of reference and syntax in *trend, larger, huger.* At the level of sound, first, by the regular, heavy, 'iambic' rhythm; and secondly, by the accented syllables lengthened by nasals and led in by the alliterating L's, with an impressive modulation of their vowels and that culminate . . . in the impact of a spatially and kinesthetically expressive dissonance upon the repeated -ger, closing a remarkable train of interlocking short sequences and exchanges." Then, in a note, Masson suggests about the vowels in "larger" and "huger" that the first is "compactness" and "implies energy, violence, extraversion" while the *u*, "non-compact graveness," implies "depth, darkness, mystery, and (as non-compact) rarifaction, loneliness, outer space. As to their kinesthetic associations, the vowel of '*la*rger' seems wide open and brutally insistent, while that of 'h*u*ger' seems hollow, secret, and profound."

63. Jakobson, in *Essays*, ed. Chatman and Levin, p. 312.

64. For a study of Chaucer's repetitions, especially of his vowel sounds, see my article "Chaucer's Assonance," *JEGP*, 71 (1972), 527–40. Quotations of Chaucer's lines are taken from *The Works of Geoffrey Chaucer*, ed. F. N. Robinson, 2nd ed. (Boston: Houghton Mifflin, 1957).

65. Baum, *Chaucer's Verse* (Durham, N. C.: Duke Univ. Press, 1961), pp. 57–58.

66. Nathaniel B. Smith also demonstrated this kind of caesural emphasis in Old Provençal and Old French poetry. See n. 17 above.

67. See, for example, Helen Gardner, *The Art of T. S. Eliot* (London: Cresset Press, 1968), p. 5.

68. From Virginia Spencer, *Alliteration in Spenser's Poetry*, to a recent treatment by Ants Oras, "Spenser and Milton: Some Parallels and Contrasts in the Handling of Sound (1956)," in *Essays*, ed. Chatman and Levin, pp. 19–33. This article appeared first in *Sound and Poetry*, ed. Northrop Frye (New York: Columbia Univ. Press, 1957), pp. 109–33. Oras has other essays of interest to students of the sound of poetry, for example, "Surrey's Technique of Phonetic Echoes: A Method and Its Background," *JEGP*, 50 (1951), 290ff., and "Lyrical Instrumentation in Marlowe," *Studies in Shakespeare*, eds. A. D. Mathews and C. M. Emery (Coral Gables, Fla., 1953), 76ff.

69. Raymond, p. 154.

70. Oras (see n. 68 above) has selected more nearly typical examples to study; see, for example, p. 223.

71. For example, see Robert Bridges, *Milton's Prosody* (Oxford: Clarendon Press, 1901), and Walter Thomas, "Milton's Heroic Line Viewed from an Historical Standpoint," *MLR*, 2 (1906/07), 289–315; 3 (1907/08), 16–39, 232–56. For a good short statement, see Kaluza, pp. 314–15.

72. See Oras, pp. 21–26: For each poet he found that on the average every 100 lines have (1) 175 stressed syllables beginning or ending with consonant clusters such as *cl*, *nd*, or *st* and (2) 91 stressed syllables beginning or ending with a vowel. But there the stylistic similarities between the two poets stop. Because the Elizabethan language of Spenser was different from Milton's seventeenth-century English, and for other reasons, Spenser has far more stressed syllables beginning with consonant clusters and Milton has far more that end with them. Furthermore, Spenser has much more alliteration, liked to employ end rhyme in a circular pattern, and "often comes close to using sound" for its own sake, while Milton is said to have slightly more assonance, the effect of which "is greater, however, since it need not compete with end rhymes."

73. See n. 67 above.

74. This conclusion supports that of Professor Oras in every way but one: he thinks that Milton has slightly more assonance than Spenser and that Milton's assonance is more effective because his does not need to compete with rhyme. My study shows Spenser using considerably more assonance as well as more alliteration. For example, the first 200 lines of *Paradise Lost* have only a small proportion of phonic echoes, although it is interesting to note that *Lycidas*, a rhyming poem, as well as *Comus*, has proportionately more of them than either *Paradise Lost* or *Paradise Regained*.

75. The English couplet, its origins and characteristics, has been studied many times and in many ways. For a good starting bibliography consult W. C. Brown, *The Triumph of Form: A Study of the Later Masters of the Heroic Couplet* (Durham: Univ. of North Carolina Press, 1948), p. 6. Besides Brown's book itself,

one of the best of the older analyses is by Ruth C. Wallerstein, "The Development of the Rhetoric and Metre of the Heroic Couplet, Especially in 1625–1645," *PMLA*, 50 (1935), 166–210, while one of the best recent analyses is by Paul J. Korshin "The Evolution of Neoclassical Poetics: Cleveland, Denham, and Waller as Poetic Theorists," *Eighteenth-Century Studies*, 2, no. 2 (Winter 1968), 102–38, which concentrates on the variety and complexity of the heroic couplet and not on rhymes or other sound effects. To Brown's bibliography one should also add Fussell, *The Theory of Prosody in Eighteenth Century England*, William B. Piper, *The Heroic Couplet* (Cleveland: Case Western Reserve Univ. Press, 1969), and A. W. Allison (see n. 77 below). Peter Thorpe, "The Nonstructure of Augustan Verse," *Papers on Language and Literature*, no. 3 (Summer 1969), 235–52, has avoided recent fine scholarship on Dryden, Pope, and their contemporaries to attack all neoclassical poetry except Pope's *Rape*.

76. Van Doren, *The Poetry of John Dryden* (New York: Harcourt, Brace, 1931), p. 69.

77. See Dryden in several essays, especially "Discourse Concerning Satire" in *The Poetical Works of John Dryden*, ed. G. R. Noyes (Boston and New York: Riverside Press Cambridge, 1909), pp. 310–20, 374, hereinafter called the Cambridge ed. See also Pope in *An Essay on Criticism*, lines 630–61; and Johnson in *Lives*, 1.58, 61, 212, 213. For a recent short study of Waller see A. W. Allison, *Toward an Augustan Poetic: Edmund Waller's "Reform" of English Poetry* (Lexington: Univ. of Kentucky Press, 1962), especially the chapter "The Reform of Our Numbers," which, although speaking of rhyme, makes no reference to internal phonic echoes.

78. The Cambridge ed., p. 319.

79. T. H. Banks, Introduction to *The Poetical Works of Sir John Denham* (New Haven: Yale Univ. Press, 1928), 30–31.

80. George Williamson, "The Rhetorical Pattern of Neo-Classical Wit," *MP*, 33 (1935), 55–82.

81. As W. C. Brown, p. 7, claims.

82. See Banks, p. 31, and n. 77 above for such references and comparisons throughout the eighteenth century.

83. See Banks, pp. 50ff., for facts about the MSS. and eds. of "Cooper's Hill." The 1668 ed. is very close to that of 1655.

84. These eleven include a four syllable [I] in two lines (345–6) and three internal [o]'s in two lines (229–30).

85. Joseph Spence, *Anecdotes, Observations, and Characters of Books and Men* (London: W. H. Carpenter, 1820), pp. 281–83.

86. A study of Banks's facing editions of "Cooper's Hill" will convince any student of Pope that he was both studying and borrowing from Denham. And then we have Pope's statement to Spence (n. 85 above) and his debt in *Windsor Forest*.

87. As W. C. Brown, p. 14, points out.

88. See Waller's "Upon His Majesty's Repairing of Paul's" and Banks, p. 163.

89. This is the opinion of Kaluza, p. 290. It should be noted, however, that Kaluza does later qualify this opinion.

90. Winters, *In Defense of Reason* (New York: The Swallow Press and W. Morrow, 1947), p. 141.

Chapter 2

1. Dedication to the *Aeneis*, 2:252. Here and throughout the chapter, unless otherwise noted, all references to Dryden's prose works will be to the two-volume Everyman edition, ed. George Watson (1962).

2. His chief statements on the sound, "harmony," language of poetry are in the Dedication to the *Aeneis*, addressed to Lord Mulgrave (1697), "A Parallel of Poetry and Painting" (1695), the Preface to the *Fables Ancient and Modern* (1700), "A discourse on the Original and Progress of Satire" (1693), the Preface to *Albion and Albanius* (1685), the Preface to *Sylvae* (1685), "An Account of the Ensuing Poem, Prefixed to *Annus Mirabilis* in a Letter to Sir Robert Howard" (1667), and the Dedication for "The Music of *The Prophetesse*" (1690).

3. 1:98.

4. 2:203.

5. See, for example, "Preface to the *Fables*," 2:275. In the Dedication to the *Aeneis*, coloring is spoken of in exactly the same words (2:242).

6. Dedication to the *Aeneis*, 2:238, for example. See the discus-

sion of Dryden and numbers in Fussell, pp. 7–8. One of Dryden's
most interesting comments on the relationship between poetry
and music is in his Dedication for "The Music of *The
Prophetesse*" (1690): "Musick and poetry have ever been acknowledged Sisters, which walking hand in hand, support each
other: As poetry is the harmony of words, so musick is that of
notes: and as poetry is a rise above prose and oratory, so is
Musick the exaltation of poetry. Both of them may well excell
apart, but sure they are most excellent when they are joined,
because nothing is wanting in either of their perfections: for thus
they appeare, like wit and beauty in the same person." For
Dryden's own poems on music, and for the tradition leading to
those poems, see Hollander, *The Untuning of the Sky*.

7. Preface to *Tyrannic Love* (1670) 1.141.

8. Preface to *Sylvae*, 2:21.

9. Preface to the *Fables*, 2:274.

10. These are Pope's words in "On Pastoral Poetry." For
evidence that Dr. Johnson used the expression in the same way,
see *Idler*, no. 6. Dryden often discussed turns, which to him
included a thought turn as well as an attractive sound. See,
especially, 2:151, 238. See also nn. 79 and 80 in chapter 1.

11. W. H. Gardner, *Hopkins*, 2:124.

12. See especially, "A Discourse on . . . Satire," 2:150, and
the Dedication to the *Aeneis*, 2:237.

13. See "An Account of . . . *Annus Mirabilis*," 1:100, and,
especially, the Preface to the *Fables*, 2:274; "A Parallel of Poetry
and Painting," 2:204; and the Dedication of the *Aeneis*, 2:234–46.

14. *Lives*, 1.342.

15. Ibid., 1.305. Although Johnson began his famous study of
Dryden by saying that "it will be difficult to prove that Dryden
ever made any great advance in literature," he then went on to
prove it: "He was the first who joined argument with poetry. He
showed us the true bounds of the translator's trade," etc.

16. See *Auden: A Collection of Critical Essays*, ed. Monroe K.
Spears (Englewood Cliffs, N. J.: Prentice-Hall, 1964), p. 40;
T. S. Eliot, *Homage to John Dryden: Three Essays on Poetry of
the Seventeenth Century*, The Hogarth Essays, no. 4 (London:
Hazell, Watson & Viney, 1924).

17. *The Autobiography of Mark Van Doren* (New York: Greenwood Press, 1958), pp. 99–100.

18. Van Doren's oft-reprinted study of Dryden, for example, devotes only a few pages to his sound effects, praising his rhythms, diction, and "music," and drawing these three conclusions about his alliteration. First, alliteration is an integral part of the poems of Dryden, binding "words, phrases, lines, couplets, paragraphs together," and "seems to have been instinctive with him, as indeed it is with most rapid and powerful English writers." Second, it assists both his sense and his sound. And third, "scarcely ten consecutive lines can be found in him wherein alliteration is not conspicuous." But nowhere does Van Doren employ the term *assonance* or the term *consonance.* Proudfoot's study of Dryden's *Aeneis* analyzes the Laocoön passage from the second book, speaking of alliteration, motion, noise, speed, and other onomatopoeic devices, but makes no reference to the frequent vowel echoes in that passage and throughout the *Aeneis.* See Van Doren, pp. 60–66, 75–76, 170, for example; and L. Proudfoot, *Dryden's "Aeneid" and Its Seventeenth Century Predecessors* (Manchester Univ. Press, 1960), pp. 255–56. See also W. C. Brown, p. 19, and a very brief statement in Mead, pp. 34–35, about alliteration in Dryden and Pope. The best guide to a study of Dryden's prosody, including his sound devices, is the monograph by Jacob Adler, *The Reach of Art: A Study of the Prosody of Pope*, Univ. of Florida Monographs, Humanities, no. 16 (Spring 1964). Although this study has been much needed by students of eighteenth-century poetry, it does not note Pope's great debt to Dryden in nearly all his prosodic effects as well as in his theories about prosody; and it says little about assonance and does not use the term *consonance:* the present chapter is indebted to my own article, "'Harmony of Numbers': Dryden's Alliteration, Consonance, Assonance," *Texas Studies in Literature and Language*, 9, no. 3 (Autumn 1967), 333–43. See also Paul Ramsey, *The Art of John Dryden* (Lexington: The Univ. of Kentucky Press, 1969), who mentions alliteration but does not discuss assonance or consonance; Ramsey's enthusiasm for Dryden is most refreshing.

19. Dedication to the *Aeneis*, 2:252.

20. For an analysis of one eighteenth-century theory about alliteration as being undesirable because, unlike rhyme, it was an element of surprise, see Fussell, pp. 50–51.

21. One could as easily select all his examples from *The Hind and the Panther*, or any other long poem by Dryden. All quotations from Dryden's poems will be from the one-volume Cambridge edition, ed. G. R. Noyes (Boston and New York: Houghton Mifflin, 1909).

22. *Essay of Dramatic Poesy*, 1:79.

23. In the Preface to *Albion and Albanius* (1685), 2:37, and in the Dedication to the *Aeneis*, 2:234ff.

24. The [k] of "vocal oak" and of "oraculously spoke" is excellent evidence that one cannot always be sure whether a consonant is final or initial: for three of the words [k] is obviously final; for *vocal* the [k] is probably unstressed initial; nevertheless, all readers will agree that it harmonizes beautifully with the other three [k]s.

25. *Lives*, 1:310.

26. "A Parallel of Poetry and Painting," 2:206.

27. "Notes and observations on Virgil's Work in English," appended to the translation of *Aeneis*. See the Cambridge edition, ed. Noyes, p. 710.

28. "Postscript to the Reader," appended to the *Aeneis*, 2:261–62.

29. Ll. 130–300.

30. Ll. 357–527.

31. See Dr. Johnson's thesis in *Lives*, 1:345, that, along with other advances in the art of poetry, Dryden was "perhaps . . . the first who joined argument with poetry."

32. Adler has demonstrated Pope's extended use of alliteration for this kind of emphasis. See especially his discussions on pp. 83, 91, 99.

33. See n. 49, chap. 1.

34. "An Account . . . prefixed to *Annus Mirabilis*" (1667), 1:100. See n. 18 for the only scholarly reference, a very brief one, to Dryden's onomatopoeia.

35. W. F. Jackson Knight, *Roman Vergil* (London: Faber, 1944), p. 243, thinks that Virgil's line depends most for its effect on "the bitter, frightening *a*" in three of its words. The same [k] is

one of the dominating sounds in an echo-laden couplet that in *The Medal* (304–5) employs animals most ironically, the mob of croaking small things being the victim of the crane Shaftesbury:

> And frogs and toads, and all the tadpole train,
> Will croak to heav'n for help from this devouring crane.

36. Knight, p. 242. Knight is, however, speaking of Virgil's line in 8.596, which differs from the one quoted only in that it has *sonitu* instead of *cursu*.

37. See Jespersen and Weinreich, chap. 1, n. 56 above.

38. For the same phonestheme and Burke's diminution, see the first *Georgic*:

> And brews for fields impetuous floods of rain,   (577)
>
> The hollow ditches fills, and floats the plain.   (512)

39. See Bolinger, e.g., chap. 1, n. 56 above.

40. Although only certain phoneticists seem agreed on the significance of this sound, see Jespersen especially, chap. 1, n. 54 above.

41. For *tw-*, a popularly recognized phonestheme, see Bolinger, chap. 1, n. 56 above. Another such couplet in the first *Georgic*, but without the second phonestheme, emphasizes the *st-* even more with an example of augmentation in the word *set*:

> For stalking cranes to set the guileful snare;
> T'inclose the stags in toils, and hunt the hare.

42. Jespersen, Weinreich, Bolinger, for example.

43. Although Adler is the only one to point out its effectiveness in *The Dunciad*, a number of phoneticists have noted its use to suggest "dark states of mind," disgust, etc., and David Masson (see chap. 1) has discussed Wilfred Owen's discovery of [ʊ], or what Masson calls the American [ʌ].

44. See above, n. 36 of chap. 1, which points out that with Dryden "*long*" rhymed with "*sung*" as well as with "*song*."

45. Many other such images of fire or light could be cited, for example, *Aeneis* 11:316–17, with five [aɪ,əɪ]'s in stressed syllables; 6.972 and 1.249 with three in each line; and a triplet in the third *Georgic* (822–23) with seven.

46. Dedication to the *Aeneis*, 2:245.

47. Ibid., p. 255.

48. K. G. Hamilton, *Two Harmonies: Poetry and Prose in the Seventeenth Century* (Oxford: Clarendon Press, 1963), pp. 5–7, who quotes Morris Croll's corroborating opinion.

49. See n. 22 above.

Chapter 3

1. Among the many studies of Pope's versification one should consult Wimsatt, "One Relation of Rhyme to Reason: Alexander Pope"; H. C. Wyld, "Observations on Pope's Versification," *MLR* (1930), 274–85, who has much on the "speed" but little on the sound effects; Edith Sitwell, *Alexander Pope* (London, 1930; New York, 1962), although her chapter "Some Notes on Pope's Poetry" is very disappointing; Rebecca Price Parkin, "Tonal Variation," in *The Poetic Workmanship of Alexander Pope* (Minneapolis: Univ. of Minnesota Press, 1955), who stresses variety in tone and does not seem to agree with Pope that his pastorals appeal to the ear; Foster Provost, "Pope's Pastorals: An Exercise in Poetic Technique," *LSU Studies*, Humanities Series, no. 5; W. P. Ker, *The Art of Poetry: Seven Lectures 1920–22* (Oxford: Clarendon Press, 1923), who emphasizes that Pope could touch his "musical instrument of the couplet in a thousand ways"; Piper (chap. 1, n. 75); John A. Jones, *Pope's Couplet Art* (Athens: Ohio Univ. Press, 1969); and Jacob Adler, *The Reach of Art: A Study in the Prosody of Pope*. Adler's book and several articles (in *PMLA*, June, 1961, for example) provide the most nearly complete such investigation of Pope's caesura, rhetorical devices, syncope, monosyllabic lines, rhymes, alliteration, and representative meter. My own study will try to avoid repeating this analysis by approaching alliteration differently; by stressing assonance, seriously neglected heretofore, and consonance, not mentioned in any study; and by pointing out new facts about Pope's onomatopoeia, his use of balanced echoes, and, especially, his alterations for the sake of sound.

2. Adler does consider it briefly—for example, p. 40, pp. 51–52, p. 96.

3. Pope's statements about prosody are found principally in his letter to Cromwell (1710); the probably spurious letter to Walsh (1706) that is very similar to the Cromwell letter; the essay "On Pastoral Poetry" (1709); and "The Guardian," no. 40 (1713). For Dryden's theories of prosody, see chapter 2 and its notes. That Pope was most interested in and conversant with Dryden's theories of prosody is further borne out by Pope's copy of Dryden annotated in Pope's handwriting and found now at the University of Illinois. The comments in the margins indicate that versification was Pope's chief interest. See, for one study of the MS., Richard D. Erlich and James Harmer, "Pope's Annotations in His Copy of Dryden's *Comedies, Tragedies, and Operas:* An Exercise in Cryptography," *Restoration and Eighteenth-Century Theatre Research*, 10 (May 1971), 14–24.

4. "Pope," in *Lives*, 2.242.

5. Wherever possible, lines quoted from Pope will be taken from the Twickenham ed., except that italicized words are not shown in italics, for obvious reasons.

6. See, for example, the first line of pt. 2 of *An Essay on Criticism*, "Of all the Causes which conspire to blind," or line 298 of the same poem, "What oft was thought, but ne'er so well expressed."

7. Chatman, "Comparing Metrical Styles," in *Style in Language*, ed. Sebeok, pp. 149–73. This essay is reprinted in *Essays*, ed. Chatman and Levin, pp. 132–55.

8. For such a comparison one can make use of the variorum *Dunciad* in the Twickenham edition, and, more particularly, of Robert M. Schmitz, *Pope's Windsor Forest 1712: A Study of the Washington University Holograph*, Washington Univ. Studies, n.s., Language and Literature, no. 21 (St. Louis: Washington Univ. Press, 1952); Earl R. Wasserman, *Pope's "Epistle to Bathurst": A Critical Reading with An Edition of the Manuscripts* (Baltimore: The John Hopkins Press, 1960); and Robert M. Schmitz, *Pope's Essay on Criticism 1709: A Study of the Bodleian Manuscript Text with Facsimiles, Transcripts, and Variants* (St. Louis: Washington Univ. Press, 1962).

9. Sherburn, "Pope at Work," in *Essays on the Eighteenth Century Presented to David Nichol Smith* (Oxford: Clarendon Press, 1945), pp. 49–64.

10. The [d] of *amaz'd* elides with the [d] of *defenceless* leaving [z] as the final sound.

11. See Johnson, *Lives*, 2.257.

12. By Adler and Chatman especially. See nn. 1 and 7 of this chapter.

13. In order to emphasize the balancing sounds, here and in certain other lines some phonic echoes are not marked.

14. But he could balance sounds in a chiasmus other than those in adjectives:

Blush in the Rose, and in the diamond blaze,

(*Moral Ep* 1.146)

Now flames the Cid, and now Perolla burns, (*Dun* 1.250)

The same their Talents, and their Tastes the same.

(*Dun* 2.380)

15. There are exceptions, of course. Already cited is one *gl*- alliteration from the holograph of *Windsor Forest* (231), "The bow'ry mazes, and the glimmering glades," but this line was not in the published poem. See also *St. Cecilia's Day*, line 78, "Glitt'ring thro' the gloomy Glades." But there is no *gl*- alliteration in any of the Pastorals or—as far as I can tell—in the *Dunciad*, while the *Rape* has one in a couplet (1.23–24). In *Autumn* the phonestheme *fl*- comes in line 86 with *fly*, *flocks*, and *flowers* and in *Winter* with *flow*, *flocks*, and *fleeces* lines 4–5.

16. See also 1.120–21; 2.3.

17. See Adler, p. 102.

18. See n. 3 of chap. 2.

19. See Johnson, *Lives*, 2.260, for a reprinting of the variants of the Tydides passage. Again near the end of Book 8 of the *Iliad*, after revising a couplet three times Pope ended with a four-syllable assonance of [aɪ,əɪ] that aids in producing the image of "vivid light." First his couplet read,

The conscious swains rejoicing at the sight
Eye the blue vault, and bless the vivid light.

Then it was altered to

The conscious shepherds gazing with delight
Eye the blue vault, and bless the glorious light.

(*u*seful)

Finally it became,

> The conscious shepherd joyful at the sight
> *Eye*s the blue vaul*t* and numbers every li*gh*t.

Pope started with an [aɪ,əɪ] assonance in each line as well as the [t] consonance and two alliterations in the second line. On his way he gave up the [v] alliteration and one [aɪ,əɪ] while toying with the parallel assonance in *blue* and *useful*. Finally he gave up his other alliteration [bl], replaced the missing [aɪ,əɪ], and ended with the very unobtrusive [t] consonance and only one other internal sound echo—the dominating four-syllable assonance of [aɪ,əɪ] in a couplet whose primary purpose was to produce the feeling of light.

20. Hagstrum, *The Sister Arts: the Tradition of Literary Pictorialism from Dryden to Gray* (Chicago: Univ. of Chicago Press, 1958).

21. Wimsatt, p. 338.

22. These odes (1687, 1697) employ not only rhyme and many internal phonic echoes but attempt slow and fast tempos, a variety of rhythms besides the iambic, and the sounds of musical instruments (trumpet, drum, flute, violin). But I have omitted discussions of them here because they have been handled so well by John Hollander (see chap. 1, n. 2 above), whose very title, *The Untuning of the Sky*, is taken from one of the odes.

Chapter 4

1. See Ralph Cohen, *The Art of Discrimination: Thomson's "The Seasons" and the Language of Criticism* (Berkeley: Univ. of California Press, 1964).

2. Scott, Wordsworth, and Hazlitt also praised Thomson but found fault with his language. See Cohen, pp. 326–39 especially.

3. See Cohen, pp. 331, 342, 361–62.

4. In Thomson's letter to Sir John Clerk, January 18, 1728, in *James Thomson (1700–1748): Letters and Documents*, ed. Alan Dugald McKillop (Lawrence: Univ. of Kansas Press, 1958), p. 59; and again in *Summer*, line 1747 (see n. 7 below).

5. By Bailey McBride, "The Poetry of James Thomson

(1700–1748)," (Diss. Univ. of Tennessee, 1966). Repetition is also an important structural technique in the poetry of Lucretius, one of Thomson's masters. See especially Rosamund E. Deutsch (chap. 1, n. 9 above).

6. At times, of course, Wordsworth—writing language hardly that of common men—did employ phonic echoes, as in these lines from the *Prelude* quoted for other reasons by Spacks, p. 110 (see n. 10):

Angling I went, or trod the trackless hills
By mists bewildered, suddenly mine eyes
Have glanced upon him distant a few steps,
In size a giant, stalking through thick fog,
His sheep like Greenland bears.

7. All quotations from *The Seasons* are taken from Otto Zippel, *Thomson's "Seasons": Critical Edition* (Berlin: Mayer and Müller, 1908). If no edition is indicated with the line number, the edition is that of 1746. All quotations from other poems by Thomson will be from J. Logie Robertson, ed., *The Complete Poetical Works of James Thomson* (London: Oxford Univ. Press, 1908).

8. There are other passages in these two poets which are similar. On the Grecian Urn is that "bold lover" to whom Keats addressed some of his greatest lines:

never canst thou kiss,
Though winning near the goal—yet, do not grieve;
She cannot fade, though thou hast not thy bliss,
For ever wilt thou love, and she be fair.

Thomson also had a frustrated lover (*Summer* 1212ff.), whose dejection he compared to that depicted in a piece of statuary:

on the Marble-Tom[b]
The well-dissembled Mourner stooping stands,
For ever silent, and for ever sad.

Here, even if we include Keats's one end rhyme with his two alliterations and two assonances of [ɪ], Thomson has more phonal repetition in his much shorter passage—three alliterations, including the [st] phonestheme and the neatly balanced [s] in "silent" and "sad," the consonance of [m], and three assonances.

9. See n. 7 above.

10. The best studies of Thomson's revisions are to be found in Zippel, Robertson, and Dugald McKillop, *The Background of Thomson's "Seasons"* (Hamden, Connecticut: Archon Books, 1961). No one of these, however, is concerned with any revision that involves altering the sounds of words. Nor is Patricia Mayer Spacks, in her fine *The Varied God: A Critical Study of Thomson's The Seasons* (Berkeley/Los Angeles: Univ. of California Press, 1959). See, for example, her chapter 6, "Description in *The Seasons.*"

11. For example, in the 1730 *Autumn* he wrote,

where astride
The lubber Power himself triumphant sits,   (555–56)

which became in 1744,

where astride
The lubber Power, in filthy Triumph sits.   (560–61)

By exchanging two words for one and shifting the accent in *triumphant* to that in *triumph*, Thomson lost one assonance but gained two.

12. Cohen, p. 341.

13. It was possible, of course, for Thomson to employ balanced sounds without restricting them to a single line as the heroic couplet nearly always did. In *Winter* he assonated the verb of one end-stopped line with the parallel verb found in the next (other echoes are not marked):

enough to light the Chace,
Or guide their daring Steps to Finland-Fairs.   (864–65)

Even in run-on lines he could alliterate the balancing nouns and consonate the balancing verbs:

I solitary court
Th'inspiring breeze; and meditate the book
Of Nature.   (*Autumn* 669–71)

14. In Kenneth Burke's system "collected, cool" would provide both an example of "alliteration" of *c–c*, even though the

first *c* is weak, and an example of consonantal chiasmus in the *l–c* (/l/–/k/) of *collected* and the *c–l* (/k/–/l/) of *cool*. See chapter 1, n. 38.

15. See, for example, the section on Dr. Johnson in chapter 5.

16. For these alterations see *Summer* (1727) 212, 214; (1744) 230, 232; *Winter* (1730) 145; (1744) 166; and *Autumn* (1730) 965; (1744) 1035.

17. For these examples see *Spring* (1744) 584; and *Winter* (1744) 150–51.

18. See chapter 1.

19. One of his most obvious attempts at rendering the nightingale's song is in *Summer*, where initial [s] occurs five times:

> Thro' the soft Silence of the listening Night,
> The sober-suited Songstress trills her Lay.   (745–46)

20. As in these lines:

> *Even Light itself*, which every thing displays
> Shone undiscover'd, till his brighter mind
> Untwisted all the shining robe of day;
> And, from the whitening undistinguish'd blaze,
> Collecting every ray into his kind,
> To the charm'd *eye* educ'd the gorgeous train
> Of Parent-Colours.   (96–102)

See also lines 5–11 and 125–31.

21. Physical brightness:

> To where the deep adorning Cyclad Isles
> In shining Prospect rise,   (2.105–6)

> Fair shine the slippery Days, enticing Skies
> Of Favour smile;   (5.532–33)

the light of virtue or knowledge:

> This Hive of Science, shedding Sweets divine,   (2.143)

> Virtues that shine the Light of Humankind,   (3.114)

> Bright rising Eras instant rushed to Light.   (5.564)

22. For Fehr, Tillotson, and the comments on the "shoreless Ocean" line, all in this paragraph, see Cohen, pp. 241–42, 361–63.

Chapter 5

1. These are the words of the "poet" in Letter XXX of *The Citizen of the World*.

2. "Tired Nature's sweet restorer, balmy Sleep" is only one of many Shakespearean echoes in the *Night Thoughts*. See, for example, the passage beginning line 67.

3. No doubt the most famous line in the *Night Thoughts* is "Procrastination is the thief of time" (392), but there are dozens of others, among them, "All men think all men mortal, but themselves" (423). Quotations from Young are taken from *The Works of the Author of the Night-Thoughts*, in three volumes, Revised and Corrected by Himself (London: Dodsley, 1802), vol. 2.

4. Here six lines again alliterate half the stressed syllables:

Let thy Pride pardon what thy nature needs,
The salutary censure of a friend.
Thou happy wretch! by blindness art thou blest.
By dotage dandled to perpetual smiles.
Know, smiler! at thy peril art thou pleas'd;
Thy pleasure is the promise of thy pain. (311–16)

5. See for example, lines 58, 371ff., 410, 416, 457–8. For Blair's lines, see the text of the ed. of 1786, as found in *A Collection of English Poems 1660–1800*, ed. Ronald S. Crane (New York and London: Harper, 1932), pp. 658–60.

6. Here the vowel of *rogues* may be close to that in *cut* rather than to the [o] of *robes*. See the *Og–rogue–clog* rhyme with Otway's contemporary Dryden (chap. 2). All quotations from the tragedies of Otway, Addison, and Rowe are taken from *British Dramatists from Dryden to Sheridan*, ed. George H. Nettleton and Arthur E. Case (Boston: Houghton Mifflin, 1939).

7. For the quotations from Butler see *Hudibras*, ed. A. R. Waller (Cambridge: Cambridge Univ. Press, 1905).

8. See also 1.1.15–16, 34–35, 421–22, 619–20, 648–49.

9. In spite of his effective use of sounds, Butler has no more than one assonance or alliteration to about six lines. Swift's "Verses on the Death of Dr. Swift" also has less than one assonance to six lines and even fewer alliterations although there are

some very striking phonic echoes in this witty poem. For Prior's octosyllabics see, for example, "On Beauty, A Riddle" or "An Epitaph," neither of which has many noticeable internal echoes. Prior did, however, employ alliteration and assonance in other types of poems, for example, in "On Exodus iii. 14 . . . An Ode."

10. The lines quoted from both the short-line poem and the ode are found in *Grongar Hill*, ed. with int. by Richard C. Boys (Baltimore: The Johns Hopkins Press, 1941), and in *Eighteenth-Century English Literature*, ed. Geoffrey Tillotson, Paul Fussell, Marshall Waingrow (New York: Harcourt, Brace and World, 1969), pp. 807–810. Both volumes reprint the octosyllabic poem from the 1761 edition and give the Pindaric version as found in Richard Savage's *Miscellaneous Poems and Translations* (1726). Boys provides the fullest and best discussion of the three versions. For an earlier treatment of the question see Garland Greever, "The Two Versions of 'Grongar Hill,'" *JEGP*, 16 (1917), 274–81, who gives one text of the little known poem but does not compare the versions or mention their phonic echoes. The ode has a number of such echoes also, for example, this four-syllable assonance: "Towers, ancient as the Mountain, crown its Brow" (73).

11. Dryden has a number of trochaic and anapaestic songs and even one in dactylic rhythm: see *An Evening's Love* (1668) 4.1.

12. Quotations from Shenstone are taken from the 1764 edition of Shenstone's *Works* as found in Crane.

13. The quotations from Watts and Cowper may be found in Crane; for Wesley's lines see *Representative Verse of Charles Wesley*, ed. Frank Baker (London: Epworth Press, 1962).

14. Much has been written about odes and other poems to or about music, especially by Hollander (see chap. 1, n. 2).

15. Quotations from Collins are taken from the first edition as found in Crane.

16. *Lives* 2.485.

17. All quotations from Gray that follow are found in H. W. Starr and J. P. Hendrickson, eds., *The Complete Poems of Thomas Gray* (Oxford: Clarendon, 1966).

18. From the widely used *Eighteenth Century Prose and Poetry*, ed. Bredvold, McKillop, Whitney, 2nd ed. (New York: Ronald, 1956), p. 412.

19. See the song in *As you Like It* 3.2, which always and often rhymes *Rosalind* with such words as *find*. In Spenser's "June" the name is never rhymed, but it does assonate in "Ah, faithless Rosalind, and voide of grace." For this pronunciation see Kökeritz, pp. 218, 477.

20. The quotations from Gay are found in A. C. Faber, ed., *The Poetical Works of John Gay* (London: Oxford Univ. Press, 1926).

21. W. C. Brown, *The Triumph of Form*, pp. 48–50, agrees that Gay was extraordinarily accomplished as a "musical" poet and says of these lines that "here the alliteration, the length of the vowels and consonants, and rhyme play variously upon the meaning. The long *l* sounds and the long vowels . . . combine to suggest in music and movement the idea of luxurious living."

22. Ibid.

23. *Poems*, ed. E. L. McAdam, Jr., with George Milne, The Yale Edition of the Works of Samuel Johnson (New Haven and London: Yale Univ. Press, 1964), 6:xiv. Quotations from Johnson's poems are from this ed.

24. Hagstrum, *Samuel Johnson's Literary Criticism* (Minneapolis: Univ. of Minneapolis Press, 1952); *The Critical Opinions of Samuel Johnson*, arranged and compiled and with an introduction by Joseph E. Brown (Princeton: Princeton Univ. Press, 1926; 1953; 1961); and Fussell, *Theory of Prosody in Eighteenth-Century England*, pp. 24–26, 41–44 especially.

25. See *Rambler* 86 for Saturday, January 12, 1751, and Fussell, especially pp. 24–49.

26. Chapter 10 of *Rasselas* (my italics).

27. My italics.

28. See chapter 1 of the present study for Churchill's slighting reference to "Apt Alliterations artful aid" (*Prophecy of Famine*, 1.85), which indicates a use of the term like that of Dr. Johnson.

29. 2.484.

30. For other initial consonant echoes that stress syntactical parallelisms, see *lute–lyre* (271), *fav'rite–friend* (297), *pride–Prudence* (336, as well as 340), and *freedom–friend* (338).

31. Bate, *From Classic to Romantic: Premises of Taste in Eighteenth-Century England* (Cambridge: Harvard Univ. Press, 1946), p. 95.

32. The *Dictionary* has almost the same words for "Consonance": "Accord of sound."

33. These statistics are compiled on the assumption that Johnson pronounced *oi* more or less as it is pronounced by most Englishmen today. Although he seldom rhymed *oi* with *i*, others in his day did.

34. The first two occurrences of initial [f] are made more noticeable by the consonance of [l]. W. C. Brown, p. 82, points out that *f* binds the couplet here but he does not note the first *f* nor the fact that the *f*'s provide vertical alliteration that is certainly effective by the second repetition.

35. In "London" see, for example, lines 172–73:

No s*e*cret island in the bou*n*[d]less mai*n*?
No p*e*aceful d*e*sart y*e*t uncl*ai*m'd by Sp*ai*n?

or lines 220–21, which begin "There ev'ry bush . . . ? There ev'ry breeze . . . "

36. See W. C. Brown, pp. 141ff., who discusses Goldsmith's vertical alliterations as well as his other acoustic effects and concludes enthusiastically that "the couplet becomes more frequently and consistently lyrical in *The Deserted Village* than in any other neoclassical poem" (p. 154).

37. See Yale ed., 6:xiv.

38. See Yale ed., 6:103n.

39. In Introduction to *London* and *The Vanity of Human Wishes* (London: Haslewood Books, 1930). See W. C. Brown, pp. 76, 85, for another defense of Johnson's poetry against the "non-lyricism" urged by Krutch.

40. P. 86.

41. For Cowper's adverse opinion about the couplet, which, with one exception, he used only in his youth, see W. C. Brown, pp. 132–41. The exception is "On the Receipt of My Mother's Picture out of Norfolk" (1790; 1798).

Chapter 6

1. W. B. Yeats, *Essays* (London: Macmillan, 1924), p. 193.

2. Strachey, *Books and Characters* (New York: Harcourt Brace, 1922), p. 78.

3. For Wordsworth, see chapter 4. Although Whitman has long passages without many phonal echoes, he consistently has more than Wordsworth, and some of the sections of *Song of Myself* or, for another example, "When Lilacs Last in the Dooryard Bloomed" have a surprising number of alliterations and even more assonances. For Whitman's alliteration see the well known lines beginning "Pre*ss* clo*se* bare-bosom'd night—pre*ss* clo*se* magnetic nourishing night." For his assonance see section forty-nine of *Song of Myself*: "I sm*e*ll the white r*o*ses sw*ee*t-sc*e*nted and gr*ow*ing, / I r*ea*ch to the l*ea*fy lips, I reach to the po*l*ish'd br*ea*sts of m*e*lons." As one would expect, a poet who used anaphora and parallelism so much could hardly avoid paralleling his sounds, as Whitman did in "filter and fiber your blood," "watching and wondering," "I witness and wait," "You shall l*i*sten . . . and f*i*lter," etc.

4. The quotations from Blake are found in *The Complete Writings of William Blake*, ed. Geoffrey Keynes (London: Oxford Univ. Press, 1966).

5. For the quotations from Housman see *The Collected Poems of A. E. Housman* (New York: Holt, Rinehart and Winston, 1966). The page number from this text is cited with each of the longer quotations.

6. See Francis Berry, *Poetry and the Physical Voice* (London: Routledge and Kegan Paul, 1962), p. 98, who claims that Milton used -*n* and -*ng* more habitually, more pervasively than any other poet in English. My own experience with the sounds in poems does not bear out Berry's conclusion, since I find many other poets favoring final nasals, for music images, for lines about sounds, for onomatopoeia of several kinds, or for ornament merely. Dryden, Pope, Byron, Shelley, Housman are only a few who might compete with Milton when one looks for effective use of final nasals.

7. For a fine discussion of this poem and the "courage" of Housman's mercenaries, see Richard Wilbur, "Round About a Poem of Housman's," in *The Moment of Poetry*, ed. Don Cameron Allen (Baltimore: Johns Hopkins Press, 1962), pp. 73–98.

8. The quotations from Byron are taken from *The Poetical Works of Lord Byron* (London: Oxford Univ. Press, 1935).

9. See, for example, D. H. Lawrence, *Studies in Classic*

American Literature (New York: Viking, 1964), p. 77; and Robert Hillyer, *First Principles of Verse* (Boston: The Writer, 1950), p. 20.

10. For a study of Poe's alliteration, assonance, and consonance, including his revisions for more phonic echoes, see an unpublished thesis by Kenneth Holland Cherry (Univ. of Tennessee, 1965). The versions of Poe's poems that show how carefully he revised can be found in *The Poems of Edgar Allen Poe*, ed. Killis Campbell (Boston: Ginn, 1917).

11. The young Keats very often echoed his phones. See especially "To Hope" (1815), whose forty-eight lines have some sixteen alliterations and thirty assonances, or the anapaestic "To Some Ladies" (1815), which frequently stresses the accent with echoes, as in "Bless Cynthia's face, the enthusiast's friend," or "Why linger you so, the wild labyrinth strolling." The mature Keats, on the other hand, wrote beautiful odes with a low proportion of phonal recurrences: for "To Autumn" see chapter 4; "Ode to Melancholy" has only twelve assonances in its eighty lines, at least four of them being hardly unique ("fade away," "beechen green," etc.); "Ode on a Grecian Urn" in fifty lines has no more than eight assonances, although four of these are polysyllabic and most effective. For more on Keats, see the comparison with Thomson in chapter 4.

12. For some treatment of Shelley's sounds, especially his vowels, see studies by Donald Reiman, for example, his *Percy Bysshe Shelley* (New York: Twayne, 1969).

13. Quotations from Browning are found in *The Selected Poetry of Robert Browning*, ed. with an int. by Kenneth L. Knickerbocker (New York: Random House [Modern Library], 1954).

14. In addition to the books cited in chapter 1, see such recent collections as Helmut Kreuzer and Rul Gunzenhauser, eds., *Mathematik und Dichtung* (Munich: Kymphenburger Verlagshandlung, 1957), and Jacob Leed, ed., *The Computer and Literary Style* (Kent, Ohio: Kent Univ. Press, 1966). Both of these were widely reviewed, for example, in *TLS*, Feb. 9, 1967.

15. Osip Brik, "Zvukovie povtory" (Sound-Figures), in *Poetika* (St. Petersburg, 1910); and Valery Bryusov, "O rifme" (On Rhyme), *Pechat i revolutsiya* (1924). See also V. Zhir-

munsky, *Rifma, ee istoria i teoriya* (Rhyme, its History and Theory) (Petrograd, 1923). For references to these and to many other books on the subject, most of them now being superseded, see the still authoritative article by René Wellek and Austin Warren in *Theory of Literature* (1942; rpt. New York: Harvest, 1956), pp. 146–74. Wellek and Warren, however, have only a casual mention of alliteration and assonance and make no mention of anything resembling consonance.

16. See *TLS*, January 25, 1968, p. 88.

17. Dale L. Plank, *Pasternak's Lyric: A Study of Sound and Imagery* (The Hague: Mouton, 1968).

18. See, for example, his paper delivered at the 1967 meeting of the Modern Language Association in Chicago, Illinois.

19. Raymond, p. 137.

20. Gardner, *Hopkins*, 1:134–35.

21. A very recent article quotes Frost's early letters ("write with the ear on the speaking voice"; "A sentence is a sound in itself on which other sounds called words are strung.") and attempts to prove that he was a "radical" formalist related to those "other" formalists of the same time—Brik, Jakobson, and Zakubinsky. See Frank Lentricchia, "Robert Frost: The Aesthetics of Voice and the Theory of Poetry," *Criticism*, 25, no. 1 (Winter 1973), 28–43.

22. Among the thickest clusters are these:

Winding across wide water, without sound.
The day is like wide water, without sound,
Stilled for the passing of her dreaming feet
Over the seas, to silent Palestine.

23. See chap. 1, n. 18.

24. See Graves, "Language Levels," *Encounter*, 26 (May 1966), 45–51.

25. Nabokov, *Pale Fire* (London: Weidenfeld and Nicolson, 1962), p. 68.

26. Ibid., p. 52.

27. See Chad Walsh, *Doors into Poetry*, for a section displaying both the early and the published versions of poems by these writers.

28. See *Auden: A Collection of Critical Essays*, ed. Spears, p. 40.

29. From "The Growth of A Poem."

30. See *Poetry and Prose of William Blake*, ed. Geoffrey Keynes (New York: Random House, 1927), p. 551.

Index